HELP!
This Animal Is
Driving Me Crazy

HELP!

This Animal Is Driving Me Crazy

Dr. Daniel F. Tortora

ΨP

A Playboy Press Book

Library of Congress Cataloging in Publication Data

Tortora, Daniel F
    Help!

    Bibliography: p.
    Includes index.
       1. Dogs—Behavior.   2. Dogs—Psychology.
I. Title.
SF433.T67   636.089′68′9   77–5457
ISBN 0–87223–491–6

To my love, Angie

Contents

Tables

Figures

Acknowledgments

The most important group of people who contributed to the creation of this book and who were indispensable to the formation of the ideas expressed in it are the pet owners. They shared their pet behavior problems with me. Without them I would never have been aware of the complex pet problems owners experience, nor would I have had the opportunity to apply experimental psychology to solving these problems.

As an experimental psychologist, I was used to the controlled atmosphere of the laboratory, where I could create the problem behavior myself and then test ways of solving it. In applying psychology to animal behavior problems, I was not given this luxury. My clients presented problems of unknown cause that had developed in the uncontrolled environment of their home. But thanks to the tutelage of my graduate mentors, Drs. M. R. Denny and Stan Ratner, I have been able to bridge this considerable gap between the laboratory and my clients' homes, thus successfully solving many pet behavior problems and learning more about animal and human behavior than I could have ever learned by confining myself solely to the laboratory.

The second most important group of people are the thousands of research psychologists who have spent their time studying animal behavior, learning, motivation, canid ethology and behavior modification. Without the knowledge they generated there could be no scientific approach to solving pet behavior problems because there would be no behavioral science. It is unfortunate that this book's scope does not permit an account of their valuable work. However, special mention must be made of Dr. Michael Fox for his numerous scientific contributions to the understanding of the dog and Drs. John P. Scott and John L. Fuller for their work on the genetic behavior of the dog. Without their guidance, I would not have been able to understand the problems my clients described.

I would also like to acknowledge the advice given me by my friends and colleagues, Drs. Peter and Diane Borchelt. They both patiently listened to my numerous case studies and shared their expertise with me.

Last and most of all, I acknowledge the help of Angela Tortora, my wife, who typed the first draft of this book, transforming it into a legible manuscript.

HELP!
This Animal Is
Driving Me Crazy

1

THE PHONE CALL

CALLER: Dr. T. Help, this dog of ours is driving me crazy!

DR. T: What seems to be the problem?

CALLER: Well, every time we try to talk, Sebastian gets hysterical.

DR. T: What do you mean by getting hysterical?

CALLER: He just barks and barks at my daughter. It's almost impossible to shut him up. We have tried everything we could think of, even tranquilizers, but he got worse.

DR. T: Could you tell me a little more about your dog—his age, sex and breed?

CALLER: He is a male miniature poodle about four years old. We've had him since he was eight weeks.

DR. T: When did the trouble start?

CALLER: The trouble started when he was about nine months old and has gotten worse ever since. It has gotten so bad that my daughter and I cannot speak to each other if Sebastian is in the room. He just barks and barks. We can't stop him no matter what we do and, God knows, we've tried everything.

(3)

DR. T: Okay, why don't I set up an appointment for you? You can tell me all about it when you come.

After scheduling the caller for an appointment, I pondered the problem. Many people, unsophisticated about animal behavior, might think that some obvious human emotion was responsible. "The dog is jealous of the attention the mother is giving to the daughter," or perhaps, "The dog disliked the daughter and was barking out of spite," they might say. Explanations using human-psychological concepts such as these have never been very useful to me. First of all, little is known about the human emotions of jealousy and spite; secondly, there is no evidence that a dog or any other animal can experience such emotions. Even if this were the explanation, what could you do about it?

After dismissing this type of explanation, I hypothesized that the caller's dog probably had a typical case of *operant* barking, that is, the dog was being rewarded in some way for barking. Consequently, he barked until he got the expected reward. The solution sounds simple: identify the reward and eliminate it. But the solution gets somewhat complicated because a reward may not be anything as obvious as a dog biscuit. In fact, very strange things can be made into rewards. Even a good whack with a newspaper can be rewarding under the right circumstances. Most people inadvertently and unknowingly reward their animal for a wide variety of behavior. Since the reward is not intentionally delivered, bad behavior gets rewarded as well as good behavior.

Suspending further ruminations about the caller's problem, I made a note to investigate potential sources of reward for barking when the caller and her daughter came for their appointment.

THE FIRST APPOINTMENT

It's been three weeks since the scheduled first appointment. My clients have missed three in a row. Each time they called, cancelled the appointment and asked for another. The excuses all seemed legitimate: the car wasn't working, or the rain made driving hazardous. However, the cancellations were too frequent for comfort. I wondered if there could be any other reason for missing appointments. Did these people really want the barking to stop? Perhaps the dog's barking served some useful function. If the mother and daughter were prone to arguing, the barking could function to distract them and prevent arguing. This would fit my first hypothesis that the barking was rewarded. It would also make it more difficult to deal with the problem since any attempts to stop the barking would lead to unknowing counter-attempts on the part of my clients to reinstate the barking. I made a note to explore this with them.

My clients arrived at 9:00 P.M. The mother was an attractive woman in her early forties and dressed stylishly. The daughter was fifteen years old. She was tall, slender and pale. She was dressed rather peculiarly for her age, in ragged and loose-fitting jeans with a hole in the knee, a flannel shirt and an army surplus overcoat that terminated well below her knees. Her hair was cropped close to her head. This was not the typical attire of a teenage girl living in the small midwestern town where my clients resided.

I invited them to take off their coats and sit down. They seated themselves but refused to take off their coats. I wondered about the girl's peculiar dress and the fact that both refused to remove their coats. Perhaps they were apprehensive about talking to a psychologist. Some people have the feeling that a psychologist can see right through them. Perhaps wearing coats could somehow prevent this. In order to break the ice, I explained to them basically what I planned to do this evening and then asked them to recount their problem.

THE PROBLEM

DR. T: To start, let's get some facts. You have a four-year-old male miniature poodle who barks a lot. Why did you wait so long to get help?

MOTHER: Well, he wasn't that bad when we first got him. He's gotten more and more cranky each year. Now he's just intolerable. All the tricks we used in the past to shut him up don't seem to work any more.

DR. T: Tell me about the tricks that used to work.

DAUGHTER: If he would bark or jump on my leg, I would get so angry I would throw a whole box of dog biscuits at him. He just sat there gobbling up the biscuits. That way I could get out of the room. By the time he finished the box, he probably forgot about me and everything was okay for a while.

DR. T: And does the biscuit trick still work?

DAUGHTER: When he's finished he looks for me and when he finds me he starts all over again, frantically barking. I can't stand the sound. The barking can go on for hours.

DR. T: Since the trick doesn't work any more, what do you do now?

DAUGHTER: I just try to avoid him. I lock myself in my room and he stays outside my door and barks. I know the biscuit thing was wrong and avoiding him is wrong, but I just don't know what to do. I know Mom and I ruined the dog, and it's our fault that he behaves this way.

Part of my initial hypothesis was confirmed. The dog was being rewarded for barking. And the reward wasn't even a subtle one.

(6)

At this point I explained to them the effects of rewarding unwanted behavior. They understood. I also tried to relieve some of the guilt they were feeling about causing the problem. Guilt obviously doesn't solve the problem. If an owner's old habits cause a problem, then part of the solution is to change his habits, not to make him feel guilty.

However, it was becoming obvious that our conversation about guilt was not succeeding. After I explained that guilt is a poor motivation for change, the daughter said, "Perhaps you're right, but I still feel terribly guilty and ashamed. I have felt this way for years."

I decided to deal with guilt at a later meeting and to continue probing the problem. In order to proceed, I had them look at my Behavior Problem Checklist (see page 103).

When people come to see me about one problem, they usually check off approximately three to five problems in the list. These problems usually cluster around the main complaint. However, my present clients proceeded to check off 50 percent of the list. Over thirty problems, all in one dog, was quite unusual. In order to devise a complete treatment plan, I had to know in detail the exact nature of all the problems, how my clients had dealt with the problems in the past and how all the separate problems fit together. They would have to live with these problems a little longer while this information was being gathered. Since they had lived with the problems for so long, a few more weeks wouldn't matter.

They were somewhat disappointed that I didn't have a miracle up my sleeve. Many of my clients think I can give them a few words of advice or wave my hand magically over their dog and their problems will dissolve. However, these clients realized, probably for the first time, the severity of their problem, and agreed to be patient.

It is interesting to note that my clients had not fully realized how bizarre their dog was. The activity of just listing the problems allowed them to look at their pet more objectively.

(7)

It also pointed to behaviors that they did not consider problematic since they had gotten used to them. After all, they came to see me about a barking dog and initially made no mention of the other problems. They would have probably been much happier if I could have just dealt with the barking and ignored the other problems. But this was not to be the case. It was quite likely that all the problems were interrelated in some way. My job was to find the cause or causes and change them.

This brought me to another issue: Who was going to do the changing? Many of my clients initially think they can turn their dogs over to me and come back to a new, remade dog. In other words, abandon the responsibility to the professional. However, my clients are told that *they* are the ones who will work with their dog. If I did it, the dog would learn to behave with me but continue to misbehave with them. It is my job to help them objectively analyze the problem, come up with new methods and teach them how to use these methods effectively. It is *their* job to use these methods consistently and accurately and report back to me about the success or problems they are having. My present clients agreed to this and we proceeded with the analysis of the problems.

Feeding and Barking

The first type of behavior we analyzed was feeding. There can be many problems involved with this behavior and other behavior problems can also be influenced by feeding. We have already seen that feeding this dog biscuits may have rewarded barking.

DR. T: Can you tell me how your dog eats his meal? What I want to know is the way he eats. Does he eat rapidly? Is he a picky eater?
DAUGHTER: Picky eater! He eats all his meals like food was

going out of style. He eats so fast that you barely put the food down and he is finished. Then he wants more. He eats so fast that he sometimes vomits after he's finished.

DR. T: How often do you feed him and how much food does he get at any one meal?

DAUGHTER: He gets one whole can of food as his main meal. But he also gets a lot of snacks throughout the day. Sometimes we give him snacks but most of the time he just takes them.

DR. T: How does he take snacks? Do you leave food out for him?

DAUGHTER: No, he has two techniques for getting snacks. He demands to get whatever we are eating or he steals food.

DR. T: How does he demand food?

DAUGHTER: Well, he just barks and barks frantically whenever my mother and I are eating something. If I am eating a cookie or something he will run up and start barking at me. He won't stop until I give him the food. It's a high-pitched whining bark that gets on my nerves. He's totally unreasonable. He won't settle for just a piece, he has to have all the food you have. If you just give him a piece, he will gobble it up and start barking again. It has gotten so bad that I can't eat anything with him around. I think I have even lost weight because of him.

DR. T: Think back to when this started. I want to trace the history of this behavior from its very beginning. Try to to focus on how the behavior changed and how you dealt with it.

DAUGHTER: Well, it could have started when he was a puppy. He used to sit by the table and beg for food. He was so cute.

MOTHER: When we first got him, he would just sit by my feet while we were eating. He would patiently wait, looking up at me, until I gave him some food. My daughter didn't

(9)

think it was right to feed the dog from the table. I agreed with her, but I couldn't resist.

DR. T: When did you notice a change in his behavior from sitting quietly to demanding?

MOTHER: It must have been when he was around seven months old. We decided that he shouldn't beg from the table so we started ignoring him.

DAUGHTER: That's when it started to get bad. When we didn't pay attention to him he would try to attract our attention. First he started jumping up and putting his paws on our laps. Sometimes he would whimper. That's when my mother would give in and give him something.

MOTHER: Yes, I felt so guilty about giving in. I vowed not to give in the next time, but the longer I ignored him, the more distracting he became until finally I couldn't ignore him any longer. I figured it would be better to give him something and have a peaceful meal.

DR. T: What did you do when he whimpered?

DAUGHTER: We would push him down and say "No!"

MOTHER: But we didn't do that all the time. Sometimes we would just give him something.

DR. T: After you pushed him down what happened?

DAUGHTER: For a while he would just go away. But when he was about a year old, he started to get more persistent. He would come right back and jump on my lap again. But now it was with all four feet. He sat in my lap and stared at me eating, sometimes whimpering. I know you're supposed to ignore him, but how can you ignore a dog sitting in your lap?

MOTHER: He would refuse to be pushed off. He held on to my arm with his front legs. And sometimes he growled at us and would try to bite if we tried to push him off.

DR. T: How did you finally get him off?

MOTHER: My daughter and I would get up from the table and call Sebastian or we would throw a piece of food on the floor. He would jump down and eat it, but as soon as he was finished, he would be back on our laps for more.

DAUGHTER: This is when he really started getting demanding. He would try to jump. If we stopped, he would whimper and then very shortly thereafter start barking. The only way we could shut him up was with food.

MOTHER: Over the years his barking for food has gotten more and more shrill. In the beginning he would bark only after he had tried everything else. Now he starts barking as soon as we sit down to eat.

DAUGHTER: No, he barks *before* we sit down to eat. If he hears anyone in the kitchen he will run in barking and continue the racket until we give him something. This really makes me lose my temper.

DR. T: How can you have a peaceful meal with him around?

DAUGHTER: We can't! It got so bad that we would try to eat when Sebastian was sleeping. We would sneak into the kitchen very quietly get the food out and then eat it fast before he discovered we were eating. That worked for a while.

DR. T: What works now?

DAUGHTER: Nothing; he became too alert. He watches us all the time. If we make a move for the kitchen, he starts barking. Even if he is sound asleep on the other side of the house, the slightest kitchen noise will send him into a barking fit. What I used to do was make a mad dash for the kitchen, grab something from the refrigerator, then run in my room, close the door and try to eat.

DR. T: What does the dog do when you do that?

DAUGHTER: He chases me, grabbing my leg and barking. If I don't get out of the kitchen fast enough, he catches me. Then he wraps his front legs around my leg and holds on and barks. I usually can't get him off. Then I wind up walking around dragging the dog on my leg for ten minutes.

(11)

DR. T: What happens if you get to your room?

DAUGHTER: Then he usually sits by my door barking. He won't stop by himself. My mother has to come over and distract him. But it's not much of a problem any more.

DR. T: How come?

DAUGHTER: We never eat at home any more. It got so bad that we decided to go to restaurants to eat all our meals. That's really weird, isn't it? The dog has driven us out of the house. We only go there to sleep. I don't understand why Sebastian is so mean. We feed him, we treat him nicely, we don't hit him, we love him and he pays us back by kicking us out in the street!

At this point I tried to explain that to try to understand their dog in terms of human behavior was inappropriate. To expect their dog to be reasonable, and to be shocked or annoyed when it is not, implies that the dog can reason. Do not expect a dog to be reasonable. This does not mean, however, that a dog is completely incomprehensible. The nature of his behavior lies in an entirely different direction.

Let's take it from the dog's perspective for a moment. For this dog, eating is an important event. He not only eats ravenously but also spends much of his time acquiring food. Food is a powerful reward. From the dog's point of view, he is only doing what he was trained to do: bark to get food. This cannot be considered "unreasonable." So far, this is not an atypical problem; it is different in severity, but not in kind.

The Behavioral Trap

If one was going to deliberately set out to train a dog to bark, you could not do a better job than the owners of this dog did. The problem was that the owners did this unintentionally and therefore the procedure was not under their conscious control. They had fallen into a "behavioral trap": i.e., every attempt to correct the situation led to further intensification of the problem. Initially the dog sat quietly under the table begging for food and occasionally received table scraps. Since the mother was more likely to notice the dog when he whimpered or made noise, the animal soon learned that noisy behavior was likely to bring rewards. When the owners started ignoring the dog's begging behavior, he quite naturally escalated the level of noise and distraction.

The owners, feeling guilty about giving in to the dog's begging, would hold out for longer and longer periods of time. But it always ended in the dog getting his reward. From the dog's perspective it was simply the old adage. "If at first you don't succeed, try and try again."

When the dog became sexually mature, at about one year old, the quite natural begging behavior of a puppy turned into the assertive demanding behavior of a mature male dog. It must be pointed out that the owners were also being trained by the dog. The owners' desire was to have a peaceful dinner. They could achieve this, at least in the beginning, by giving in to the barking. This is the behavioral trap: the dog trains the owners to give in, while the owners train the dog to bark. The consequences of this trap are inevitable. This is a recipe for creating a monster.

Mothers of whining, demanding children will recognize the same trap, with a few changes in the scenario. Change the dog to a child, change the barking to whining, and there you have it: a recipe for creating a brat. In fact, I have never met a child who doesn't whine at least a little. No matter how conscientious the parent is, in moments of weakness, fatigue or strain, he or she is likely to reward the behavior that is most upsetting. But it does not follow that the situation is hopeless. All that is needed in fact is an understanding of the pattern. Then one can be on guard against it and take appropriate measures to correct it.

THE CLIENTS

After explaining this notion of the behavioral trap to my clients, I wondered how many of the other problems could be similarly explained. If their characteristic response to problematic behavior was to unintentionally reward the dog, it was quite possible that this could be the cause of all their problems. However, to make an a priori judgment without the facts would be a mistake. I explained this to my clients and gave them a homework assignment. They were to note the exact time every problem occurred, describe the problem, describe what transpired before the problem behavior, what they did to correct the behavior and what the dog's reaction was to this correction. In other words, they were to write a detailed behavioral diary of their day-to-day problems with the dog.

I explained to them that it would take a number of meetings to get the entire picture. They agreed to be patient and to be conscientious about the diary. Our next appointment was in five days, which would give them enough time to get the needed data. When they asked what to do when the dog started acting up, I told them to do what they used to do, except this time they were to record in the diary exactly what they did and the dog's reaction. I knew that they would not be able to fully follow this instruction. They had already begun to understand something about the dog's behavior, the way they handled problems and the effect of unintentional reward. This served to defuse some of their anxiety and guilt. As the session neared its end, they were speaking about the dog's problems with more objectivity.

At this point I felt it important to deal with a very critical issue, that is, why would anyone want to keep such a dog? My clients, probably for the first time, had a conception of the severity of their dog's problem. We had discussed the fact that the treatment could take a long time and be somewhat expensive. With this information in mind, I told them that there were other potential solutions. The dog could be "put to sleep," or they could try to find a new owner for the dog. Both of these solutions could be less time-consuming and troublesome. The question was, how did they feel about these solutions?

DAUGHTER: I don't like either of the solutions. We can't consider putting Sebastian to sleep. He is our dog. He is part of the family. No matter how bad he gets we couldn't do that. Besides, that would be like giving up. Since we caused the problem, I feel it is our responsibility to correct it. If we can't correct it, then we'll just have to live with it, somehow.

MOTHER: I agree partly with my daughter. I feel so guilty every time we look at Sebastian. We made him that way. And despite all the trouble he makes, we still love him. We just couldn't put him to sleep. Dr. T., you talked to us about guilt earlier and told us that it is not a good motive for doing something. Well, I can't tell you how guilty I would feel if Sebastian had to be put to sleep because of the way we treated him.

DR. T: You said you agreed partially with your daughter.

MOTHER: When it comes to finding Sebastian a new home, I feel that maybe on a farm, where he could run, he could get better somehow. Perhaps with someone else he could start acting more normal.

DAUGHTER: But that would also be giving up. We caused the problem and it is our responsibility to correct it. I would just hate it if we gave him away without at least trying. It's admitting failure. Besides, who would take such a crazy dog? Anyone who would want a dog like that would probably be crazy. Sebastian would go from the frying pan into the fire. And it wouldn't be right to lie about his problems, hoping that they wouldn't show up with

(15)

another person. Dr. T., how do you think he would act with someone else?

DR. T: It depends on who that someone else is. Your dog would probably be okay for a week or two with a new owner. This is called the "honeymoon effect." But when the honeymoon is over, he will start to try his old tricks. Since the tricks are very powerful, it is likely that they will work with a new owner. If that happens, Sebastian will get rewarded for his bad behavior and the whole cycle starts all over again. However, if a new owner really knew how to handle dog behavior problems, then it is possible that he or she could take advantage of the honeymoon effect and start rewarding good behavior.

DAUGHTER: Well, I want to try first. I don't like giving up and I don't like failure.

The daughter's desire to deal with the dog's problems, while admirable, was worrying me. This desire did not seem to be motivated by a true concern for the dog, but rather by guilt and fear of failure. I explained this to them and tried to deal with the notions of success and failure.

The daughter appeared to be a person doomed to failure in any activity she chose. (I determined this from independent conversations with the daughter and her mother.) Her goals were unrealistic; she set them too high to be attained in any reasonable period of time. She needed to be rewarded for her attempts to help her dog. And in this case her reward would most logically be an improvement in the dog's behavior. Unfortunately, the daughter defined improvement as complete cure, the removal of all aberrant behavior. As this could take months, the daughter would be likely to give up and experience failure before this time.

In order to overcome this attitude, I explained the notion of subgoals: i.e., partial goals that can be attained fairly quickly. Consequently, instead of shooting for the complete elimina-

(16)

tion of barking, the aim would be to eliminate some portion of the barking. The idea is to try during the first week to get the barking to three-quarters of its original level, try for more the second week and so on. With a subgoal as the aim, you begin with the problem that is most easily and rapidly changed. Then, as you succeed with the easier one, proceed to the more difficult problems. However, I was not sure that the barking problem was going to be the easiest. Perhaps it would be better to deal with another behavioral problem first.

I gave my clients a second homework assignment. They were to take my Behavior Problem Checklist (see page 103) and rate the problems in order of priority. The daughter was also asked to write her subgoals for the elimination of barking. I wanted to see if she understood how subgoals worked.

After my clients left, I wondered how long it would take to untangle the entire case. Since we had gotten over the preliminaries we could move faster in subsequent meetings. My subgoals were as follows: (a) completely outline the problems in the next two meetings; (b) get enough information in the second meeting so that tentative treatment plans could be described by the third meeting; (c) elaborate and define the treatment plan for subsequent meetings. I hoped that the entire procedure would not take longer than eight meetings, or four to five weeks. I had no illusions that the problems would be solved in this period of time. I estimated that this could take from six to eight months. What I wanted was to arm my clients with enough knowledge so that they could continue on their own, developing new treatment plans and modifying old plans as needed.

THE SECOND APPOINTMENT

It has been one week since the first meeting. During this time my clients have called me twice. The first call concerned the behavioral diary. The second call had to do with a minor altercation between the dog and the daughter.

My clients arrived at 9:00 P.M. sharp. This time both were willing to take off their coats. I hypothesized that they were feeling more comfortable with me. They did appear generally more relaxed and seemed eager to start the session. The daughter especially seemed to be in better spirits.

THE PROBLEM INTENSIFIED

DR. T: How did it go last week? Were you able to keep the behavioral diary?

MOTHER: We were able to do it for a couple of days, then Sebastian was taken to the vet to get his stomach fixed again. This time he got into my jewelry box and ate a number of earrings and a brooch. He is okay now.

DR. T: I see on your Behavior Problem Checklist that you have checked the eating of non-nutritional substances. Could you tell me a little more about this?

DAUGHTER: He eats everything. We have to take him to the vet at least three to four times a year.

DR. T: I have to know more about what you mean by "eating." Does he chew on things in the house and accidentally swallow or does he actually *eat* these things? Also, what does he eat?

DAUGHTER: When he swallows something it is not an accident. My mother's jewelry wasn't even damaged. There weren't any teeth marks on any of it. He just swallowed the jewelry.

MOTHER: He doesn't seem to have any favorites. In the past four years he has eaten tissues, soap, nails, glass, chicken bones, tacks, garbage, pine cones, pebbles and candles.

DAUGHTER: He also has eaten my ring and glasses, pens, the

toothpaste tube and combs. He also has the disgusting habit of eating his own waste.

DR. T: Does he eat any typical things like old shoes or chew up the furniture?

DAUGHTER: No, he's never chewed the furniture. He occasionally gets my shoe but if I chase him he runs away and drops the shoe without damaging it. He seems to eat only small stuff.

DR. T: What I need to know is the whole sequence of behavior. How does he get the items? When he has something in his mouth, what do you do about it? How do you feel when you think he's got something?

MOTHER: Well, I get very nervous. He's somewhat of a sickly dog and all I see is another trip to the vet. That can get pretty expensive. So when we think he's got something we try to look in his mouth and take it away from him.

DAUGHTER: Let's start from the beginning. Sebastian usually finds these things on the floor, or outside on the ground. We try to be careful about dropping things but if something is on the floor, he will find it. Sometimes he will take things off my desk or from a chair.

DR. T: Does he eat everything that is near him, like a vacuum cleaner?

DAUGHTER: No, many times he just ignores things or walks over them. He could be lying right near something and completely ignore it. But if you go to pick it up, he will immediately grab it and hold it in his mouth. He is sneaky too. We were walking him a couple of days ago and I suspected that he had picked up a pebble, but every time I looked in his mouth there was nothing there. Then he started moving his jaws and drooling like he had something. The next time I looked under his tongue. There it was! He was hiding the pebble under his tongue.

(19)

Guarding

DR. T: You say he grabs things only when you pick up the items; this could be "guarding." Many dogs have this problem. The only difference here is that your dog swallows what he is guarding.

DAUGHTER: He picks things up even if you have no intention of taking the thing away. If you just walk in his direction or if you get close to him by mistake he will do the same thing.

DR. T: What do you do if you notice that he has something? How do you take it away?

DAUGHTER: It wasn't always this bad. If my mother noticed he had something, she would panic and tell me to take it away. Then I would usually hit him and say, "No." Then we gave him something else to chew on, like a bone or a hard dog biscuit. We figured he just wanted to chew on something and if we gave him something good, he wouldn't pay attention to the uneatable stuff.

DR. T: What do you do now?

DAUGHTER: Now, he runs away from me. Then everything explodes. My mother starts screaming and we both chase him around the house. He's gotten very hard to catch. At first, I could pry his mouth open but now he's gotten much worse. He tries to bite me, so my mother opens his mouth while I hold him. It is at this time that he sometimes swallows what he has in his mouth.

MOTHER: Now when he has something, he makes a beeline for my room and hides under the bed. It's impossible to get to him. He just barks, snarls and snaps.

DR. T: What do you do?

MOTHER: We call him. We try to distract him from the thing he has in his mouth.

DR. T: How do you distract him?

DAUGHTER: We say something like, "Do you want to go out?" Then we get his leash or throw a ball or get his favorite toy. Sometimes I go to the kitchen and operate the can opener to make him think I am opening a can of food. That worked for a while, but when he came to the kitchen he started barking and wouldn't stop until I gave him something.

DR. T: Does this kitchen trick still work?

DAUGHTER: No. The only way we can distract him now is to give him food or cookies or a bone. Then he drops what he has and eats the treat. If we are not fast enough, he will gobble up the treat and then immediately pick up the thing again. Sometimes he keeps his foot on the object while he eats the treat.

DR. T: You said that initially you would take an item away from Sebastian and then hit him. Where do you hit him, how often and how hard? Also, when do you hit him?

DAUGHTER: Since I am the one who did all the disciplining, I should answer the question. I hated having to be the one but someone had to do it.

DR. T: Tell me exactly what you did. Some people use a rolled-up newspaper or magazine as a spanking tool. Is this what you used?

DAUGHTER: Sometimes, but a newspaper wasn't always available. I usually just hit him with my hand.

DR. T: Where did you hit him?

DAUGHTER: No special place. Whatever was closest, I guess. You see, when I got the thing out of his mouth, many times he would break away from me, and then I would chase him and get him in the rear end. If he tried to bite me, then he would get it in the face.

DR. T: How hard did you hit Sebastian?

DAUGHTER: That varied too. But usually it wasn't very hard.

MOTHER: I think we'd better tell the doctor the whole story. You see, my daughter loses her temper a lot. And when

(21)

you lose your temper, you hit a lot harder than you think, and then you don't calm down for hours.

DAUGHTER: This has always been a sore point with us. My mother and sister don't believe in hitting the dog. The arguments got so bad that my sister would beat me up if I hit Sebastian. But someone had to do it. I think that Sebastian acts the way he does because my mother coddles him. She thinks that Sebastian's problems came from me hitting him.

MOTHER: You don't just hit him. You beat him and even kick him.

DR. T: How do you feel when you hit the dog?

DAUGHTER: I feel angry. I am angry at Sebastian and I am angry at my mother and sister for coddling him, and I end up with the responsibility for disciplining him. Let's settle this once and for all. Let's ask the doctor who is at fault. Who do you think was guilty?

I explained that the concept of guilt or fault was not appropriate. This was not a trial. We were here to analyze the problem and find a solution. It was important to discover the cause-and-effect relationships that led to the development of the problem. Each of the family members, including the dog, probably had a causal part in the creation and maintenance of the situation.

The manner in which they tried to correct the situation made the problems worse. But they could not help this. What was important was to determine present causes and eliminate them. The development of the problem, the past causes, are important only as a source of instruction so as not to repeat the cycle all over again.

I explained that guarding things is probably normal behavior in dogs. One had only to watch TV natural history films of wild dogs, wolves and other canines to see guarding behavior in the raw.

(22)

The domestic dog still possesses this genetic program for guarding. However, generations of domestication have reduced its intensity and made it more unpredictable.

So we start with a dog guarding inappropriate objects. The next step toward disaster came with my clients' attempt to change this behavior by using punishment. Punishment can result in escalation. If a little punishment doesn't work, then hit harder, scream louder. In addition, punishment is usually administered when the person is angry and has lost any semblance of sound judgment. Finally, hitting an animal will quite naturally cause the animal to fear you and consequently run away or attack you. If you then chase the animal or hit it some more for attacking you, you establish a vicious cycle. Each attack leads to more punishment, which leads to more attack. Each chase leads to more running away, which leads to more chasing. The behavioral trap is set. The results are inevitable.

This is exactly what happened to my clients. The daughter's anger at the dog and her mother and sister contributed to the escalation of the problem. The next step in escalation came from the mother. In order to avoid having to resort to punishing, she tried to cajole or distract the dog away from the guarded object. However, this served to reward the animal for the very behavior that they wanted to eliminate. Thus, behaving as if they were going to take the dog out served as a reward for guarding. When this trick stopped working, the daughter escalated the reward. She operated the can opener in the kitchen. This was eventually followed by giving the dog food on demand. We already know how rewarding food is to this dog. This can opener trick had two results: First, it served to reward the guarding, and second, it served to associate the guarding with the other behavioral problem of demanding food. The second behavioral trap was set and sprung. This resulted in the ultimate situation: the owners handing biscuits to the dog while he was under the bed guarding the objects. The dog would guard the object, then they would reward him, and in return he would continue to guard.

This analysis leaves unexplained two aspects of this dog's bizarre feeding behavior. First, why did the dog eat such an amazing variety of objects? There seemed to be no connection between these items, except that they were all small. The answer was that the object had to be small enough to carry and guard easily and it had to be easily available.

The second question was, why did the dog persist in consuming these objects? Why didn't he just stop at guarding them? It was quite unlikely that the dog was eating these things for nutritional or gustatory reasons. In order to answer this question, more information was needed concerning the dog's eating behavior during its daily meal. You will recall that this dog eats his meal very rapidly. So rapidly, in fact, that he occasionally vomits. The question was, does this dog guard his food?

DR. T: I am interested in how your dog eats his daily meal. You say that he eats so fast that he occasionally vomits. Can you predict when he will vomit and when he won't?

DAUGHTER: He doesn't vomit if we just put the food down and immediately leave the room. But if we have to go into the kitchen for some reason or if we don't leave, that's when he's likely to vomit. It's as if he thinks we are going to take his food away. If we go up to him while he's eating, he huddles down over his food and gobbles it down in two bites. I don't understand why he would think we were going to take his food away when we just gave it to him.

MOTHER: I have noticed another thing. A couple of days ago, I fed Sebastian, then went out of the kitchen and waited about fifteen minutes before reentering. When I returned, he was sitting at the other end of the kitchen and his food was untouched. I walked over to him to see what was the matter. Sebastian jumped up, ran to his food dish and started eating.

DR. T: What did you do then?

MOTHER: Well, of course I left immediately.

DR. T: When you returned had he finished his meal?

MOTHER: No, that was the funny part. I came back a few minutes later and he was just sitting there. I think he was waiting for me to return. This time I just stayed by the kitchen door and he finished his meal.

All the pieces fit. Sebastian was swallowing inedible objects because of a queer set of associations. After the can opener trick, guarding had become closely associated with eating and, consequently, swallowing. Rapid bulk swallowing had been associated with the presence of the owners. This association was so strong that the mere sight of the mother influenced the dog's eating. All these associations caused the dog to swallow what he had in his mouth when the owners approached him. When it was suspected that the dog had something in his mouth, he was chased, caught, held tightly or cornered. It is surprising that the dog didn't swallow more objects.

At this point, I felt that we had a pretty good handle on both the feeding and barking problems. We had also determined how the two were related. But the dog had a number of other problems: drinking, fighting, fear, elimination, exploring, care of the body surface, resting and operant (see list, page 103).

It was becoming more probable that all these had a common cause. Since any organism is a functioning, integrated whole, it was possible that these aberrant behaviors of Sebastian's were interrelated. Suppressing one behavior could be analogous to squeezing an inflated balloon. Since a balloon is a closed system, squeezing one part causes the other parts to expand.

Suppressing one problem could lead to a reduction in one behavior and an exaggeration of some or all of the others. There are a number of techniques available for reducing problem behavior. The question was whether to use them or not.

I decided to exhaust the behavioral checklist. The only way to proceed was to get a complete picture of all the behaviors and try to deduce all possible interrelations. Then a treatment plan could be created and an estimate made about the potential effects of the plan. If such an estimate was supported by the results, then there would be evidence to continue. If unexpected results occurred, then the plan could be changed. This empirical approach to solving problems is the basis of the scientific method.

I explained to my clients how we were going to proceed and went into some details outlining the scientific method. This was necessary for two reasons. First, the more scientific their thinking became, the more objective would be their analysis of the problems and the faster we could proceed. And second, eventually these people would be dealing with their dog without my assistance. If future problems arose, they would need such skills.

Elimination

The next problem I decided to deal with in depth was elimination. As with feeding and barking, I was interested in all aspects of this behavior.

DR. T: I would like to deal with your dog's elimination problem. Tell me, how frequently do you take him for a walk?

DAUGHTER: Oh, we take him out all the time and he still goes in the house.

MOTHER: He has ruined two carpets. We used to have wall-to-wall carpeting but now we just have bare floors. I don't understand this problem at all. I can see now how we could have rewarded the barking and eating, but he never gets food if he soils.

DR. T: What do you mean by "taking him out all the time"? Twice a day? Three times a day?

DAUGHTER: I can take him out ten times a day and he still soils in the house. He does go when we are out but it seems like he always saves some for inside. I think he does it on purpose, just to annoy me. I know what you said about attributing human motives to dogs, but I still think he does it out of spite. He knows it disgusts me.

MOTHER: My daughter has taken him out a lot. But most days he gets taken out three times. In the morning around 6:00 A.M., 3:00 P.M. in the afternoon and in the evening at 10:00 P.M. That should be enough, shouldn't it?

DR. T: Yes, it should. Could you tell me about his soiling behavior in the house? Does this occur every day? When and where does it occur? Does your dog both defecate and urinate in the house?

DAUGHTER: He does everything, everywhere. For example, a couple of weeks ago, Sebastian had diarrhea. So I took him out at least six times. I had paper all over the floors. When we went to bed, I went to my room and Sebastian went to my mother's room, where he always sleeps. We put paper on the floor in her bedroom too. At about 2:00 or 3:00 A.M., I woke up because I heard a strange sound. I turned and there was Sebastian squatting by my left ear, defecating. Now, Dr. T., you have to realize that Sebastian had to go out of my mom's room, walk over all those papers, push open my door, jump on my bed, and then squat by my ear. If that's not spite, I don't know what is.

DR. T: That's quite a story. What did you do? Does he do that all the time?

DAUGHTER: God, no! He only did it once. When it happened I was so surprised and shocked, I didn't know what to do.

(27)

I guess I just started screaming. But later I wanted to kill the dog. If it wasn't for my mother intervening, I would have.

MOTHER: Well, you gave him some pretty good kicks anyway.

DR. T: It seems to me that that would have been the last straw.

DAUGHTER: It almost was but I got over it in a few days. Since then, I always keep my door closed and it has never happened again.

DR. T: Since it has not happened again, it makes it difficult to determine the cause. It is possible that your dog was sleeping on your bed when he had the urge. However, since you have solved the problem by keeping your door closed at night, it would be more meaningful to explore other aspects of your dog's elimination problem. Dogs usually give some signs when they are about to go. Some dogs will sniff and walk in circles before they defecate or sniff a vertical object before they lift their leg. What signs does your dog give?

DAUGHTER: He doesn't give any signs. I'll just be walking in the hall and find him squatting. He doesn't lift his leg, he squats when he urinates. Dr. T., I think this could be important: My mother thinks that this squatting posture is cute.

MOTHER: Well, it does look cute to me.

DAUGHTER: And you make a big fuss. Talking baby talk to him. Then I have to come in and discipline him.

DR. T: How do you discipline him?

DAUGHTER: We tried a number of ways. I read somewhere that if you keep him caged up, he won't dirty the cage. We did this when he was a puppy. But it didn't work. He would just go and get it all over himself. This is when my mother started making a big fuss over him.

DR. T: What do you mean by fuss?

DAUGHTER: Well, she would talk baby talk to him, and wash and comb him.

(28)

MOTHER: I felt so guilty about him being locked up for so
long in a small box. He looked so sad. You know how
a puppy can look. I just wanted him to know that we
loved him.

DR. T: What do you do now?

DAUGHTER: I hit him on the rear.

DR. T: Some people think that they can bring their dog to
the place where it has soiled and punish the dog. Do
you do this?

DAUGHTER: Sometimes, but other times I catch him in the
act.

DR. T: What does Sebastian do when you hit him?

DAUGHTER: He does what he always does when I hit him. He
jumps up and holds on to my leg with his front paws.

DR. T: Then what?

DAUGHTER: I used to hit him when he held my leg. I couldn't
stand that. But if I hit him he tried to bite me. Now I
just wait till he gets tired and lets go. Once I walked
around the house for at least two minutes with him
attached to my leg.

MOTHER: That's not what usually happens. You usually yell
for me to get him off.

DR. T: And what do you do to get him off?

MOTHER: I try to distract him. I call to him or bounce a
ball. I say, "Come on, Sebastian, let's go see what
Mommy's got," or "Come on, Sebastian, let's go get a
Milk Bone." Then he lets go and runs into the kitchen
barking. I have to give him a dog biscuit or he won't
stop barking.

My clients had managed to find a way to reward defecation
and urination. This was done in two ways. When Sebastian
was a puppy, the reward was attention. As an adult, the dog's
reward was food. It would be instructive to trace the origin
of the problem. It all started with confining the puppy to a

(29)

small box. This may sound cruel, like some kind of solitary confinement, and basically it is. However, my clients were not intentionally being cruel. They were simply following the advice that many owners of new puppies have gotten through so-called dog books or other sources. This canned advice belongs with all other canned advice, in the garbage can.

Confinement as a treatment for an incontinent puppy or adult dog is based on partial information. The notion is that dogs will not soil where they sleep. If one looks at adult wild canines, you will notice that they keep their den or sleeping quarters clean. Wild canine bitches keep their den free of the waste produced by their offspring by removing or eating it. They defecate and urinate to mark their territory, but it would make little sense to mark where you are sleeping.

There are two false assumptions about using confinement treatment on a puppy. The first is that a puppy is a miniature adult, with all the innate behaviors fully developed. This is obviously false, since it's the bitch who keeps the nest clean. Thus, the puppies must be dirtying the nest. The second false assumption is that domestic dogs are just tame copies of their wild cousins. Generations of domestic breeding have had a variety of effects. One effect is to make the behavior of the domestic dog as a species more variable. Thus, some dogs will have strong inhibitions about dirtying their sleeping area; others will have no inhibitions at all.

My clients obviously confined their puppy for long periods. This had two effects. Since the puppy was confined for long periods, he would have to soil this area. Then the puppy got covered with his own waste. This would have the effect of reducing whatever aversion the puppy may innately have had to his own waste. You will be able to appreciate this if you will reflect on how pungent the smell of a hospital is when you first enter and how this strong smell seems to fade with time in the hospital. The second effect of confining the puppy was to deprive him of the attention and care he needed. Thus, any attention given by the mother was rewarding to the puppy. The only way the puppy could get this attention was to get himself dirty.

Later on, when the dog was an adult, another mechanism for reward was used: the establishment of a behavioral ritual. The ritual never varied. The dog would defecate or urinate. The mother would think the posture was cute and consequently attend to the dog. The daughter would punish the dog. The dog would hold on to the daughter's leg. The mother would reward the dog by distraction or food. This ritual was repeated day after day.

My clients did not realize they were rewarding elimination for two reasons. First, the mother did not understand that giving attention was a reward. Second, the food reward came at the *end* of a behavioral sequence that began with elimination. The puppy was in fact being trained to eliminate in the house and also being trained to attack the daughter.

After explaining the origin of their dog's elimination problem to my clients, I told them that this problem would probably be the most difficult to stop. Both the elimination and barking were part of a long-standing behavioral ritual that involved ingrained habits on the part of the owners as well as the dog. In order to reduce these problems it would be necessary to change the owners' behavior that supported the problems. Just telling the owners what they were doing wrong was not enough. For example, if you are overweight you know what you are doing wrong. You eat too much. But just being told to stop eating rarely works. The owners had to gradually learn to undo old, ingrained habits. And they had to be rewarded for this gradual change.

In order to determine where we were, I made an inventory of what problems had already been dealt with. We had discussed feeding, barking and elimination. We had also covered fighting and fear when we talked about the guarding and eating inedible objects and the effects of punishment. The exploring problem was related to the excessive chewing and mouthing of things. What remained to be discussed was excessively rapid drinking, bizarre behavior rituals, lack of obedience, excitability, excessive hair chewing and sexual behavior.

It was getting late, my clients seemed tired and so was I. I told them what was left to be covered and we agreed to deal with these problems at the next meeting. I scheduled them for an appointment in three days. In the meantime they were to continue making a daily diary of their dog's problem behavior. They were to think about the problems that we had gone over to see if there was any important aspects we had failed to uncover. They were also to think about the problems that had yet to be discussed. This would help to organize their thoughts and allow us to get the information more expeditiously. They agreed.

I promised to outline a tentative treatment plan at the end of the next meeting. I felt this was possible because I had already been entertaining some hypotheses and formulating some treatment plans during this meeting. They felt good about this and seemed to be relieved that at least someone else was sharing their problem.

REVIEW OF THE PROBLEM

As I later went over the pages of notes, I thought of how complex this case seemed to be and how this would make treatment more difficult. Complex problems sometimes need complex solutions, but if these became too complex, my clients were bound to make mistakes that could generate new problems.

As I thought about the potential solution, I had the uneasy feeling that I had not been told the whole story. There were a number of clues that led me to suspect some deeper problems.

The first was the girl's appearance. A fifteen-year-old doesn't dress the way she did. Perhaps this was an attempt to appear unconcerned with frivolities, which would be consistent with her inordinate fixation on responsibility. Yet I noted she did not deal with her dog's problems responsibly. She continually got angry and threw temper tantrums. She also seemed to harbor much hostility toward her mother and sister. Many times this hostility seemed to be directed at the dog. She seemed to accept the responsibility for the dog's discipline grudgingly, as if it was forced upon her by what she perceived as her mother's and sister's lack of responsibility. This would lead her to displace more of her aggressions onto the dog.

Until now her feeling toward her father had not been discussed. I had learned that the father died four years ago and that the younger daughter and the father were very close and the daughter was extremely depressed about her father's death, feeling somehow responsible for it. Since the dog was four years old, the family must have gotten the dog about the time of the father's death. In this case the dog could symbolize a wide variety of things. His close association with the death could be a constant reminder to the mother. The daughter could associate the dog with the first time responsibility was thrust upon her by the death of her father.

The mother's behavior also concerned me. She did agree to remove her coat at our second meeting, but she did not remove her gloves. She seemed to be a very anxious woman who was barely coping with her life. If she had so much trouble handling the dog problem, how much trouble would she have handling the problems of two teenage girls, especially after a death? She also seemed to invest an extreme amount of emotion in the dog, but considerably less emotion toward the problems the dog was causing.

It was possible that the dog's problems served a very useful function. By being so disruptive, the dog became the focus of the family's attention. This would divert attention away from

(33)

the interpersonal problems that the mother and daughter might be experiencing. They could discuss why the dog did this or that, argue about who was at fault in creating the situation, and argue about how to deal with the dog's problems. Thus they were not dealing with their own problems or feelings toward each other.

Another, more devastating, function could be that the dog enacted the hostility the mother and daughter felt toward each other. The mother did not seem to be able to express anger and hostility. However, she could have unintentionally trained the dog to attack the daughter as well as unintentionally trained the daughter to bring on this attack. And, as already discussed, the daughter could be displacing her feeling of aggression for her mother onto the dog. The dog in fact becomes an unintentional messenger of hostility.

The magnitude of the potential number of alternative explanations fatigued me. If my ruminations bore any semblance to reality, then the dog's problems could be very difficult to solve. I made a note to explore some of these issues at the next meeting.

THE THIRD APPOINTMENT

It had been three days since our last meeting. I wondered about the prognosis of my clients' problems. If my speculations were correct, the prognosis was not hopeful.

My clients arrived at 7:00 P.M. Both seemed to be in good spirits. They took their coats off and seated themselves before I suggested it. This was a sign that they were more comfortable. The mother had also removed her gloves. I noticed a difference in the way they were seated. In the past meetings they sat back from the table. The daughter usually kept her hands in her pockets. The mother usually kept her hands clasped together on her lap. This time they sat close to the table. The daughter leaned forward with her elbows leisurely placed on the table. The mother still clasped her hands but her grip appeared to be looser. She also leaned forward.

I fixed myself a cup of coffee and as usual offered them some. I had done this during the previous meetings but they always refused. This time, however, they accepted my offer. All of these were signs that my clients were feeling more comfortable with me, a necessary condition if I was to explore some of the more delicate issues concerning the feelings felt toward each other and the father's death. Of course I would explore those areas only to the extent that it related to the problems with their dog.

THE PROBLEM AGAIN

DAUGHTER: I tried a little experiment yesterday. I think I found out something about Sebastian's barking.

DR. T: Good. Tell me about it.

DAUGHTER: I was thinking back to a couple of months ago when my mother took a trip. I was alone with Sebastian for two weeks. That was the most pleasant two weeks I had in years. Sebastian was no problem at all.

DR. T: How did he behave during that time?

DAUGHTER: He slept most of the time. He hardly barked at all. Come to think of it, I don't seem to have trouble with Sebastian when I'm alone with him. It's when my mother and I are together that the trouble starts.

MOTHER: I found the same thing. When I'm alone with Sebastian I don't remember him being a bother at all. I never realized this until just now. I guess I only think about him when he is causing trouble. That's when he draws my attention.

DR. T: It appears that an important stimulus for the barking is when you are together.

(35)

DAUGHTER: That's where my experiment comes in. Yesterday I was alone with Sebastian all day. He was quietly lazing around. I was thinking about the notion of a behavioral ritual. I tried to go over in my mind the exact sequence of events that happens when Sebastian starts barking or attacking me. It came to me that he doesn't start until I call my mother for help.

DR. T: If he doesn't start until you call your mother, then why do you call her for help?

DAUGHTER: I try to anticipate problems. If I am going to the kitchen or if Sebastian is starting to pester me, then I tell my mother to call him. I hope that this will distract him away from me.

DR. T: Tell me more about your experiment.

DAUGHTER: As I said, Sebastian was resting quietly and I said, "Mom, call Sebastian." My mother wasn't home at the time. Sebastian jumped up and immediately started barking at me and looking around the house for my mother. He eventually settled down and I went into another room and said, "Mom, get this dog away from me." He came running from the other room, barking.

DR. T: It's possible that just hearing your voice could cause him to bark. Did you try saying something else?

DAUGHTER: Yes. I figured that too, so I read aloud from the Bible and he didn't bark. Then I said things like "Apples are sweet" and "Have a banana" and Sebastian didn't bark. It just seems to be those words.

DR. T: That could be, or it could be your tone of voice.

MOTHER: That's possible. When I returned home, I said what I usually say and Sebastian started his happy fits and then started barking at my daughter.

DAUGHTER: All that evening and all day today we vowed not to raise our voices. We just whispered to each other or we would pass notes. He was fine until this afternoon.

DR. T: What happened then?

DAUGHTER: He followed me all day. He seemed to be waiting for me to make a mistake. But I was careful. Then I was lying on the couch reading and he came up and sat there just staring at me. He seemed to be spoiling for a fight.

DR. T: What did you do?

DAUGHTER: I tried to ignore him. I turned my back to him and kept reading but I could feel his eyes just staring at me. Then he started a very low whimper and then a low growl. I couldn't stand it. As soon as I said, "Mom," he was all over me, barking and holding.

DR. T: That was an interesting experiment. It tells me a lot more about your dog's barking problem.

Not only was this dog trained to bark and attack the daughter, but he did it on command. It is not unusual or difficult to train a dog to do this. What was different here was that the command to attack was given by the victim. What was most hopeful was that the daughter was starting to think more scientifically and was viewing Sebastian's problems more objectively.

I thought it important to continue with the rest of the problems.

Drinking and Foot-Chewing

DR. T: I would like to deal with the rest of the problems. Let's start with drinking.

DAUGHTER: Yes, he drinks all the time. We got him one of those gallon drinking bowls, you know, the really large one for big dogs. We have to fill it at least two times a day. He also drinks from the toilet bowl.

DR. T: What would happen if you didn't leave so much water around all day?

DAUGHTER: Then he would bark at his water dish or push it around the kitchen and whimper. He won't stop until we give him water. Then he drinks so much that he has to urinate an hour later.

DR. T: What would happen if you picked up the water dish?

DAUGHTER: I don't know; we never tried it.

DR. T: Okay, try this since you walk your dog three times a day. Give him a measured quantity of water about a half hour before each walk. After he finishes the water, remove the dish.

DAUGHTER: What if he doesn't finish?

DR. T: Give him sixteen ounces at a time and about eight minutes to finish the water. If he doesn't finish it, then pick up the dish. He doesn't get any water until the next watering period.

DAUGHTER: Then he will drink from the toilet.

DR. T: Keep the bathroom door closed.

MOTHER: I am afraid that he will get dehydrated or something.

DR. T: Don't worry about that. Forty-eight ounces of water a day is enough for any dog. It's possible that your dog is urinating in the house because he is drinking too much. Restricting his water intake will restrict his output to the period of time during his walk.

DAUGHTER: If he gets frustrated about not having water, I am afraid that something else might happen.

DR. T: What's that?

DAUGHTER: He will probably start chewing on his feet. He seems to do this when he is frustrated or when we ignore him.

DR. T: That brings us to the care-of-the-body-surface behavior. How does your dog chew on his feet?

DAUGHTER: He bites the hair on his front feet with his front teeth. You know, like dogs bite parts of their body when they have fleas.

DR. T: So he doesn't chew on his feet like a bone; he nibbles with his incisors.

DAUGHTER: Yes, but this nibbling causes a lot of damage.

(38)

Sometimes he nibbles all the hair off his feet. His feet become red and sore. He sometimes bites himself so hard that he bleeds.

DR. T: And what do you do when he starts chewing his feet?

DAUGHTER: We have done a lot of things. We tried punishing him, distracting him with a toy, or giving him something else to chew on like a bone. We can't ignore him or he will bite his feet raw.

DR. T: What happens if you punish him?

DAUGHTER: The same routine that happens when we try to punish him for other things. He grabs my leg. Then my mother has to get him off me. You know, he really must be crazy; he guards his feet like he guards his food or an uneatable object.

DR. T: What happens if you approach him while he is chewing his feet?

DAUGHTER: That's the funny part. He puts his foot in his mouth and growls. The growling sounds so dumb. It's sort of a muffled sound. If I get closer he will try to get up with his foot in his mouth. Then he hobbles away on three legs, trying to get under the table or my mother's bed.

DR. T: You're right, that is very peculiar behavior. I have had cases of hair-chewing before, but never one like this. Tell me, what do you do to stop him?

DAUGHTER: We don't punish him any more. I try not to walk up to him. Sometimes I tell my mother to call to him. Sometimes I throw dog biscuits to him. This usually stops him for a while. He gets so interested in the food, he forgets about his feet. I guess this means that we are rewarding him for chewing his feet?

Dr. T: That's right. You're starting to get the point. I'd like to know a little more about the history of this behavior. Some dogs will suck on parts of their body when they are puppies. Was this so in Sebastian's case?

DAUGHTER: Yes, Sebastian did that. He would suck on his feet. It didn't seem to be too bad and my mother thought it was so cute.

MOTHER: He was like a little baby sucking on his thumb.

DAUGHTER: This is when my mother started her baby talk. She would say, "Ah, look at the little baby sucking on his thumb. Come to Mama." I can't stand it when she talks baby talk to him. She still does it.

DR. T: Then you would pick Sebastian up and pet him?

MOTHER: Yes, I would hold him in my arms like a baby and talk to him or pet him. He just lay there quietly sucking his paws. Do you think that's why he chews his feet now?

DR. T: Yes. But that's not really important now. You couldn't know that your attention to Sebastian when he was a puppy would lead to his present problems.

MOTHER: I guess so, but it seems as if we have done everything wrong with this dog.

DR. T: Let's focus on the present and the future. Past mistakes are important only because they tell us what *not* to do in the future.

MOTHER: Maybe so, but I don't see any way to stop him.

DR. T: The key to many of your problems including this one is to get strong inhibitory control over your dog's behavior. He must stop whatever he is doing when you say, "No." We will be starting this inhibitory training with your dog's feeding problems. The whole idea is for the word "no" to stop Sebastian without your having to approach him.

The drinking problem may have started as a reaction to stress. My clients' household was probably a very stressful environment for everyone concerned. There were obviously arguments between the daughter, mother and older sister. The father's death probably resulted in a large amount of emotional turmoil. And, finally, the dog was treated inconsistently. He would alternately be punished, rewarded, kicked, yelled at and coddled. All this would lead to a very stressful environment indeed. There is ample research evidence concerning the effect of stress on behavior. We know from laboratory studies that stress from frustration or fear can cause excessive drinking. This is called polydipsia. I was hoping that as my clients learned to deal with their dog correctly, this would reduce some of the drinking problem.

The drinking problem had similarities to the feeding problem. The dog would demand water by barking or pushing his bowl around. He had learned that this behavior was rewarded by water. The technique of giving the dog a measured amount of water at a definite time and for a prescribed duration and ignoring his demands at other times would reduce this behavior. This would also restrict the dog's intake of water, which would go a long way in decreasing the frequency of urination. We would arrange it so that the dog would urinate when he was outside for a walk. This would allow the owners to start rewarding the correct elimination behavior with praise or a dog biscuit.

The foot-biting problem had aspects that were similar to the feeding and guarding problems. The way this dog bit and guarded his feet was uncommon. However, self-abusive behavior is not in itself uncommon. At first the behavior is not serious enough to cause damage, but is unusual enough to attract attention. Then the dog is rewarded with attention for this behavior. A key aspect of the pattern is that the dog is ignored much of the time and so resorts to self-abuse in order to attract attention. The caretakers will learn to ignore this low-level abuse as they get used to it. Then the behavior will become more intense or violent until again it is rewarded by attention. At the same time the nerves in the abused portion of the body are becoming desensitized. Thus the dog does not feel the pain that comes from such abuse. In my clients' case, the dog would actually bite his foot until it bled.

Sebastian's reward was attention, distraction and feeding. The problem went one step further in that it became associated, quite naturally, with the other reward-getting behaviors. Thus the dog would guard his own foot and even carry it off if approached. I'm sure he would have swallowed his foot if it wasn't attached to his leg. I explained this to my clients and then we proceeded to discuss the rest of the problems.

Sexual Behavior

Next we dealt with sexual behavior. One component of sexual behavior in a dog is foreleg holding, i.e., the male dog will grasp its partner and start copulation. This grasping behavior is similar to Sebastian's response when he was punished.

DR. T: You have checked sexual behavior on the Behavior Problem Checklist. Tell me, has your dog ever directed his sexual activities toward inanimate objects or people?

DAUGHTER: Yes. He has done both. When he was a puppy he used to masturbate on the bathroom rug and towels. But he doesn't do that any more.

DR. T: What about people?

DAUGHTER: This was a sore point between my sister and me. I hated it when he would grab your arm or leg, but my sister didn't care. She even encouraged it.

DR. T: How did your sister encourage it?

DAUGHTER: She would put her arm down so Sebastian could get it. Then she would call him and slap her arm. Sebastian would run up and jump on her arm. My sister just stayed there and let him do it. I think my sister did it just to annoy me.

DR. T: What makes you say that?

DAUGHTER: She knew how I hated it and she would do it all the more. Sometimes when we were together she would call Sebastian and tell him to do it. Or she would come into my room and tell Sebastian to do it. She was just trying to drive me crazy.

DR. T: Did Sebastian ever mount you?

DAUGHTER: My sister taught him to mount me on command. She would say, "Sebastian, let's go get her," then Sebastian would run up and grab my arm or leg. My sister always got a big kick out of watching me struggle to keep the dog off me.

DR. T: How did you deal with that?

DAUGHTER: I couldn't. My sister was bigger and older than me. She hit me if I hit the dog.

DR. T: How did you get the dog off you?

DAUGHTER: My mother had to stop it. She would come and distract the dog or something. If she wasn't home, I just had to stand it until Sebastian got tired.

DR. T: I take it that you and your sister are not friends.

DAUGHTER: Friends! We are mortal enemies. She still teases me when she comes home from college.

MOTHER: I guess I should have stepped in, but at that time I was too preoccupied with my own troubles to do anything. I don't think I knew about it until much later.

DR. T: So basically, your sister taught the dog to mount you. Then the mounting became part of the other problems like feeding, guarding and so forth.

DAUGHTER: That's what it looks like.

DR. T: What do you do now that your sister is away at college?

DAUGHTER: I tried hitting Sebastian, but he tried to bite me. So I just wait till he gets tired. I end up dragging him around the house.

Dr. T: When is he likely to mount you?

DAUGHTER: We have discussed this before. He mounts me after he starts barking, when I try to hit him, or when I refuse to give him food.

It now became apparent that the holding problem previously discussed started with this misdirected sexual behavior. The older sister first taught the dog to mount herself and then taught the dog to mount her sister. The mother inadvertently continued this training by rewarding the dog by distracting his attention with food.

It was clearer than ever that this dog had become the messenger of the family's hostility.

Obedience

DR. T: I would like to talk about obedience. Does your dog sit, lie down and come upon command?

DAUGHTER: He knows tricks but he doesn't do them right.

DR. T: What do you mean by that?

DAUGHTER: He knows about ten commands. We taught him to sit, lie down, sit on his hind legs, roll over, jump in the air, lie down on his back and play dead, lie down and put his paws on his head, walk, sneeze and cough.

DR. T: That sounds as if he's pretty well trained.

DAUGHTER: It's not as good as it sounds. You see, he does all these tricks at once in rapid succession. Then he runs to the kitchen and barks for food.

DR. T: How do you start the sequence?

DAUGHTER: All you have to say is, "Sit." Then he takes over. He finishes with a sneeze and a cough and finally barking. He does it so fast that it is hard to see all the tricks.

DR. T: I guess he performs these tricks in the same sequence that he was taught.

DAUGHTER: That's right. Very early he started anticipating my next command. Now he does them all like he's impatient to get it over with and get the treat. Another thing, he growls while he is performing, as if to say that he really doesn't want to perform.

DR. T: How did you reward him when you were teaching him?

DAUGHTER: We always gave him a dog biscuit.

DR. T: Did you reward him after every trick?

DAUGHTER: At first we did. But then it was easier to give him a treat at the end.

DR. T: Well, that's some behavioral ritual! Does he have any other rituals?

MOTHER: I guess his happy fits are behavioral rituals.

DR. T: What are "happy fits"?

MOTHER: When I get home or when I pet him he rolls over on his back, shakes from side to side, and sneezes repeatedly.

DR. T: What do you do when he goes into happy fits?

MOTHER: I talk to him and pet him on the belly. I say, "Oh, what a good boy."

DAUGHTER: She always uses that baby talk to talk to him.

DR. T: Tell me, does your dog go into happy fits when you distract him from your daughter, such as those times when he has been barking and holding?

MOTHER: Oh, yes. All the time. Any time I call him he will come to me and go into a happy fit. I think he is so cute when he does that. If I am angry at him for causing trouble and he does that, I lose all my anger. I guess he really knows how to control me.

DR. T: You are controlling each other. Sebastian's happy fits reward you and you reward Sebastian's happy fits.

Some people would be surprised to hear that this troublesome dog knew so many tricks. I personally was not. This was the final piece of the puzzle. The dog was a superior learner. He could learn long sequences of behavior, as easily as he learned all the aberrant behaviors. Perhaps if the dog was not so bright, he would not have acquired all these problems. However, the dog's "intelligence" had its positive side. Whatever could be learned in the first place could also be unlearned. By reversing the requirements for reward or turning the tables on the dog we might be able to change these patterns. The more "intelligent" the dog, the more rapid the reversal of behavior.

The happy fits confirmed my hypothesis that the mother's distraction techniques were rewarding for the dog. An added complication was that the dog's reaction to the mother's distraction rewarded the mother's behavior. I have found many times in my practice that when the dog starts improving, the clients experience ambivalent emotions, happy that the dog is getting better, but experiencing a sense of loss. They have lost their puppy. Their dog starts acting like a mature, healthy dog and my clients are disappointed. It is at this point that they have to decide what they want, the puppy or the adult dog.

I talked to the mother and explained that this might happen. She seemed to understand and was willing to give up some of that "cute" behavior that she liked so much in her dog. The question was, could she do it? There was so much pressure against it.

ANALYSIS OF THE PROBLEM

Before we start detailing some of the solutions to this dog's problems it would be interesting to get a complete picture of his day-to-day behavior.

My clients would get up early in the morning, approximately 5:00 or 5:30 A.M., in the hope that they could catch the dog before he soiled in the house. Invariably, they would be disappointed. The dog would have defecated and urinated somewhere in the house. They had tried to prevent this by taking the dog out late the night before but this seldom worked. This was not the best way to start the day, but they had gotten used to it. Now two things could happen: they could ignore the problem, clean it up and take the dog out, or they could punish the dog. They would do one or the other depending on how angry and frustrated they were feeling that day. If the daughter punished the dog, this would lead to an altercation between the dog and the daughter.

After getting dressed they would go to a restaurant for breakfast. Not for the enjoyment of eating out, but to avoid the constant high-pitched barking of their dog while they were eating. They ate all their meals in restaurants for the same reason, namely, to escape the continuous demands of their dog. They initially resented this, but they had gotten used to it.

When the mother and daughter were home together, they were constantly subjected to the dog's demands for food and water. They would succumb to these demands. The dog would then eat or drink so rapidly that he would vomit. Another mess had to be cleaned up.

The interaction at home between the mother and daughter had to be constrained. The dog would bark at and attack the daughter if she approached or spoke to the mother. In order to maintain peace mother and daughter would limit their conversation. This must have been difficult, for both were highly verbal people.

They would have to be constantly on guard to prevent any small object from reaching the dog. The dog would guard and swallow small objects. This caused a great deal of anxiety since the dog's health was in danger and the veterinary bills would pile up.

The dog's health was not perfect. In addition to the obvious stomach problems the dog had a weak back and was prone to slipped discs. He also had a habit of chewing his paws raw when frustrated. They would try to avoid frustrating him, but it became impossible.

(47)

They had tried and failed numerous times to solve these problems. They had tried punishment, bribery and a variety of other tricks. Every time a new solution was tried it led to a further intensification of the problems. The daughter had experienced complete failure in her attempts to discipline the dog. They had gotten to the point where the dog was no longer a pleasure, but a constant source of irritation and guilt. Even the attempts to control the dog by teaching it tricks had met with failure. However, my clients were too neurotically attached to their dog to give up. They felt responsible somehow for the problems.

In some respects, they were correct. The causes of this dog's problems were numerous but it all boiled down to the way my clients went about trying to solve the problems. They did not intentionally cause these problems, so there was no need for guilt. Ignorance was one of the culprits: ignorance of the effects of reward and punishment; ignorance of the innate behavior of a dog. Decisions based on ignorance were bound to be in error. The other culprit was the disruptive home life caused by the father's death.

The Genesis of the Problem

The problem began to fester four years before when my clients purchased a cute miniature poodle. The family, a mother and two girls, had just finished recovering from the death of their father when their first dog, a springer spaniel, was run over. This occurred when the younger daughter had taken the dog for a walk. The dog had broken the clasp on the leash and run into the street. After a number of near misses the dog was hit by a car and killed. The older daughter persisted in blaming her sister for being irresponsible and causing the dog's death.

Soon after the death of the first dog a new puppy was obtained. It was to to be the younger daughter's responsibility to

(48)

care for the dog. The mother hoped that this new charge would alleviate some of the pain and guilt the daughter was feeling. However, because of her own problems and new responsibilities, she was unable to guide her daughter in the formidable job of raising a puppy. The daughter did not accept this puppy with the normal joy of a child with a new dog, but with fear and resentment. She had already been told by her sister that she couldn't handle this responsibility, so she would have to prove that she could, or she would be a failure. She felt a natural resentment for this added burden, but couldn't express this since that would be admitting that her sister was right. She would show her sister that she could take care of a dog.

In addition to the daughter's guilt and resentment there were feelings of hostility. It is not unusual for children after the death of a parent to feel hostility toward the remaining parent. The daughter's hostility toward her mother and sister was probably directed at the dog. The mother's hostility toward her daughters was taken out in a number of ways: Failure to help the daughter with her new responsibility, perhaps even getting the dog in the first place, could have been indirect hostile actions. The mother also persisted in doing things that would exaggerate the dog's problems. All these factors were working against the normal development of the children as well as the dog. I am not saying that these factors were the cause of the dog's pathology, but they did influence the setting in which the direct causes expressed themselves. The direct causes of the problems were my clients' behavior toward the dog.

In my opinion, the two main direct causative factors were related to feeding and sexual behavior. This established an appeasement ritual, which always followed the same pattern. The dog would initially do something that my clients did not like. He would bark or guard an object or eliminate. Then the dog would be punished by the daughter. The dog's reaction to punishment was to hold on to the daughter and bite her if she tried to hit him. Then the mother, in her attempts to help the daughter, would call to the dog and distract him or give him food. This served to reward the holding as well as the behavior that led to holding. Thus all the aberrant behaviors were trained by the appeasement ritual. The first step toward a solution would lie in breaking up this ritual. I decided to start with the feeding problem, and as this was solved we would work on the remaining problems.

THE SOLUTION

The solution to my clients' problems, as well as a large number of other problems I have dealt with in my practice, is described under the appropriate heading in the body of this book. I have done this to prevent you, the reader, from blindly applying solutions that may be inappropriate to your problems. Now there is no way I can prevent you from reading ahead. However, I would like to caution you against applying the solutions I outline without reading the entire book. Applying the wrong solutions to your problem is like taking the wrong medicine for an illness. The medicine, even though it is beneficial for treatment of one illness, may do nothing, or acutely intensify the symptoms of another illness. Before treatment, a good diagnosis is necessary.

The remainder of this book is designed to teach you, the reader, to be your own behavioral diagnostician. In order to do this you will learn about the innate behavior of your dog. You must be aware of the similarities and differences between humans and dogs so that you will conceptualize your dog's behavior in his terms and not yours. (I have repeatedly made reference to not interpreting your dog's problems in human terms.)

After that, you will learn something about "learning."

One of my clients' basic problems was that they did not recognize that they had actually trained their dog to do the things it did. To be a good behavioral diagnostician you must be able to identify the effects of reward and punishment. You will also have to know how to use them effectively. This is where goal-setting comes into play. My clients repeatedly failed in their attempts to solve their problems. They would invariably set standards that couldn't be reached in a meaningful period of time. Then they would get disappointed, give up or try something else. Without appropriate subgoals and a way to measure your progress you are likely to fail.

With that under your belt, you can proceed with the analysis of your dog's problem. You will learn how to apply the Behavior Problem Checklist and the ROCKS method. (See page 205.) You are going to be responsible for the treatment. So it is important for you to know as much as possible before you start.

2

WHAT IS AN ANIMAL PSYCHOLOGIST?

Since the goal of this book is to help you learn how to deal with your pet's problems, it would be helpful for you to know what you are getting into.

Many people, when they first hear that I am an animal psychologist, say such things as "Oh, I didn't know there was a psychologist for animals" or "How can you psychoanalyze a dog?" or "Do you put it on a couch or something?" or "I thought psychology had to do with people. What do psychologists know about animals?" or "I don't understand. Dogs don't talk, do they? How do you talk to them? Do you analyze their dreams?"

The picture they usually have of a psychologist comes from the media. They see Bob Newhart sitting in a chair in his office with his client unloading his problems, or a middle-aged fatherly-looking man with white beard sitting in a paneled office attempting to help his client understand his problem. He will do this using ink blots, free association or analysis of dreams. A third image is that of a conservatively dressed middle-aged woman who appears periodically on TV talk shows. She usually brings a list of questions for the moderator to answer. From his answers she will be able to determine some hidden secret about his personality.

All these images are partially correct.

Some psychologists sit in offices and listen to their clients' problems. Other psychologists try to help their clients understand the hidden nature of the problems by using a variety of techniques, from paper and pencil tests to ink blots. They are all engaged in a common activity: behavioral diagnosis and treatment. Their methods may differ but they have a common goal, to alleviate human suffering and help their clients lead happier, more fulfilling and meaningful lives.

Consequently, when you put the word animal in front of psychologist, it conjures up strange associations. How can an animal tell you about his problems? How can you get this animal to understand what he is doing or feeling?

The answer is that you do and you don't! An animal psychologist has the same goals as other psychologists. The difference is that he deals with different problems, using different techniques, drawing from different information, and most of all he has a decidedly different outlook.

An animal psychologist is first and foremost a behaviorist. In order for you to deal with your pets' problems *you*, too, have to adopt a behaviorist's outlook. You have to stop trying to figure out what your dog is thinking or feeling and start paying attention to what your dog is *doing*. The behaviorist does not ask, "Does this dog *like* his owners?" Instead, he asks, "Does this dog *bite* his owners?" Thus, if you see your dog voraciously consuming his food, a nonbehaviorist observation would be to say that he must really be hungry. A behaviorist observation would be that the dog had his last meal twenty-four hours ago and he is eating his food very rapidly. Notice that there is no statement about hunger, just a statement about what happened before the dog ate and a description of how he is eating.

This must seem like a peculiar orientation indeed. To completely ignore what you are confident is going on inside the animal and focus totally on what the animal actually does is foreign to the normal way of talking about and thinking about behavior. So what is the benefit of such an orientation? Where does it get you?

One benefit of this kind of focus is that it makes your observations more objective, that is, more in accord with what you are actually seeing. There is no way that you can ever directly observe someone else's inner behavior such as anger, frustration, fear, love, attachment or thinking. All you can see is what the other is doing. Then, you infer from your own reaction what is going on inside that person. An example: You see a young man running toward you with his arms waving in the air. What is happening? Is he running to you or away from something behind him? If you notice that a lion is also running in the same direction about ten feet behind the young man, you might postulate that he is afraid and is running away. If you notice a beautiful girl running toward the young man, then you might postulate an entirely different motive. Notice what is most important to your interpretation of the event: the stimulus for the action and the actual behavior. If you confine yourself to these two aspects you will tend not to make errors of interpretation.

Another benefit from looking at behavior as a behaviorist is that it improves the reliability of your communication. We never really know what someone else is feeling; we can only guess how we would feel in the same situation. However, another person may not feel the same emotion in that situation. So in order to communicate effectively, we must restrict our observation to what actually happened without interpretation.

This does not mean that a behaviorist never interprets behavior. In fact, the behaviorist almost always interprets what he is seeing. However, he tries very hard to separate his observations from his interpretations.

Distinguishing between observation and interpretation allows the behaviorist one extra luxury. That is, someone else can observe the behavior and verify what is happening. The two observers may disagree on interpretation, but if they stick to observable acts they can agree on what actually happened. If you see a man sitting at a table, pen in hand, rubbing his beard, you can agree that he is rubbing his chin but you may disagree as to whether he is thinking or whether his beard is itchy.

So a behaviorist pays close attention to what the animal is actually doing. The final benefit of this is that you can actually measure what you are seeing. This is very important to diagnosing and treating a behavioral problem. By actually measuring problem behavior you can tell just how bad the problem is to begin with, and exactly how much progress you are making in your treatment program. You can precisely determine how much better or worse the problem has gotten.

Imagine that you have the misfortune to be hospitalized. You will notice how much probing and poking and feeling is going on, in an attempt to measure how your body is reacting. The doctor uses everything from a thermometer to complex chemical tests. If he gives you a pill to lower your blood pressure and your pressure goes up or stays the same, he can stop the pill. Just imagine a doctor who depends solely on his vague impression of how you feel.

The same method is used for treating a behavioral problem, but the measurement instrument for behavior is much simpler. You use your senses, paper and pencil and sometimes a watch. If your dog barks you can count how many times the barking

(55)

occurs over a period of time. Or you can time how long it takes for your dog to start or stop barking. These are easy, but important, measurements. The only problem that might arise is knowing exactly what to count or when to start and stop timing. We will deal with this later in the book.

Different Facts and Techniques

An animal psychologist uses a different set of facts and techniques to deal with the peculiar set of problems he encounters. It is important for you to know these different facts and techniques so that you can apply them to treating your dog's problems.

A typical clinical psychologist's day-to-day activities involve diagnosing and treating human psychological problems. However, there is another group of psychologists who don't actually treat behavior; they study it. This group, of which I am a member, is known as experimental psychologists. Experimental psychologists can usually be found in behavioral laboratories at universities and colleges around the country. Their goal is to establish the facts and prove or disprove new behavioral theories and techniques. Many new behavioral theories and techniques are tried out first on animals before they are tested on humans. In many cases we have determined that a given technique is applicable to animals even if it has not been proven that it works with people. In order to understand your pet, it would be helpful to be acquainted with this new information.

The three areas or specialties of experimental psychology that have information most important to you as you try to understand your pet are comparative psychology, animal learning and behavior therapy. Each of these disciplines has developed powerful techniques for dealing with animals.

THE ORIGIN OF THE DOG

Current theories and evidence indicate that the dog was domesticated from the wolf, probably in Denmark, about 8000 B.C. This means that the dog has lived with man for some ten thousand years, or some four thousand to eight thousand generations of dogs to be changed in directions to suit man's needs or fancy.

You can imagine how the first dogs could have come about. About 8000 B.C. man was beginning to live in primitive agricultural communities. Since wolves are pack-hunters as well as scavengers, they probably started hanging around the villages to get food scraps. It is not uncommon for primitive people to adopt small young animals as pets. This is what must have happened to the wolf cubs. Since wolves are by nature social animals who live in packs, this transition from the wolf to the human pack would not have been hard. And, since wolves are naturally territorial, the pet wolves would establish a territory around the village and would be sensitive to the approach of strange animals, wild wolves or humans. This must have been a decided advantage to the villagers.

At the same time it must have been necessary to distinguish the wild wolves from their tame counterparts. The villagers must have bred for a different-looking wolf. The first dog characteristic was a curlier tail. Also, the villagers must have chosen for adoption animals that could be more easily controlled—small or medium-sized wolves with smaller and less dangerous teeth.

Thus, the basic traits of the domestic dog were established. Each village had its own type of dog, somewhat different from the other villages'. Perhaps this was because of village pride or perhaps it was due to random mutation. The dogs would have occasionally been bred back to their original ancestors, the wolves, to maintain the health and strength of the breed. This is still done by Alaskan Eskimos. In fact, the original dogs must have looked much like the contemporary Alaskan Eskimo dog.

Even with the great variety of dogs existing today, some of which look more like shaggy guinea pigs than dogs, there are still strong behavioral ties to wolves. Thus, studying wolves can tell us something about the behavior of present-day dogs. When we go over the Behavior Problem Checklist we will be using this knowledge to give us a handle on what is normal behavior for your pet.

GENETICS AND YOUR DOG

Some people think that a dog's behavior is learned. Either the owners have taught the dog what it knows or the dog has learned how to act like a dog from its mother, or by watching other dogs. This is wrong for a number of reasons. First of all, most dog owners have no idea, or only a vague idea, of how a dog is supposed to act. Nevertheless, almost all dogs all over the world have unmistakable similarities in their behavior. When was the last time you saw someone trying to teach his male dog to lift his leg when urinating?

It is possible that the mother dog teaches her pup some of the things it has to know to be a dog, or that a puppy learns by copying the behavior of other dogs. However, a little reflection will tell you that this cannot be the whole story. Many puppies are rejected by their mothers at birth and raised, cared for and bottle-fed by their human owners. These puppies may have some behavioral problems, but in general they act like other dogs. This is true also for dogs who are raised in complete isolation from other members of their species.

Other people suggest just the opposite hypothesis: that is, all the dog's behavior is inherited. They maintain that certain breeds of dogs are innately aggressive, destructive or good with children. A little reflection about the behavior of dogs you have known will demonstrate the fallacy of this belief. A good dog will learn to adjust his behavior to suit his owner's behavior. The dog will fit in naturally to the patterns of the family. If the family's patterns are aberrant it is likely that the dog's behavior will be the same. This is not to say that there aren't genetic differences between breeds of dogs; however, an individual dog's behavior will be a result of the interaction of his genetic predispositions and the demands of his environment.

The responsibility for good or bad behavior cannot rest solely on environment or genetics. This is a very difficult concept to get across. After I explain this to people they say, "I understand all that, but don't you think that the owners cause the problem?" or "Yes, I know what you mean, but aren't the problems people are experiencing with their pet primarily caused by inbreeding by the dog breeders?"

Let's take an example to see how interaction of genetics and environment works. An environmental event that many dogs commonly encounter is being struck by their owners. As a general rule, I recommend not hitting your dog. This is not only because of the commonly held belief that your dog will learn to fear you; I recommend this also because the behavioral effects of hitting a dog depend on your animal's predisposed genetic reaction to aggression. Thus, a naturally timid dog can develop into a shy and fearful one as a consequence of being hit. Other dogs can react to being struck by becoming terrors. The results are not unpredictable. They are a function of the interaction between the genetic predisposition and the environmental event.

To know exactly what the result of an environmental event will be on your dog, you must know something about his genetic predisposition. Comparative psychologists spend their time doing laboratory studies on the genetics of behavior. As the name implies, their basic goal is to compare the behavior of various animal species to determine how the genetics of these different species lead to different behavior. Two comparative psychologists named John Paul Scott and John L. Fuller made an extensive study of the genetics of dog behavior. We will examine what they found later on in the chapter. For the present, we address the question, what can be inherited?

What Can Be Inherited?

Most people realize that many of the physical attributes of their pets are inherited. We have some solid facts concerning the inheritance of coat color, coat length and body size. The variables have been manipulated for years by dog breeders to produce the wide range of dog breeds available today. This selective breeding has produced everything from the short-haired Mexican Chihuahua, which can weigh less than a pound, to the long-haired St. Bernard, which can weigh in at 185 pounds. Colors include white, red, brown and spotted. This is a tribute to the ingenuity and creativity of people specializing in breeding dogs. However, even though genetic manipulation has been so successful, there are some limitations. A breeder can breed only for a characteristic that is already present. How many of you have seen a blue dog?

It is interesting to note that present breeders have focused almost exclusively on looks and have ignored to a large extent the behavior of the breed. A glance at the AKC description of different breeds will convince you of this. Large sections are devoted to how the "ideal" dog should look, with only lip service given to its behavior. This was not always true. At present, dogs' primary commercial value is based on the appeal to potential pet-owners, and so there is a premium on looks. However, in the past when dogs had important commercial value for what they did, that is, hunting or herding, more attention was given to the dog's behavior.

There is another reason breeders have ignored behavior. Many physical attributes such as coat length or color follow simple Mendelian inheritance principles. For example, coat length is controlled by a single gene. Short coats are dominant over long ones. This means that if a short- and long-coat dog mate, all their offspring (the mutts) will have short hair. If the mutts mate they will produce, in the long run, one pure-breed short-hair, one pure-breed long-hair, and two mutts with short hair. Thus 75 percent of the mutts' offspring will have short hair. Figure 1 shows how Mendelian principles apply to hair length. So for coat length, color and in some respects body size it is easy to determine the outcome of any mating.

But what about behavior? To my knowledge no behavioral characteristic follows simple Mendelian principles. Instead, another genetic mechanism, called pleiotrophy or manifold effects, is operating. Unfortunately, we do not understand how this mechanism works. All that can be said with certainty is that there is probably a different genetic combination for each different behavior. What we do know is that any one behavior is probably the result of many genes. This of course leaves breeders at a loss when they try to select for a particular behavior.

Genetics and Behavior

We are all familiar with the behavioral descriptions of different breeds of dogs. Chihuahuas are supposed to be nervous, snippy dogs, German shepherds, protective, St. Bernards, benign and placid. Miniature dogs are characterized as nervous and fearful whereas large dogs are considered to be aggressive, protective and generally calmer.

We will deal with behavioral differences of different breeds later on. For now I would like to discuss what behavior is inherited. Can a dog inherit protectiveness or nervousness? The answer is No. What kind of behavior is nervousness? This

Figure 1. Inheritance of Coat Length

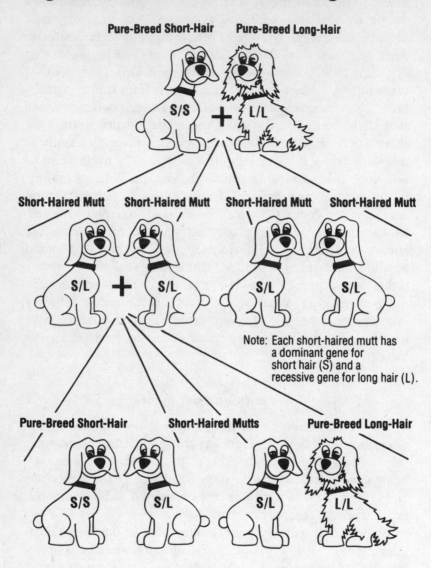

Pure-Breed Short-Hair   Pure-Breed Long-Hair

S/S + L/L

Short-Haired Mutt   Short-Haired Mutt   Short-Haired Mutt   Short-Haired Mutt

S/L + S/L   S/L   S/L

Note: Each short-haired mutt has
a dominant gene for
short hair (S) and a
recessive gene for long hair (L).

Pure-Breed Short-Hair   Short-Haired Mutts   Pure-Breed Long-Hair

S/S   S/L   S/L   L/L

could mean very different things to different people. It could mean too much barking, running around or something else. Animals inherit specific tendencies to behave in specific ways and not general characteristics such as protectiveness. The question is, what are these tendencies?

There are at least three types of inherited behaviors that vary in their complexity: reflexes, tropisms and fixed-action patterns. The simplest is the reflex. Reflexes occur without necessarily going through the brain. There is just a stimulus and a reaction. An example in humans is the patella reflex. Hit your kneecap in the right place and your knee will jerk. You don't have to think about it. In fact, it helps if you don't. A shark has a jaw-closing reflex: pressure on its teeth automatically causes its jaw muscles to close. Dogs have many reflexes, which sometimes change as the dog gets older. According to Michael Fox, director of the Humane Society, for example, a puppy may have up to twenty-six different reflex reactions when it is born. If you pinch a puppy's hind foot, it will withdraw the pinched foot and extend the other hind foot. If you turn a puppy's head to one side it will extend the legs on that side and pull in the legs on the opposite side. If you touch a puppy on the lips this will produce sucking movements. The puppy doesn't think about what is happening to it. It just reacts. For complete list of all reflexes see page 71.

A more complex type of inherited behavior is the tropism. In this type of behavior an animal automatically moves toward or away from some source of stimulation. There is no volition involved. The animal has to do what it does; its genetic program gives it no choice. The best example of this is the behavior of moths and other insects near a bright light. These bugs will repeatedly smash into the light until they are exhausted or die. There is no thought, no choice. Dogs have tropisms as well. Puppies and adult dogs will automatically approach sources of mild stimulation, while avoiding sources of intense stimulation. Puppies especially seek contact with warm objects such as the mother's body.

The most complex inherited behavior has been commonly called an instinct. Konrad Lorenz, a European naturalist, ethologist and Nobel Prize-winner, renamed these fixed-action patterns (FAPs). Unlike the reflexes and tropisms, FAPs are chains of responses. Sometimes these chains are very long and can last for days; other chains can run off in a few seconds. FAPs may be compared to computer programs. In order for the program to work each step in the program (each instruction to the animal) must be preceded by the previous step. Of course this is just an analogy; a dog is far more complex and flexible than any computer. An animal may stop its program and start another; computers do not have this option.

Just as dogs differ in size, color and shape, so do their genetic programs. And just as we can recognize these different shapes as dogs, the individual genetic program differences are enough alike to be grouped together as dog programs. This grouping is called species typical behavior.

An example of species typical behavior in the dog is the male urination pattern. If you watch two dogs approach each other you will see a genetically organized behavioral ritual that almost all dogs go through. The dogs will start sniffing each other's hind-quarters. Then one dog will lift his leg and urinate on an upright object. Then the other dog will sniff the object and urinate, and so on until the ritual ends. Each one of the behavior classifications in the Behavior Problem Checklist (page 103) contains a number of genetically organized behavioral rituals. We will describe these rituals in greater detail in the next chapter. It is important that you learn to recognize these patterns. Many of the problems I encounter in my practice are the results of owners having misinterpreted their animals' FAPs.

Humans have their own reflexes, tropisms and fixed-action

patterns. There is no reason why we, the human animal, should be deprived of genetically organized behavior, when all other animals have them. However, genetic behaviors are modified by learning, cultural factors, experience and language to a great extent. This is why it is wrong to interpret your dog's behavior using human terms such as anger, spite and jealousy. It is quite unlikely that your dog, with his different genetic programs and different experiences and upbringing, could possibly experience the same emotion as you do in the same situation. Consequently, it is better to understand your dog in his terms rather than in yours.

Breeds and Genetics

A quick glance through many popular dog books will acquaint you with the amazing variety of shapes and sizes of this animal. Each shape or size has been specially bred to increase the capacity of the dog to perform specialized tasks. The Saluki, which were used originally by the Egyptians to hunt gazelle, were bred for their long legs. The short-legged terriers were bred to creep into small ground nests and drive out small animals like foxes and badgers. The bloodhounds, with their sensitive noses, were used to track wounded beasts and later thieves who had stolen meat. In short, modern breeds of dogs are all specialists.

The ancestor of all modern dogs, the wolf, is a generalist. Any predator that specialized on only one prey would soon perish due to the normal variations of nature. Physically, the wolf has only a few noticeable differences from dogs: heavier coats and somewhat thicker skin in special areas of the body, such as the cheek and under and in back of the neck. These physical characteristics protected the animal from the environment, and also served to minimize the damage inflicted during fights for dominance. The head of the wolf is doglike with ears erect. Their large, hairy heads and long, hairy legs are different from most dogs'. The wolf is a powerful, rugged animal not specialized in any one activity.

Since the wolf is a generalist, it has the capacity to perform a variety of tasks. This allowed primitive man to select one characteristic and exaggerate it. The natural history of this generalist can shed some light upon some of the problems owners have with their pets.

Of major significance is the fact that wolves live as members of a social group or pack. This probably helped greatly in domesticating the wolf. However, it can cause some problems. In most if not all social groups of animals there exists a hierarchy, or pecking order. (The phrase "pecking order" comes from the study of chicken behavior: high-ranking chickens could peck lower-ranking chickens, but not vice versa.) Every pack has its dominant or alpha male.

In good human-canine relationships, the owner will be the alpha member and the dog will be submissive. The problem arises when this is reversed. A very dominant dog can cause a variety of problems, most of which result in the owner getting bitten or attacked. And once the dog has become dominant he will fight to maintain his position. This does not mean that you must constantly battle your pet for dominance. Very subtle things can be done to establish and maintain dominance. We will explore these techniques later, under Fighting, in the Behavior Problem Checklist.

Another set of problems with pet dogs that has its origins in their wolf ancestry is the reaction to inappropriate stimuli. The wolf's structure and behavior evolved to meet the demands of the environment in which it lived. This environment is called a niche, which means that the wolf's behavior fits its environment the way a key fits a lock. Man succeeded in changing the structure and behavior of the dog during a period of ten thousand years. However, in the last fifty to one hundred years man's environment has changed drastically. One hundred years is much too short a time for a comparable change in the dog's genetically organized behavior. So we take a dog with its ancestral roots in the free-ranging wolf and raise it in an apartment. This does not necessarily make a dog"unhappy," as some people contend. What it does is to cause some of the dog's genetically organized behavior to respond to minimal stimuli. A client's pet Samoyed, a hunter, is a case in point. This animal lived on the thirty-fifth floor of an apartment building. It persisted in hunting specks of dust and shadows. It was rather funny to see this dog crouch down and stalk its own shadow. Our hunter would leap at his shadow, causing it to move away, and create quite a lot of damage in the process. I have seen many problems such as this in my practice.

Selective breeding has also caused some problems, especially when a dog has been bred for one purpose and is placed in an environment that doesn't support this purpose. When you breed a dog for show, the main purpose is that the dog look good. So two good-looking dogs, champions, will be mated. The problem with this is that looks and behavior are unrelated. Scott and Fuller have done numerous studies to determine the relation between body type and behavior. They used five breeds of dogs that were quite different in color, size, shape and behavior. These were cocker spaniels, basenjis, beagles, shelties and fox terriers. Precise measurements of various body dimensions and behavior were taken. By cross breeding these dogs they could determine the genetics of the body structure and behavior. They found that contrary to popular opinion, body structure and behavior were genetically separate. There were factors that predicted the behavior of the offspring and factors that predicted the looks of the offspring. But these factors did not affect each other.

When man domesticates an animal he usually pays attention to one or two characteristics and ignores the rest. This allows man to control and standardize those characteristics he is interested in. But what happens to the characteristics he ignores? They become more variable. An animal in the wild is pressured by its environment to develop certain of its characteristics. This does not make all wild animals identical. In fact, there is an optimum amount of variability for any species in any particular environment.

Breeders pay very close attention to the dogs' looks, so the appearance of breeds has been standardized. But little if any attention is paid to the behavior of the breed and so it has become variable. It is not possible to predict how a particular breed will act, especially very popular breeds that have been subject to mass production. The best way to select a pet is to observe its behavior. Don't make your choice merely because it is a member of a specific breed and has champion lines. The major source of problems, other than health problems, that an owner faces is behavioral in nature. Of course, people usually select a puppy for adoption. Therefore it is necessary to know the relation between puppy behavior and adult behavior. This brings us to behavior development.

3

DEVELOPMENT OF BEHAVIOR

A puppy is usually chosen on the basis of a brief observation that will take from two to five minutes, depending on the patience of the salesman and your ability to be assertive. There is usually one representative of each breed displayed in the pet shop, so 90 to 100 percent of your choice depends upon looks. However, the best way to choose a puppy would be to decide on the breed you want—from a visit to a pet shop or looking at a dog book—and then to go to a place that specializes in that breed, such as a registered breeder. This way, all the puppies would look pretty much the same and you could focus on behavior.

But what behavior do you focus on? One thing we know about puppies is that as they grow older their behavior changes in certain predictable ways. The newborn puppy is in a stage of development called the neonatal period for the first fourteen days of life. During this period its eyes are closed and all its behavior is directed to one function, that of obtaining nutrition by nursing. The puppy is not self-sufficient. It needs its mother for food, to maintain its temperature and even to urinate and defecate. Its mother must lick its hindquarters to stimulate that reflex. The puppy can be considered a bundle of reflexes and tropisms all directed toward maintaining its bodily needs through its mother.

A summary of these reflexes is presented in Table 1, on page 71.

What you are able to observe during the neonatal period is the relative activity of the puppies. Perhaps you will also be able to identify neurological damage if the puppy doesn't exhibit the appropriate reflexes at the right time. However, this would not be the best time to choose a puppy.

As the puppy gets older, some of its reflexes disappear and others develop. About fourteen days of age, puppies open their eyes and enter the transitional stage. This lasts for about seven days, or until the puppy is twenty to twenty-one days old. During this period the puppy is profoundly reorganizing its behavior and beginning to sense more of the environment. It can also move around on its own. The table shows how some new behavior starts.

The most important period for you as an owner is one which begins at three weeks of age and ends at twelve weeks. During this time the puppy forms permanent social relations. This is called the imprinting period. Most students of dog behavior fix seven weeks of age as the optimal imprinting time. It is the time in your dog's life when it is most susceptible to its caretakers. If during this time the dog has been isolated in a cage, it will not be able to form social relations with you or other dogs. If your puppy is kept exclusively with dogs then it will not be able to easily form a bond with its human owners. Thus it is best for a pet during this period to have plenty of human contact but also to have contact with other dogs.

Unfortunately, this does not always happen. My clients from the previous chapter kept their dog in a cage during this period. They were told that this was the best way to housebreak their dog. The result of that deprivation was devastating. I have

TABLE 1. SUMMARY OF PUPPY REFLEXES

Age (in days)	Stimulus	Response
1–15	1. *Crossed extensor:* Pinch one hind foot between your fingers.	The pinched foot withdraws while the other foot extends.
1–17	2. *Magnus:* Turn the head to one side.	The legs on the side to which the head is turned extend while the others withdraw.
1–13	3. *Rooting:* Form a cup with your hand and touch both sides of the puppy's muzzle with the cupped hand.	The puppy will crawl forward maintaining contact with the cupped hand.
1–22	4. *Urination:* Tickling or stroking external genitalia.	Puppy will urinate.
1–4	5. *Breathing:* Rubbing the puppy's underbelly.	Causes the puppy to take a breath.
1–18	6. *Head Turning:* Stroking one side of the face or behind the ear.	Head is turned toward the side of stimulation.
1–19	7. *Touch Muscle:* Stroking skin on back.	Rapid contraction of skin.
1–15	8. *Pain Withdrawal:* Pinching foot between toes.	Withdrawal of limb, distress cries.
1	9. *Touch Blink Reflex:* Touching of closed eye.	The muscles around the eye contract in a blink.

TABLE 1. SUMMARY OF PUPPY REFLEXES (Continued)

Age (in days)	Stimulus	Response
4	10. *Light Blink Reflex:* Light shining in eyes.	The eyes blink.
1–4	11. *Flexor Dominance:* Animal is picked up by back of neck.	All legs curl into body.
4–18	12. *Extensor Dominance:* Puppy is picked up by back of neck.	All four legs extend outward.
Placing: 5 days Supporting: 10 days	13. *Forelimb Placing and Supporting:* Lowering a blindfolded puppy to table surface.	Forelegs extend to hold weight of puppy when they touch surface.
Placing: 8 days Supporting: 15 days	14. *Hindlimb Placing and Supporting:* Lowering blindfolded puppy to table surface.	Hindlegs extend to hold weight of puppy when they touch surface.
15 days	15. *Sitting Upright.*	Puppy is able to balance while sitting.
21 days	16. *Standing Upright.*	Puppy is able to stand on all fours.
24 days	17. *Auditory Startle:* Loud sudden noise such as clapping of hands.	The legs and head are pulled in toward the body, and eyes blink.
24 days	18. *Auditory Orientation:* A sound stimulus to side of puppy.	Head is turned toward the source of the sound.
24 days	19. *Visual Orientation:* A light or a moving object to side of puppy.	The head is turned toward source of visual stimulation.
27 days	20. *Visual Cliff:* The puppy is placed on the edge of table or bed.	Puppy hesitates or pulls back from edge; will not step off edge.

had other clients who kept their new puppy separated from an older dog in the house. They did this because they felt the older dog would somehow hurt the puppy. When the puppy matured, it was allowed to interact with the older dog. The result was immediate and sustained fighting. The new dog would continually try to attack the older dog. This was a very difficult problem to solve. We had to build in behaviors that would have been normally present if the dogs had been put together during the period of socialization.

The last two periods are the juvenile period, from twelve weeks to six months, and adulthood, when any tendencies seen in the socialization period become more fixed. It is during the juvenile period that your puppy is most susceptible to change, so problem behavior should be discouraged and good behavior encouraged. If this is not done at this point, it becomes much harder although not impossible to change. An example would be aggressive food guarding. Many puppies during the juvenile period will aggressively snap and bite if you approach while they are eating or chewing a bone. This is natural. You have the best opportunity to change this behavior when your puppy is still relatively small. His teeth although sharp are not formidable. You could stand a few bites by this little monster while you teach him to allow you and every member of the family to take food or a bone away from him. A procedure for doing this is given later on. Then you can eliminate these problems before they get worse. Remember, if problems are not corrected, they will grow as your dog grows. Biting is a problem that is directly proportional to the length of your dog's teeth. Running away is a problem that is directly proportional to the length of your dog's legs.

Up to this point we have been talking about what your dog is born with, his genetically organized behavior. However, this is not the whole story. Whatever behavior patterns your dog has because of genetic endowment usually can be modified through learning. Just as a sculptor shapes his clay, so do the processes of learning shape behavior. And what is the clay of behavior? What is modified by the environment? The answer is genetically organized behavior.

So the principles of learning can be used to change your dog's genetically organized behavior. But this is not as simple as rewarding good behavior and punishing the bad. Genetics has not only set limitations on your dog's ability to act, but also on what he can learn and most importantly *how* he can learn. Rewards and punishments must be dealt appropriately, as some will be effective with certain behaviors but not with others. And some of these differences will depend on breed. If you don't believe this, try to punish an aggressive terrier by hitting him. The animal doesn't cower, he attacks ferociously.

You might say that learning is genetically organized. In order to understand how to deal with problem behavior, you must understand how the principles of learning work for your dog. Psychologists have been studying animal learning since the late 1800s, and it is one of the most extensively researched fields in American psychology. This allows us to apply hard scientific fact to changing your dog's problem behavior. The next section of this chapter deals with what is known in this area.

THE TECHNOLOGY OF CHANGING BEHAVIOR

"If I reward my dog, isn't it bribing him for doing what he is supposed to do?'

Many people have asked me this question. They somehow feel that correct behavior should be done for its own sake, without the addition of some extraneous reward. They say, "He knows what's right and what pleases me. I don't see why that isn't enough. Why do I have to give him a dog biscuit?"

These people are on a responsibility trip. They feel they

have to do things which do not get rewarded, so why should their dog get special favors. But a reward is not a special favor, nor is it a bribe when administered correctly.

We are all rewarded mildly for many of the day-to-day things we do. Take, for example, riding an elevator. One approaches the elevator, pushes the button and waits for the elevator to arrive. When it arrives, the door opens, you enter, push your floor, the door closes and the elevator moves. I contend that every step along the way is rewarded. If you think of reward as anything that keeps you doing something, then pushing the button is first rewarded by the illumination of the elevator light and then rewarded by the arrival of the elevator. Pushing the floor button is rewarded by closing of the door and movement of the elevator in the appropriate direction. You can test this statement by observing the effects of not being rewarded. When you are not rewarded when you expect to be, you get frustrated. This certainly happens when the elevator is malfunctioning.

You would never say that the elevator is bribing you for pressing its buttons. But the activity of the elevator is rewarding your behavior. Your dog also goes through sequences of behavior. Many of your dog's sequences are unlearned, that is, they are fixed-action patterns. The successful completion of any fixed-action pattern is a reward for your dog. A bird dog that is on the prowl is rewarded by the performance of the search and the finding of the prey.

So your dog's environment is rewarding his behavior all the time. But what about the more common rewards like a dog biscuit or praise? Of course these may be used to control your dog's behavior. If you use them correctly you will have a well-behaved dog. However, if you use them incorrectly, they can cause as many problems as they can correct.

One way to use food as a reward incorrectly is to always reward everything your dog does with food. This will make your dog a chow hound. He will always expect food for doing something. If you run out of dog biscuits he may get frustrated and refuse to listen to you. I have heard numerous times, "My dog only listens to me if I have a dog biscuit in my hand. If I am empty-handed, he just ignores me." You will remember that Sebastian would rapidly perform all his tricks and then demand food. In fact, food is being used as a bribe. The dog will do everything for food. This is like the person who does everything for money. He never participates in anything just because it is fun or interesting; it must pay off monetarily.

The solution to this bribery trap is to vary the types of reward. Sexual behavior is rewarding. A chance to explore is rewarding, especially if your dog hasn't explored anything recently. Care of the body surface can be rewarding. Many dogs like to be petted, scratched and rubbed. Resting can be rewarding to a tired dog. Giving a pregnant bitch nesting materials can reward a variety of behaviors. Even the opportunity to eliminate is rewarding. It is even possible that fighting and biting can be a reward for an aggressive, dominant dog.

In all of these examples, there are two common threads. First, the reward follows a natural behavior sequence and is itself a natural behavior. Eating food comes at the end of a feeding sequence. Copulation comes at the end of a mating sequence. Defecation and urination come at the end of an elimination or marking sequence. Biting attacks may come at the end of a dominance or territorial defense sequence.

The second common aspect is that the dog must be in the right state for the behavior to be rewarding. Food works best when your dog is hungry; care of the body surface, if your dog is itchy. In fact, what behavior will be the reward and what behavior is going to be rewarded depends on your dog's current state. You can reward exploring with food if your dog is hungry. Or you can reward eating when your dog is full by giving him an opportunity to explore some novel and interesting place. Any time you deprive your dog of doing something he likes for a long time, then doing that thing becomes rewarding.

You can use this knowledge to train your dog to do almost anything without ever giving him a dog biscuit. The key is to know what your dog likes to do and then let him do it when he does something you like. This is how I trained my dog to sit and stay for long periods. My toy schnauzer is not very fond of food. You might say he eats to live rather than lives to eat. However, he loves to be outdoors. To train him to sit and stay, I made a rule that he had to sit quietly for a few seconds before I opened the door. In other words, sitting was rewarded by going out. If he got up I would close the door and he would have to sit down again. He got out only if he sat down on command and remained seated until I said "Okay." He will now sit for long periods on command. He never bolts out of the door but politely waits for my okay. When he is outside, I reward him for sitting with praise, a pat, a scratch, a piece of cheese, and the opportunity to run free and chase something or to explore. I consciously vary the reward and seize every opportunity to reward him for sitting or some other behavior. Of course, my dog is obedient, he does what I tell him to do, including an elaborate set of tricks and commands, because if he does, he knows he can do something he likes to do.

Unintentional Reward, or Without Really Wanting to, You Can Train Your Dog to Bite Your Face

With so many things that can be rewards for your dog, it is not surprising that many people give rewards to their pets unintentionally. If you unwittingly reward your dog for doing things you like, you will feel as though your dog knows how to please you. In reality, you have trained him to do what you like, but many people feel good in believing that their dog is consciously trying to please them.

This unintentional reward can have bad side effects. If you

reward your dog for doing something that displeases you, you will believe that your dog is consciously trying to hurt you. In reality, you may actually have unintentionally trained your dog to displease you.

I have had numerous cases where unintentional reward was the cause of the problem. My clients in the first chapter unintentionally rewarded an entire range of problem behaviors. In another case a dog had the habit of jumping through glass storm doors. The dog had occasionally jumped through the bottom screen of the door. In order to prevent this, my clients would make a dash to the door when the bell rang, and open it before he leaped through the screen. They were not always successful. The dog has learned to dash toward the door with them; the reward was getting outside. During the winter, when the glass was replaced, he did the same thing, breaking the glass but not hurting himself. He soon learned to dive through other windows, smashing them to get out. The whole incident could have been avoided if my clients were aware of how they were training their dog.

Unconscious Reward, or Without Really Knowing It, You Can Train Your Dog to Bite Your Mother-in-Law

Another way undesirable behavior can be trained is through unconscious reward. This is somewhat different from the unintentional type. Using unconscious reward, you train your dog to act out what you consciously cannot do or are unable to accept. My clients in the first chapter trained their dog to act out the hostility they felt toward each other. Instead of being hostile toward each other, they trained their dog to be hostile for them. You might say that the dog had an uncanny sensitivity to these people's feelings. However, a simpled explanation is that the dog was unconsciously trained by the mother to bother the daughter.

When the cause of the problem is unconscious reward it is

much harder to treat. The owners have to recognize their unconscious motives in order to deal with the problem. A recent case of mine illustrates this point. The problem was with a one-hundred-pound male German shepherd who persisted in mounting the male owner's sister. The husband had recently married and the dog made no attempts to mount his new wife. The wife and her sister-in-law were good friends on the surface. However, after the marriage the sister-in-law persisted in coming to the house during the day and telling the new wife how to handle things. The wife unconsciously resented this intrusion. She worked out her resentment by unconsciously rewarding the dog for mounting her sister-in-law by making a big fuss. She would bring him into the kitchen, scold him and then try to calm him down. Her scolding always tended to be on the mild side. She would say, "How many times have I told you not to do that? Now you be a good boy." With this, the dog's ears pricked up and his tail wagged. Then she would say, "Calm down, be a good boy" and stroked him gently on the head. Her attention, and saying "good boy," which was previously associated with reward, all served to reward the dog when it mounted the sister-in-law.

This resulted in a number of benefits for the wife. Since the dog was her husband's, and he would not part with his pet, she could not be blamed for its behavior. The sister-in-law found the dog's behavior disgusting and curtailed her visits. She would visit only when the husband was home. At those times, she would not offer advice to the wife. Thus, the wife got back at her annoying sister-in-law, removed the source of the problem and came out smelling like a rose. She, too, was disgusted by the behavior and would not tolerate it. She could sympathize with her sister-in-law's plight but at the same time get in the final dig. She could suggest that it must be something her sister-in-law was doing that stimulated and encouraged the dog's amorous attentions.

The solution to this problem was to get the wife and the

sister-in-law to come to terms about who was running the house. After that, the mounting behavior could be changed. Without a change in the relationship between the sister-in-law and the wife there was no hope of changing the dog's behavior.

So unintentional or unconscious rewards can have powerful effects. They can be the cause of many behavioral aberrations the dog exhibits. The dogs in these cases are not abnormal, vicious or hypersexual. They are just doing what they perceive to be expected of them. The only way to prevent these types of problems from developing is to always be conscious of the rewards you are dispensing and reward only desirable behavior. In order to do this effectively, you must know some of the Rules for Effective Reward (see page 82).

THE NATURAL TENDENCY

When I tell my clients about unintentional or unconscious reward, they say, "I understand that, but it doesn't happen with me." What they don't understand is that it is a natural human and animal tendency to notice primarily only things that are salient, things that stand out from the crowd. This leads to two natural reward tendencies in people even if they are sophisticated about the effects of reward.

The first is to ignore good behavior. When your dog is quiet, nice or pleasing you, you have the tendency to ignore him. Since most people with problem dogs have only a few complaints, most of their dog's behavior is acceptable. Try this. Watch your dog for a whole day and take note of what he does that you consider good or at least neutral. Then take note of how many times you pay attention to your dog when he is being good. Use a lined piece of paper for this. At the left side of the paper write the names of the behaviors. At the right record how many times you intentionally reward your dog for these behaviors per day. If you do this conscientiously, you will notice that you ignore most of your animal's good behavior.

The second natural tendency is to notice bad behavior. When your animal is chewing, biting, barking, and so forth, you generally pay attention to him. This is because the bad behaviors stand out. You might say that these are attention-getting behaviors for your dog. Do the same thing with bad behaviors as you did with good behaviors. Write the names of the behaviors that bother you on the left side of the paper, then how many times you pay attention to them, and finally the type of attention.

Now, compare the two lists. If you find that you pay attention to good behavior far more than bad behavior then you are doing fine. However, you are more likely to find just the opposite. The highest density of attention is paid to bad behavior. This means that you are teaching your dog to bother you.

This imbalance in the density of attention, with the scale tipped toward bad behavior, has another effect. For one thing, it makes ignoring a bad behavior ineffective. Many of my clients have said, "But I have tried to ignore the problem and it got worse." That is because they totally ignored their dog. The only way to make ignoring bad behavior effective is to, at the same time, pay more attention to the behavior that pleases you.

The third effect of focusing on bad behavior is the possibility of creating a masochistic dog, that is, a dog who seeks to be punished. You can make hitting, punching, or otherwise hurting your dog a reward if this is the only attention he gets and if he really needs attention.

An example of this is a case I had of a male schnauzer who would defecate on his female owner's bed every time she entertained a boyfriend. The owner was sure that her dog was jealous of her boyfriend. However, there was a much simpler explanation. The owner usually attended to her dog when she was alone. But like most people she attended to bad behavior more than good behavior. One of the dog's bad habits was defecating on the bed. She had pretty much cured the dog of this until one weekend when her boyfriend stayed over. The dog started all over again. From then on the dog would defecate on the bed whenever she entertained.

The key to this case was the shift in the density of reward. When she was entertaining she forgot completely about her dog. The dog would run through many of the other attention-getting behaviors before he would finally defecate on the bed—something that obviously had to be attended to. Since she interpreted this behavior as jealousy she didn't punish her dog but lavishly attended to him after he defecated in order to make him less jealous. Of course what happened was the problem got worse. It finally reached the point that as soon as her boyfriend entered the house the dog would dash to the bed and defecate.

RULES FOR EFFECTIVE REWARD

It has probably become obvious by now that reward is not as simple as giving your dog a biscuit. There are many types of reward and there are many ways you can unintentionally train your dog to bother you. To have a happy, well-adjusted and trouble-free dog you must master the correct way to reward. This is outlined in the four simple rules below:

1. Reward must be under your conscious, intentional control. In order to do this you must start paying attention to your own behavior as well as that of your dog. Ask yourself the following: What do I usually do when my dog pleases or bothers me? Is my behavior a reward for my dog's behavior? If so, do I want to reward this behavior?

2. Reward, to be effective, must immediately follow the

behavior that you want to reward. The longer the delay, the more likely your reward will be ineffective. This is because your dog might do something else in the meantime and then that other behavior will get rewarded. For example, if your dog brings you your newspaper and you take it and wait, he is likely to jump up on you or nuzzle your arm. If you then reward him, it is the jumping or arm nuzzling that is being rewarded and not newspaper retrieving.

3. The reward should suit the behavior as much as possible. Reward your dog for sitting quietly by the door by giving him an opportunity to go out. This will allow you to take advantage of the numerous things your dog likes to do. You can make them rewards for pleasing or good behavior. This means you will be training your dog whenever you are with him.

4. The reward for any one behavior should be as varied as possible. This will prevent your dog from becoming a chow hound. For example, when he sits on command, sometimes he will get food, other times he will get a drink, or get to play with a ball, or a scratch behind the ear. Keep in mind that many things will reward your dog. In fact, a reward can be defined as anything that increases the behavior it follows.

PUNISHMENT

Reward is the technique used to strengthen behavior. However, there is another commonly used technique, punishment, used to decrease undesirable behavior. This technique has been subject to many heated debates. Some people advocate strong punitive discipline for bad behavior, others suggest that punishment is cruel and debasing and should never be used under any circumstances. Still others say that punishment is usually bad and should only be used as a last resort.

This debate has gone on for years in reference to child-rearing and penology, as well as to pet behavior problems.

The questions are moral ones that you can only answer for yourself. However, science has addressed itself to the problem. There are thousands of studies concerning the effectiveness of punishment as a technique for changing behavior. Most of this research has been carried out on animals. In order for you to make an intelligent decision on this issue it would be best to examine the results of this research.

Motives for Punishment

In order for you to know whether you should be using punishment at all, there are a number of questions that you must ask yourself. All of these revolve around how you feel when you punish your dog. This may seem irrelevant but it bears directly on whether you should be using punishment. Punishing with the wrong emotions almost invariably leads to unexpected and usually undesirable results.

Punishment Out of Anger

There are many emotions that seem to accompany punishment but the most common is anger. For example, you have just purchased a brand-new living room set. It has taken you years to replace the old, beat-up furniture. When your dog was a puppy he chewed on the old furniture but you didn't care. It was beat up anyway and he was just a puppy. Before you go out to dinner to celebrate your new purchase, you take your obedient adult dog around to each of the new pieces. Pointing to the furniture, you say, "No, stay off," confident that your command will be heeded.When you return home everything seems to be all right except that the sofa has hairs and footprints on it, and one button has been pulled out and is dangling by a thread. You clean the sofa and repair the button. Before you go to work in the morning you go through the same, "No, stay off" routine, this time a little more vigorously.

(84)

You return home about 5:00 P.M. As you enter you notice some cotton stuffing on the floor. When you enter the living room your fears are confirmed. There is a great gaping hole in your sofa where the button used to be. Stuffing is all over the place. You turn to your dog, your eyes turning red. You grab the nearest object, an umbrella, and you chase him. The fact that he is running away makes you even more angry. You corner him in the hall and mumble, "This dog is going to learn a lesson he will never forget," as you start beating him, shouting "No" with every hit. You stop only when the umbrella breaks.

This sequence is typical. You lose your head and proceed to beat your dog until something happens to stop you—your weapon breaks, you get tired, the dog attacks you or someone stops you. You are not thinking, merely reacting. You can't stop until you have dissipated the anger.

Usually people who follow this pattern either don't get angry and therefore don't punish, or they go into a blind rage and punish vigorously. For them, punishment is an expression of their anger. They would never think of punishing when they are not angry.

Now punishment can be effective when used properly. But you must use your head. To vent your anger in this way achieves nothing positive. All your dog knows is that you returned home and attacked him. He cannot associate his misdeed with your attack.

What is worse, this type of punishment can lead to a variety of bad results. For one thing, your dog could attack you, a very natural reaction. It is called *pain-elicited aggression* and has been demonstrated numerous times in the laboratory. If your dog attacks you and he is large enough he can seriously injure you. If he isn't large enough, this attack will increase your rage and you could seriously injure him both physically and psychologically.

Punishment Out of Vengeance

You might feel that your dog should get hurt. After all, look what he has done to you. But punishing out of vengeance is even worse than punishing out of anger. When you are in a rage, you have merely lost control. But vengeance is a combination of anger and calculation. You can think up really creative ways to hurt your pet. I had one client who would tie his dog up and pour scalding water on it when the dog transgressed. He felt totally justified in his actions. When I asked him if the dog stopped misbehaving, the answer was "No." So why did he continue this torture? His answer was typical: "Well, he had to be punished, didn't he?"

Punishment Out of Righteous Indignation

This form of punishment is like saying that your dog has transgressed and it must "pay its debt to society." In this case the punisher is not concerned with the consequences of punishment. They don't ask whether the punishment worked, that is, whether it stopped the undesirable behavior. Nor do they ask what the side effects may be. Many times the side effects are worse than the original problem. But the righteous punisher feels that it is morally right for misdeeds to be punished.

This is the same type of pseudologic that permeates our present penal system. The notion is that the guilty must be punished. It does not matter that the punishment seldom works and almost always leads to further crime.

Punishment Because It Feels So Good

When I confront some of my clients with the fact that their punishment techniques are ineffective, some of them say, "Maybe it didn't do the dog any good, but it made me feel great."

For these people the dog becomes a convenient target on which to vent their pent-up aggressions. This is called *displace-*

ment. Since the dog has misbehaved they feel that they have a right to beat it. But what has really happened is the boss is on your back, the kids are screaming and your mother-in-law won't leave you alone—so, hit your dog, he can't talk back. This type of punishment, like the others, is usually ineffective and invariably leads to side effects that are worse than the original problem.

Punishment Out of Fear

Surprisingly, many of my clients who abuse their dogs are truly afraid of them. They feel that if they don't dominate the dog by rough and severe treatment, one day the dog will turn on them. The sad fact is that they are creating the very conditions necessary to cause their dog to do just that. It is a self-fulfilling prophecy.

They know that one day the dog will turn into a savage beast. So they beat the dog and this turns it into the savage beast they feared in the first place and confirms their prophecy. This justifies the severe treatment and leads to more of the same. But there is no escaping the ultimate outcome, a severe attack by the dog.

Punishment without Malice

Punishment can be thought of as bad-tasting medicine. You don't administer this medicine because you are angry, vengeful or for any other negative feeling. You give it because it is necessary to cure the illness. And you administer punishment for only one reason, to stop the troublesome behavior of your pet. Just as your doctor would stop an ineffective medicine, so you should stop an ineffective punishment.

The analogy between punishment and medicine goes even further. A medicine has an effective dosage and so does punishment. Overdosing can cause serious problems. Both punishment and medicine have a prescribed routine for administration. If you don't follow the routine you can create other problems or render the attempted remedy ineffective. In addition, many medicines have side effects, even if you follow the instructions carefully. So does punishment. The key is to administer the punishment so as to minimize the side effects and maximize the effectiveness.

If you can't handle punishment without malice, anger, jealousy, hatred, displacement, spite, vengeance, fear or righteous indignation or if you like to hurt things, then don't use it. Stop reading this section; it will only waste your time.

There is only one emotion that should appropriately accompany punishment: sorrow for your dog. All the other emotions will lead you to apply punishment ineffectively, inappropriately and incorrectly. This can only lead to a worsening of the problem.

The Characteristics of a Good Punishment

You probably feel by now that it is better not to use punishment at all. But there are times when one or two correctly administered punishments can do wonders to eliminate problem behavior rapidly. Please notice that I said one or two punishments. If you find yourself repeatedly administering the punishment, even if you have the best intentions, it probably means that your punishment technique is ineffective.

Laboratory research with animals has shown that there are seven characteristics of effective punishment. Examine the following Rules of Punishment to see if your punishment procedures need to be corrected.

Rule No. 1: *Punishment should be immediate.*

For punishment to be most effective it must be given immediately after the problem behavior starts. Even a short delay can make it ineffective. There are two reasons for this: first, the reason for punishment is to prevent your dog from misbehaving again. Thus, you want to punish the very beginning of the behavior sequence. If you wait too long, you will wind up punishing the end of the sequence just as the dog is finished. Take stealing food from the table as an example. The sequence is usually one in which your dog enters the room, gets up on the table or counter, picks up the food, brings it to the floor and eats. If you wait too long, you will punish eating when you want to punish jumping onto the table. This will result in your dog going through the sequence much more rapidly so he can get the food and eat it before you discover him. Or it will result in your dog hiding somewhere while he eats. The best time to punish this sequence is a second before your dog gets the food, just as he is jumping up and reaching for it.

The second reason waiting too long makes punishment ineffective is that you wind up punishing intervening behavior. This is especially likely if there is a very long time between the problem behavior and the punishment. Let's take property damage as an example. One of my clients had a problem with their dog unraveling the toilet paper in the bathroom. They would usually discover the products of the transgression sometime after the dog was finished. They would then drag the dog into the bathroom, vigorously shake him and say, "No." This never worked. In the time between the transgression and the punishment the dog had performed many other behaviors, the last of which was coming to my clients when they called him. My clients were, in actuality, punishing their dog for coming when called. This resulted in a dog who persisted in chewing the toilet paper but who would run away when called.

This brings me to another point. You can *never* punish a *product* of behavior. Many problem behaviors leave telltale signs. If your dog chews furniture then the damage is evident. If your dog defecates in undesirable places, then the fecal matter is the product. You can figure out what misbehavior occurred. However, it is already too long after the deed to punish the behavior. Your dog will not get the message. For example, rubbing your dog's nose in his waste is not only revolting, it is completely ineffective. You have discovered the waste too long after it was produced for you to punish this behavior.

When I explain this to my clients many of them counter with what they believe to be cogent arguments.

ARGUMENT NO. 1   "But he knows he did something wrong." "He looks guilty when I say, 'What did you do?'"

What my clients have mistaken for knowledge of the act or guilt is the association of punishment to the words, "What did you do?" Every time they punish their dog they would invariably say those words. Thus, the words strike fear in the dog without his knowing what he did. If you don't believe this say these words when your dog hasn't done anything wrong. If he cowers and acts guilty that will prove the point.

ARGUMENT NO. 2   "I don't have to say a word. If he has done something wrong and I just look at him, he runs."

This is a similar situation to argument No. 1. However, in this case your bodily signs of anger or frustration have been associated with punishment. This is a very easy association for your dog to make. After all, he is a nonverbal animal. His genetics have programmed him to attend carefully to your posture, tone of voice and movement patterns. When you are angry and about to punish all these nonverbal cues change. Your dog will perceive these changes readily and be afraid of you. But he still doesn't know that he has done something wrong.

ARGUMENT NO. 3   "All I have to do is enter the room. If he has done something wrong, he cowers, even before I discover what it was that he did."

This may really look as if your dog has knowledge of his transgression and feels guilty, but it is still an association. In this case the association is between the product of the transgression and punishment. If your dog defecates in the house and then later you bring him up to it and wallop him, he will associate his fecal matter and your presence with punishment. His waste in and of itself doesn't signal punishment, but his waste plus you is the signal of an impending spanking. Thus, when you enter the room that contains his waste he cowers. He fears being punished by you, but this punishment will not be associated with the behavior of defecating.

Rule No. 2: *Punishment should be an effective dose the first time you use it.*

Sometimes out of kindness my clients have started using such a mild punishment on their dog that it would not suppress the behavior. Then they slowly increase the level. This can result in teaching your dog to endure intense physical pain to get what he wants. I am not suggesting that you beat your dog severely, just use a punishment that is mildly aversive and avoid the escalating punishment trap.

The escalating punishment trap means that you keep increasing the intensity of the punishment as your dog gets used to lower levels of punishment. This happens when you punish frequently and start at too low an intensity. If you are going to use punishment you should control it; it should not control you.

Rule No. 3: *Punishment should be ecologically valid.*

This means that the punishment should fit the crime. This does *not* mean that really bad behavior should get really severe punishment, but that your dog should experience the natural consequences of his acts.

Your dog gets punished by his environment all the time. If he approaches and sniffs a lit candle he burns his nose. He won't do that again. If he tries to catch a cat he will usually get a good, painful swat across the face. Next time he will show more respect for the cat. If he runs into a thorn bush, he gets stuck. If he bites a bee he gets stung. All these are ecologically valid environmental punishments.

You can arrange it so that your dog receives ecologically valid punishments. Many people have a difficult time leaving their house because their dog makes a mad dash for the door and runs out between their legs. The ecologically valid punishment for this behavior is to close the door just as he is about to get to it. This takes a little practice and works best with a door that opens out. But a few bumps in the head will teach your dog not to run out.

Rule No. 4: *If at all possible, the punishment should be administered by the environment and not you.*

This is related to the ecological validity of the punishment. If you administer the punishment then you become the bad guy. However, a little creative intervention can go a long way to helping the environment teach your dog the limits on his behavior.

One way to go about this I call Creative Booby-trapping. For example, clients of mine had a German shepherd who had learned to open the refrigerator and raid it. It was impossible to punish this behavior since the dog only raided the refrigerator when my clients were at work. The solution was to booby-trap the refrigerator. We did this by piling pots and pans on top of the door so that they would fall and make a loud noise when the dog started to open the door.

Other booby traps involved placing two large inflated balloons in a cabinet that the dog habitually opened. Two mouse-trap triggers with a pin taped to them were attached by strings to the cabinet door. The first trigger would activate if the door was opened six inches, the second activated at ten inches. This was easy to do by adjusting the length of the strings. There was no need for the second trigger. After the first explosion the dog never opened the door again.

For Creative Booby-trapping to be effective there should be no sign of it. Don't let your dog see you set up your dirty tricks or he might learn to associate that new cue with the trap. The point of the procedure is for your dog to learn that parts of his environment are dangerous and should be avoided.

Rule No. 5: *Punishment should be consistent and associated only to the problem behavior.*

One reason for letting the environment perform the punishment is that if you carry it out, your dog will associate you with the punishment and become afraid of you. For punishment to work best, your dog should only associate it with his transgression. If your dog could talk, he would say to himself, "If I do this I always get punished whether my master is here or not."

Punishment should be like a "bolt from heaven" preceded by the word "no." The dog should feel that wherever you are, you will know that he has transgressed and will punish him. If you give away the fact that he is going to be punished by yelling or running after him, then he will be able to predict the punishment by these cues and not associate his act with punishment.

In order to accomplish this you must be somewhat sneaky. For example, clients of mine had a toy poodle that persisted in urinating in their bed. To stop this they tried to bring him to the spot and push his nose in it and whack him. The dog continued to urinate but also would run and hide when they called to him signaling his punishment. They would say, "Come here, I want to show you what you did!" This was consistently associated with the spanking, so the dog would make a beeline under the nearest table and defend himself viciously, growling and nipping at the feet of anyone who would approach. This led them to try to coax the dog out with sweet talk, "Come on out, we won't hurt you," and sometimes food. This of course rewarded the vicious behavior. Then, as soon as they got the dog they would take him to the bed and spank him. This sequence set up an association of the sweet talk and food with punishment. Consequently, the dog got very aggressive

(93)

when he was fed and when anyone tried to speak nicely to him. They had given up trying to stop the dog from urinating on the bed and kept their bedroom door closed. However, if they forgot to close the door the dog would invariably urinate.

The solution was for the owners to intentionally open their bedroom door, then station themselves so they could watch their room and dog carefully and inconspicuously. When the dog entered the room, they were to sneak up as quietly as possible and peek in. As soon as the dog jumped on the bed they were to scream "no" loudly and throw a pillow at him. The noise and commotion would be enough punishment. This technique worked in three trials. The dog learned that urination caused punishment, no matter whether his owners were in the room or not. Thus, the key to this technique is to be sneaky:

1. When you suspect that your dog is transgressing, sneak up quietly. If he is doing something wrong, yell "no" and throw something.

2. If he is about to do something, don't stop him. Wait till the instant he starts and then punish.

3. If he has already done something and you missed it, then forget it. It's too late! Pay better attention next time.

When I tell this to my clients, they often say, "I can't watch him all the time." They are right. If they tried to, they would probably fail. You have to arrange the situation so that your dog will perform his bad behavior when you are ready to watch him. If he steals food from the table, then conspicuously place food (preferably something you don't mind losing) on the table and leave the room. Then, sneak back and watch from a good vantage point. The instant your dog transgresses, bust in and punish.

I personally have used modern technology to spy on my clients' dogs. TV cameras and electronic sensors can record when the animal is transgressing and enable you to time your punishment perfectly.

Rule No. 6: *For punishment to be most effective it should be used as infrequently as possible. Also, try to use a different punishment each time.*

This is to prevent your dog from getting used to the punishment. If he should get used to it, then you would have no choice but to escalate and you will wind up beating your dog severely when it isn't necessary.

Most dog-training books give suggestions for punishment— everything from a rolled-up newspaper to cans with pebbles in them that can be thrown at the dog, squirt guns, and so forth. All these punishments can be effective but they invariably suffer from overuse.

So, how do you punish infrequently when your dog is misbehaving frequently? This is accomplished by applying the punishment at exactly the right time as mentioned in Rule No. 5. This will make the punishment very effective and result in eliminating the problem behavior in two or three trials.

Rule No. 7: *If you have to punish your dog then find a way to reward him later on.*

If you personally have punished your dog, he has reason to fear you. To counterbalance this, you must teach him to associate your presence with some reward. Some time after the punishment, call your dog and reward him with praise, attention and food for coming to you. Then give him a command and reward him. However, never reward your dog immediately after you have punished him, no matter how sorry you feel. If you do that it will result in his associating punishment with reward. This can lead him to misbehave and earn a punishment in order to get a reward. And if your punishment is not very severe, rewarding immediately after punishment can even train him to enjoy the punishment itself.

In summary, use punishment and reward to eliminate unwanted behavior and train desirable behavior. The most effective combination is to punish the bad behavior and reward behavior that is exactly opposite. For example, if your dog jumps up on you when you enter the house, punish the jumping. But be sure to reward lying down if he should be in this position when you enter. If your dog bolts out of the door when it is open, punish this by closing the door and reward sitting quietly by the door by opening it and letting him out. If your dog eliminates in the house, punish this but reward him if he eliminates outside.

Think of it as if you have an unlimited supply of reward but a very limited supply of punishment. Find every opportunity to reward desirable behaviors and behaviors that are opposite to the problem behaviors. Use punishment only when you are sure that you can apply it at exactly the right time.

CONDITIONING

Reward and punishment are important ways your dog learns. But these are not the only ways. Habits are formed through repeated practice of the same response in the same situation. In fact, all you need for learning to occur is that *the response occur consistently, excluding all other possible responses to a stimulus.* The rule is: What is being noticed becomes a signal for what is being done.

Your dog notices many aspects of his environment—time of day, noises, changes in atmospheric pressure and your nonverbal and verbal cues. This is why many people say things like, "My dog knows when my husband is about to come home a half hour before he arrives." "He gets very excited, passes and stares at the door until my husband enters." This is not an example of ESP in the dog. Since the husband arrives at the same time every day, the stimuli that occur around that time become associated with the excitement of the husband's arrival. The fact that the dog gets so excited thirty minutes early means that his internal body clock is a little fast. Similarly, your dog is able to discriminate your footsteps or the sound of your car from all others.

Your dog may seem to know when you are about to take him for a walk without you saying a word. When you put your coat on he will jump, get excited and run around. Some dogs will bring their leash. This is because you are a creature of habit and when you intend to take your dog out you will act somewhat differently from those times when you are just going out alone.

Your body cues—posture, movements and tone of voice —are signals for your dog. We humans have been trained for years to pay attention to what someone says, sometimes ignoring how that person is acting. Your dog does not have that handicap. Since he can't talk he pays attention to movement patterns. Since these patterns signal how you feel, your dog may be a better predictor of your behavior than your friend or even yourself. This is why your dog appears sometimes to know what is on your mind.

These cues or signals through conditioning can set off your dog's genetically organized patterns of behavior (fixed-action patterns). If you pair a consistent verbal command with the fixed-action patterns you will eventually achieve verbal control over these genetically organized behaviors. Your dog will learn to obey even if you don't reward him. However, reward serves to make your dog pay attention more closely to your commands.

An example of this is training your dog to defecate on command. Anyone who has walked a dog knows how much trouble it is when he refuses to perform. You walk and walk and it seems that he has to find just the right place. This can be a problem, especially if you live in the city and must curb your dog. The solution is simple, however. Wait until your dog really has to go. Then take him out. Just as he squats, say, "Hurry up," or some other appropriate phrase. If you do this consistently then the words will be a signal to defecate.

Similarly, if you say "Attack" as your dog is barking and growling, "Eat" just before your dog takes a bite, "Speak" just before he barks, "Sit" just as he is sitting, "Come here" as he approaches you, "Jump" as he jumps, "Back up" as he backs up, "Vomit" just before he throws up, "Sneeze" as he sneezes or "Cough" as he coughs, your verbal command will eventually cue these behaviors.

The key is to arrange the environment so that the fixed-action pattern is elicited. Then, give the command just before your dog acts. This is the premise behind many of the obedience or training routines found in dog-training manuals. When you push down on the dog's rump and pull up on his neck, you are forcing the dog to sit. If you say "sit" at the same time then he learns to sit on command.

However, this rule also leads to many obedience problems. How many times have you heard someone who is chasing after his dog in the park say "Come here." He is in fact training the dog to run away on command. Or consider a dog who is in the habit of jumping on people. The owner enters the house and the dog starts jumping. The owner keeps saying, "Get down." Or when your dog gets something you don't want him to have, you try to take it away and he grabs it and you wind up having a tug of war. All the time you are saying "Give me that" as he is pulling it away. How many times have you yelled "Shut up" or "Be quiet" as your dog continuously barked? This leads many owners to say that their dog just doesn't obey, when in fact he is obeying perfectly. He jumps when they say "Get down," and runs away when they say "Come here."

The solution is to make sure that your dog performs the act that you are commanding him to do. If your dog gets loose, instead of chasing him, run the other way. When he starts chasing you, yell "Come here." If your dog jumps, say "Get down," and then push him to the floor.

The sections on the genetics and animal learning tell you something about how your dog behaves naturally and how these natural behaviors can be changed. The last section on behavior therapy or behavior modification will tell you how to apply these techniques.

4

TYPES OF PROBLEMS

In my practice I see a variety of behavior problems in dogs and an equal variety of complaints from owners. Sometimes the problem behaviors and the complaints match, but often they do not. Sometimes the owners recognize that there is something wrong but they just can't put their finger on it. At other times the owners have definite complaints about behaviors that are perfectly normal and ignore the real problems. Still other times the owners have correctly identified some problem behaviors, the ones that stand out, but the more subtle problems are ignored.

The reason for this confusion is twofold. First, many owners persist in interpreting their dogs' behavior in human terms. We can tell to some degree what abnormal behavior looks like in a human. You may not be able to give a scientific name to a problem you see but you certainly can tell that it is strange or abnormal. The reason you can identify abnormal behavior in humans is that it stands out. It violates the norms of behavior. It is different. Now the norms for dog behavior are quite different than for human behavior. And since we interact with many people but with few dogs, we do not know the norms for dog behavior. Thus you use the next best thing, that is, your experience with humans and you interpret your dog in these terms.

The second reason for this confusion relates to our incomplete knowledge of abnormal behavior. Many people are familiar with some of the psychological jargon used to describe abnormal behavior, words like neurotic, psychotic, schizophrenic, manic depressive, split personality and so forth. However, these words are never really well defined. So many of my clients will use these terms to diagnose the problem. They will say, "I think my dog has a split personality. Sometimes he is good, but other times he is vicious. I can't tell how he is going to act." They want me to confirm or refute their diagnosis and get frustrated when I tell them that this term is a human diagnostic category and is meaningless when applied to a dog.

This error is not restricted to the lay public. I recently read a book on dogs written by a veterinarian. Approximately 30 percent of the book was directed toward problem behaviors. The veterinarian classified the problem behaviors using the traditional human-oriented categories. He had sections for schizophrenia, psychopathic dogs, manic depressive dogs, types of neurosis in dogs and so forth. This is ridiculous. First of all, these categories were not designed for dogs but for humans. Second, giving a dog a label such as schizophrenic or neurotic tells you nothing about treatment. We don't know very much about how to treat human schizophrenia, let alone in dogs. The only time a label is of any value is when there is a definite prescribed treatment that goes with the label, a treatment that has been scientifically proven to be effective. Otherwise the label becomes a delusion. The labeler thinks he has done something by giving the problem a label when he has done nothing but fool himself.

What we need is a way to categorize problem behavior that

tells us something about how to treat the problem. The first step is to determine if there is a problem. The best way to find out is to answer the question, "Does my dog's behavior bother me or a member or my family or the neighbors?" You have a problem if the answer is yes. If you answer no to this question then whether your dog is acting "normal" or not is totally irrelevant. If you can live comfortably with your dog's behavior, then don't worry about it. But if your dog is annoying, bothering and/or displeasing you or someone else, it is time to think about changing the behavior.

Once you have decided that you have a problem the next question is, What is the problem? Following is the Behavior Problem Checklist alluded to earlier in the book. You will notice that the checklist is organized in two dimensions. Down the left side are behavior classifications. They describe the various behaviors that your dog can engage in. Each behavior classification is a general name of a fixed-action pattern (genetically organized sequence of behavior). The end of the sequence, or the goal of the pattern, is the consummatory act. Thus the mounting of a female by a male is the consummatory act of sexual behavior. However, there are other behaviors related to sexual behavior besides the consummatory act. Some of these occur before the act and lead up to it. These are called appetitive components. The appetitive component to copulation is the elaborate sequence called courtship. Sometimes problems can occur with these components as well. Later on we will describe the sequence of behaviors for each type of behavior. This will give you some idea about "normal" behavior in a dog.

Across the top of the checklist are the three ways in which the behavior classifications can cause problems. The behavior can occur too much, a response excess. Thus, dogs can drink and eat too much, have too much fear, scratch too much and so forth. Techniques can be used to reduce the behavior to normal levels.

(102)

TABLE 2. BEHAVIOR PROBLEM CHECKLIST

Behavior Class	Problem Response Excess TOO MUCH BEHAVIOR	Problem Response Deficit TOO LITTLE BEHAVIOR	Problem Inappropriate Stimulus Control WRONG BEHAVIOR
Feeding	hyperphagia: excessive eating or excessively rapid eating leading to vomiting; hiding food	anorexia: eating deficit leading to inanition; also food preferences leading to deficiency	pica: eating of non-nutritional substances such as paint, hair, waste
Drinking	polydipsia: excessive drinking or excessive rate of drinking (stress-induced)	adipsia: deficit in rate or quantity of fluid consumption	unusual gustatory preferences for certain dangerous liquids; drinking from toilet and alcoholism
Sexual	hypersexuality: heightened sexual arousal in the presence of minimal eliciting stimuli; excessive courtship	impotence: failure in lordosis for female; improper positioning for male; diminished sexual activity; abbreviated courtship	masturbation: sexual behavior directed at humans; mounting female inappropriately
Fighting	conspecific dominance problems between owner and pet (guarding objects; dominance attack)	lack of protectiveness when necessary; excessive submissive behavior interfering with other behavior (submissive micturition)	guarding objects or places from members of family; attacking strangers; *overprotectiveness* without control
Fear	fear-biting: excessive fear reaction to normally fear-producing objects; uncontrollability	lack of appropriate fear of dangerous objects	phobias: thunderstorms; noises; being alone; enclosed places; open spaces

TABLE 2. BEHAVIOR PROBLEM CHECKLIST (Continued)

Behavior Class	Problem Response Excess	Problem Response Deficit	Problem Inappropriate Stimulus Control
Eliminating	encopresis and enuresis: involuntary defecation and urination; excessive micturition during walk	overcontrol of defecation and urination due to excessive punitive training ("takes too long to go")	soiling problems in home; litter box problems
Exploring	puppy behavior in adult dogs; excessive chewing and mouthing objects; getting into things; distractability	inattentive to environmental stimuli	lack of fear of dangerous objects; attention to irrelevant cues
Care of Body Surface	excessive hair chewing or scratching leading to damage; excessive care seeking	incomplete grooming practices	clawing objects in home; conditioned scratching
Care of Young	failure to wean	failure to groom or feed young; attacking, killing, eating young	adopting objects or other species as young
Resting	lazy	hyperkinesis; excitability	resting on couch or table when not allowed; unusual sleep cycles
Operant	bizarre behavior rituals; barking and whining	lack of obedience; no owner control over behavior	failure to differentiate commands; failure to generalize commands
Nesting	guarding objects or places; hoarding objects and/or food in nest	failure to build or establish maternal nest	nest site in inconvenient place

Conversely, there can be a response deficit when a dog does not perform enough of the behavior. Your dog could be a picky eater and thus eat too little, he could have too little fear of dangerous objects and so forth. If this is the case, then techniques to increase the behavior are employed.

Finally, your dog could be performing quite normally but at the wrong time or place or to the wrong stimuli. My clients in the first chapter had a dog who ate the wrong things. A dog who mounts you is acting normally but to the wrong stimuli. Defecating is normal but becomes a problem when it occurs in the wrong place, such as on your brand-new rug.

In order to tell what is normal and what is not, we will go over the checklist one behavior at a time, describing the natural behavior sequences and the ways that these behaviors can go wrong. Make a note on the checklist if some of the problems refer to your dog. In the next chapter I will describe how to analyze these problems and develop a treatment plan to correct them. But first we must know what the problem is.

FEEDING
Consummatory Component

Needless to say, feeding is a very important behavior for any living organism. Natural selection worked on the dog's early ancestor, the wolf, to refine a sequence of prey-catching and eating best suited to its environment and the type of prey it habitually eats. The wolves that were most successful in catching and eating prey would be the ones most likely to survive and pass on their genetic edge to their progeny. So in order to get an idea of the "normal" feeding of dogs we must examine the feeding patterns in wolves.

When people think of feeding they usually think of the

consummatory component, that is, the seizing of food in the mouth and swallowing. The dog and wolf are quite similar in this respect. For semiliquid foods such as canned dog food, "the dog or wolf stands with his tail down seizing part of the food in his teeth, releasing it and lowering his head suddenly to shift the food to the back of the mouth, and gulping it quickly. . . . They deal with bones and tough pieces of meat by lying down, holding the food in their paws, and either tearing off strips with their front teeth or gnawing on the object with their heavy back teeth."* These patterns seem to have remained for the most part unchanged from the wolf to the dog even with eight thousand to ten thousand years of selective breeding and domestication.

Another part of the dog's ingestive behavior seems to have remained the same: the relation between quantity of food eaten and hunger. For many animals the quantity of food eaten is directly related to the time of the last meal. However, the dog and wolf, like other predators, can go for long periods, at least a week or more, without food, and not suffer serious harm. When they get food, they will usually eat rapidly without chewing, filling their large gullet with large chunks of food. This allows them to go for long durations without eating and also allows them to return to the den and vomit the food back to feed the puppies. Thus a dog, like a wolf, will not naturally limit the quantity of food it eats. It will eat whatever is available and be ready for more. One couple commented that their German shepherd, after being fed two large cans of dog food, proceeded to eat five pounds of choice ground beef and four pounds of steak they had set out for the evening barbecue. The dog ate this in the few minutes it took to go to the backyard and light the fire on the barbecue. They didn't bother to protect the food because they figured that their dog would be full and not interested in eating again.

* From *Genetics and Social Behavior of the Dog* by John Paul Scott and John L. Fuller (Chicago: University of Chicago Press, 1965), p. 72.

This is the reason many city dogs are overweight. The owners feel that if their dog is willing to eat more he must still be hungry, so they overfeed their pet. Since the dog does not naturally limit his intake he will continue to eat. The best way to combat this hyperphagia is to give your dog a measured quantity of food. The amount should be related to the size of your dog. Follow the recommendations on the dog food package or can. If your dog gains weight with the recommended amount, then reduce it by 10 percent. Continue on this limited food intake for two weeks, weighing your dog periodically. If he continues to gain, reduce the amount by another 10 percent. If he loses weight, continue on that regime until he is at his ideal weight. Your dog will probably level off near his ideal weight. If he continues to lose then increase the quantity by 5 percent. By going back and forth you will be able to determine the correct quantity of food. The dog food companies recommend a certain quantity of food but this is based on a generalized or average figure. It is quite likely that this will not fit your dog. Many apartment dwellers with inactive dogs are quite surprised to find out how little their dog needs to eat in order to be healthy. However, if your dog is on a limited diet, make sure that he is getting the minimum amount of vitamins and minerals he needs. You may have to supplement his food with specially prepared vitamins and minerals. These can be obtained from your veterinarian or pet supply store.

Extensive eating and overweight are sometimes caused because owners do not understand their dog's genetically organized eating habits. Consequently this problem is easy to correct, just by controlling the amount of food given. However, excessive rapid eating and vomiting are somewhat more difficult to understand and control. As I have already pointed out, dogs and wolves naturally eat rather rapidly. A number of things will tend to increase your dog's rate of eating. His eating behavior can be influenced by the presence of another dog eating at the same time. This is called social facilitation. Barring any competition for food, puppies tend to eat more rapidly and greater quantities if they are fed in groups than if they are fed alone. If your dog had to compete for food with another dog this would lead him to increase his speed of eating. The best way to handle this is to feed your dogs separately out of different dishes and perhaps even in different rooms.

Sometimes excessive rapid eating can lead to vomiting; however, if your dog habitually vomits after he eats then he should be checked by your veterinarian. If there is no physical reason for the vomiting then you can apply the psychological solutions.

Vomiting can be caused by many psychological reasons. Vomiting food is a fixed-action pattern of bitches which is elicited by the begging behavior of her puppies. Puppies will naturally run to the returning mother with their tails wagging rapidly, leap up, paw and lick the mother's face. This causes the mother to regurgitate. This is a natural feeding behavior and if your bitch does this you shouldn't be concerned. However, this natural pattern can go awry. A client of mine had an adult female collie who would vomit on young children, especially if the children would pet her around the head, mouth or belly. My clients thought that she resented children and that vomiting was her way of getting back at them. However, this was not the case. The dog had simply generalized her natural puppy feeding pattern.

Vomiting can also be conditioned. Remember the rule "What is being noticed can be a signal for what is being done." Another couple had a dog who would vomit only in the bathroom. This problem started when the dog had a severe stomach ailment that caused him to vomit. My clients would put the dog into the bathroom right after eating or if they felt he was about to vomit. Thus the dog vomited only in the bathroom. This made it easier to clean but it also served to condition the vomiting. After the dog was cured of the stomach ailment he persisted in vomiting in the bathroom. Of course this behavior had been rewarded since the dog would be released and given much attention after his vomiting. We determined that it took from three to five minutes for the dog to vomit after he was placed in the bathroom. I had my clients place the dog in the bathroom, then release him in thirty seconds and given attention and food. The time was slowly increased until the dog was spending five minutes without vomiting. This was easily increased to thirty minutes. The vomiting never recurred.

Vomiting can be conditioned to a variety of signals. I have treated a dog that would vomit when gently stroked on the belly. The owner would invariably do this to soothe the dog when it was sick.

Appetitive Component

Most people focus on the consummatory component of feeding; however, there are other elements involved. The start of the feeding sequence is the appetitive component of hunting. The appetitive component is less stereotyped and more susceptible to genetic and environmental change than is the consummatory component.

Pet dogs rarely hunt for food. But if they did they would probably hunt somewhat like the wolf. Wolves will occasionally hunt alone but for the most part hunt in packs. The exact pattern of hunting depends upon the size of the pack and the type of prey. Wolves usually hunt large-hoofed animals such as deer, moose, caribou and mountain sheep. They have also been known to kill domestic cattle and sheep. The pattern is to select a victim from the herd. Usually weaker, slower, less healthy animals are caught. The wolves will then dash at the animal, avoiding the head and snapping at the hindquarters. This attack stimulates the rest of the pack to join in so that the victim cannot successfully avoid all of them. After

(109)

the kill the wolves will tear great chunks from the carcass and guard it, threatening and attacking any other member of the pack that attempts to take it away. The most dominant wolf usually eats first and is the most aggressive when guarding, frequently removing food from more submissive animals.

Guarding food is a genetically organized behavior. However, it can be very troublesome when your pet guards his food. The amount of food-guarding is directly related to the dominance status of your dog in the household. He may not guard his food from you but may attack your spouse. Guarding also increases as the dog's food becomes more solid. Your dog may not guard his semiliquid food but he will get ferocious when he has a fresh bone. Guarding seems to be related to the chewing, gnawing and tearing behavior when your dog is eating. Many people tolerate this guarding behavior because they think that it is natural and will just leave the dog alone when he is eating something. They are right about such behavior being genetically organized, but they are wrong about ignoring it.

About 40 percent of my cases involve excessive guarding in which the family pet will viciously attack some or any member of the household who happens to approach while the dog is chewing or eating. My clients in the first chapter managed to not only tolerate this but also increase it by reward. This behavior should be corrected immediately when it shows itself. The best time is when the dog is a puppy. Your puppy's teeth are small and he can do less damage. However, it can be corrected when your dog is an adult, although it is a lot more dangerous.

A puppy should be tested for guarding before you accept him, and also periodically (every few weeks) after you bring him home. He should be tested with every member of the family. If he starts guarding, take the item away and return it to him when he is quiet. You may need a good pair of heavy leather gloves for this technique. If he guards food then spoon- or hand-feed him. He should get food only if he behaves. If he growls stop feeding him for a few minutes, then start again. If he growls three times in a row then he misses that meal. This should be done by every member of the family. The goal is for anyone to be able to approach him and remove anything from his mouth.

Guarding food has not changed much from the time of the wolf. A wolf that didn't guard lost its food and would be less likely to survive. For the dog, guarding food is not as important, so this behavior has become more variable. Some animals never guard while others guard ferociously.

Hunting, which occurs earlier than guarding, has been subject to much genetic manipulation. As I have already mentioned, dogs don't have to hunt for food. However, many dogs have been bred for special kinds of hunting behaviors. The Saluki, for instance, is a very fast runner. Bird dogs use a variety of their senses. The pointer will freeze in a stalking position when the prey is located. However, this selective breeding may cause problems. Bird dogs are highly stimulated by birds and can become chicken killers. Shepherd breeds are stimulated by the smell of sheep and occasionally become sheep killers.

The group attack of the hunting wolf can become a serious problem to owners who have a number of dogs. These dogs will naturally form a pack. If one member of the group attacks someone, including the owner, it could stimulate the other dogs to join in. If you must have a group of dogs, make sure you are dominant.

Response Deficit

So far we have talked about behavioral excesses of feeding. The opposite condition, that is, a feeding behavior deficit, is less common. There are two types of deficits. One, called anorexia nervosa, is a complete lack of eating. The second type results from unusually specific food preferences. If your dog refuses to eat, the first step is to have him checked by a veterinarian in order to rule out a bodily cause. Once this is ruled out, then psychological causes can be entertained.

Your dog may refuse to eat if there is a complete and drastic change in his environment, for instance, when he is taken on a trip, boarded in a kennel, or at the death or departure of a member of the household. When this happens the owners say that the dog misses its old surroundings or is mourning for the departed loved one. This may be partially correct but in a different sense from the way the owners mean it. In fact, the dog has been conditioned to eat in the presence of certain environmental signals such as his own home or the presence of his owner. If you remove these signals, eating stops.

A personal example will illustrate the point. A number of years ago I had a small green parrot. This parrot was friendly to me but persisted in biting my kids. The bite was not serious and the kids thought it was fun to play "Bite me if you can" with the parrot. They would stick their fingers and pencils in the cage and pull them out before the parrot could get them. My son, being the youngest, got a great pleasure from sneaking up and scaring the parrot when it wasn't looking. Consequently, the parrot was always on the lookout for him, fluttering madly when he approached. This teasing and taunting occurred while the parrot ate, drank and thrived in the household.

We were planning a two-week vacation and arranged for a trustworthy neighbor to feed and water the parrot in our absence. Four days after we left, I received a frantic call from our neighbor. The parrot was dying. It refused to eat and drink. Our neighbor had taken it to the vet but nothing physical was wrong. What had happened was that feeding and drinking had been associated with the constant taunting by my kids. When we left, the house was quiet and the parrot stopped eating. It did not miss the kids; it missed its normal environment.

(112)

The solution was simple. To the astonishment of my neighbor, I asked her to bother the animal, bang on the cage, make a lot of noise, reach in and poke it and chase it around the cage. This procedure worked like a charm.

In order to prevent this separation anorexia the best technique is to expose your dog to a variety of cues while he is eating. Make sure he eats in a variety of places when he is a puppy. The greater variety the less likely your dog will associate any one thing with eating. When your dog is an adult, you can correct the problem by exposing him to a graded series of changes while feeding. Make sure that your dog eats well at each step before introducing him to the new step.

Finicky eaters have a similar but milder form of the same problem. Such eaters have usually been fed the same food prepared in the same way all their lives. One client of mine had a Pekinese who would eat only broiled lamb with garlic. If the lamb was not seasoned exactly right, the dog would turn its nose up and refuse to eat. This would send my client into a panic. Sometimes she would discard the meal and recook a new batch of lamb. When people hear of such behavior they say that the dog is spoiled. A more accurate analysis is that the dog's eating behavior had been conditioned to a very limited set of smell and taste cues.

The best way to prevent this is to make sure your dog gets a variety of foods as a puppy. The dog food manufacturers would like you not to do this. Read a puppy food container to see proof of this. They would prefer you to buy only their puppy chow. Then the dog would get conditioned to their particular taste, their secret ingredient. You are then stuck with that brand. So feed your puppy as great a variety of foods and brands as possible, prepared in a variety of ways.

If your dog is already stuck on a food, then introduce new foods mixed up in the preferred food. At first use just a small amount of the new, mixed up with the preferred. Then progressively increase the concentration of new food. Eventually your

(113)

dog will be eating the new food as well as the old. Do this with each new food you introduce.

Inappropriate Control

You will recall that my clients in the first chapter not only had a problem with feeding excess but also had inappropriate control. Their dog would guard and eat a whole variety of nonfood items. This is not a very common problem, however. A more common one is stealing food, especially with larger dogs who can jump up on tables and counters and open refrigerators and cabinets. But although the behavior is natural it does not have to occur. You can control this behavior by letting the environment punish the dog for stealing. The dog should learn that food on the table is dangerous and distasteful, while food in its dish is safe and tastes good.

The technique I have usually used for dogs who steal food is to condition the food with an unpleasant taste, usually powdered Chinese hot mustard. The technique is to fold the mustard powder into the food and then place it on the counter in plain sight. Then bring the dog to the counter, show him the food, and say, "Don't touch." Put the food back on the counter and leave the room. The dog usually jumps up and gets the food. The first bite with hot mustard is usually enough. Then some unadulterated food of the same type is placed in the dog dish with the command, "Okay, now you can eat." Do this on every counter and table where your dog is likely to steal food and always follow it with untreated food in his plate. Your dog will learn that food on the counter is unpalatable but food in his plate is okay. He will also learn not to eat food that you tell him not to eat and to eat food you tell him is all right.

You can also pair an unpleasant experience with the stealing of the taboo food. This experience can range from a loud noise to a mousetrap. The key is that the experience be paired only with the food and not your presence or some other cue. If you place a mousetrap on top of the food, your dog could learn not to eat food with a mousetrap on it. However, a loud noise is far more effective. It can be sounded from a distance without any cues to give it away. I have used a starter pistol, which is very loud and very effective. The procedure is as before: place the food on the counter, show the food to the dog, say, "Don't touch" and leave the room. But here you must secretly watch your dog. The second he jumps up, fire the pistol. Your dog will drop the food and back away. Then wait a minute. Reenter and put the good food in his dish saying, "Okay, eat it." If you do this in every location where your dog steals food he will quickly learn the consequences of this action. But remember, never tip him off to what you are about to do. For example, one client of mine persisted in showing the dog the pistol and saying, "You know what is going to happen if you try it." In this way the starter pistol became the cue. Consequently, the dog feared guns but continued stealing.

I used this technique very effectively on the dog described in the first chapter. But in that case I paired the nonfood items with loud noise. Since the dog stole food and ate his own waste, I paired both these items with the hot Chinese mustard. His own waste was always baited but the food was only baited when in a taboo location. Then good food was placed in his dish and he was allowed to eat. In one week the dog had stopped demanding food and refused to eat anything not preceded by the words "Okay, you can eat it." We tested this by placing a juicy rare hamburger on the floor in front of him. He did not touch the hamburger for fifteen minutes. When he was given the command, "Okay, you can eat it," he ate it immediately.

(115)

DRINKING

Unlike feeding, drinking does not have an elaborate sequence of behaviors leading up to it. This makes sense when you consider the differences in the availability of food and water for the wolf. Food is much less available and must be hunted; thus the wolf had to develop a hunting sequence. Water is more commonly available in the temperate and colder climates where wolves range so no special water-finding sequence has evolved.

Wolves and dogs appear to drink water the same way. They will stand tail down and scoop up water or liquid food with their tongues. The general availability of water probably accounts for the lack of guarding when it comes to drinking. I have never seen or heard of a case of a dog guarding its water.

The most common problem with drinking is polydipsia, or too much drinking. This usually is accompanied by elimination problems, with the dog urinating in the house.

Excessive drinking can have a physiological cause and any sudden increase in your dog's water consumption should immediately precipitate a visit to your veterinarian. After the bodily causes have been ruled out the psychological ones should be considered.

One of the most common causes of excessive drinking is stress—either physical or psychological. Psychological stress can result from fear, frustration, confinement or excessive emotionality in the household. A household that is constantly exploding into activity can cause even a calm dog to get nervous and suffer from stress. You can imagine what this would do to some of the more excitable breeds.

Other types of stress involve conflicting demands on the dog by the same person or by two members of the same household. My clients in the first chapter were a case in point. The stress in their household came from the hostility between the sisters and the mother, and the double messages given to the dog. The dog was taught to attack the daughter and was both rewarded and punished for doing this. This conflict led to excessive drinking, excessive barking, demand for water and consequent urinating in the house.

This excessive drinking led eventually to conditioned drinking. If you recall, the dog would drink only when someone was present. The closer the owner came, the faster he drank.

The solution to stress-induced drinking is obviously to reduce the stress. In my clients' case this was accomplished by getting control of the other problem behaviors and thus reducing the general level of conflict.

The other solution to excessive conditioned drinking is to give your dog a measured quantity of water, at a specific time each day. This satisfies the dog's drinking habit and also allows you to predict when he will urinate. The change from water continuously available to water available in prescribed amounts only at certain times has solved many a urinary problem in my practice.

Adipsia, or deficit in the amount drunk, is usually caused by a physiological problem. So check immediately with your veterinarian. However, on rare occasions adipsia will accompany anorexia, or lack of eating. This condition can be caused by a dramatic change in the dog's surroundings or the departure of a significant person or animal. This is because your dog's eating and sometimes drinking becomes conditioned to his usual surroundings. The dog will usually get over it in about a week. Since a healthy dog can live without food and water for more than a week, there is no need for concern. The best rule is act as normal as possible. The more you cater to the problem the more you will change the environment and your own behavior.

A much more unusual problem relates to dogs who develop a taste for dangerous liquids. I have had only one case like this. The dog persisted in opening the kitchen cabinet and drinking the dish detergent. The detergent had a pleasant lemony aroma and perhaps the dog liked the taste. However, it was more likely that the dog was trained to do this, since the owners gave the dog attention in response to his deeds, which in turn rewarded this unusual drinking habit.

A more common drinking problem relates to alcoholism in dogs. Normally dogs find the taste and smell of alcohol unpleasant. However, it is possible to train a dog to drink alcohol. I have seen two such cases.

One was a Chihuahua who was intentionally trained to drink. The owner accomplished this by giving the dog grasshoppers, a drink made of crème de menthe and heavy cream. Apparently the dog found the sweet taste acceptable. The owner also found it amusing to watch his dog stagger around, drunk. Consequently he slowly increased the concentration of alcohol in the dog's drink until the dog was actually able to drink dry martinis. The dog actually developed a physiological and psychological dependence on the alcohol. He would constantly bark at the bar and demand a drink. This prompted the owner to seek help. He didn't mind the dog drinking but he could not stand the racket the dog would make if he was refused a drink. In other words, the owner wanted a polite drinker.

The solution was to break the dog's taste for alcohol and never give it a drink again. After the dog was dried out, it was given emetine, which can cause serious side effects and should only be used with the advice of a veterinarian. This chemical causes illness and vomiting in combination with alcohol. A few such drinks conditioned the dog to have a distaste for alcohol.

The second case of alcoholism was unintentionally caused by the owner. The dog, a male Airedale, had been given Mogen David wine for years by the owner, an elderly woman. This wine has a sweet syrupy taste that probably masked the alcohol. There was no problem until some wine was spilled in the cabinet. From that time the dog persisted in opening the cabinet, spilling the wine and drinking it. He had learned to remove the top of the bottle by chewing it. The elderly owner lived alone so the wine could not be stored in an inaccessible location. The owner found total abstinence an untenable solution. She liked a nip herself once a day, but the problems of continually cleaning up the mess became unmanageable.

The solution again was simple: adulterate the wine. This time I used quinine, a bitter-tasting substance. The bitter wine was left in its usual location. When the dog went for his nightcap he got an unpleasant surprise. After two bottles of bitter wine the problem stopped and didn't recur. This was possible because the dog was not being rewarded for drinking wine by attention. The reward was the taste. A simple modification of the taste modified the behavior.

However, it is not always that simple. If the alcohol drinking was maintained by attention, changing taste would have only a temporary effect. If the dog still got attention he would learn to drink the bitter-tasting substance.

SEXUAL BEHAVIOR

Sexual behavior, like the other behaviors in the matrix, can be broken down into three main components. First, there are behaviors that serve to find and attract a mate. The copulatory sequence occurs once a mate is found. Finally, some behaviors serve to signal that the copulatory act is completed.

The finding and attracting of a mate is very important for animals who are solitary. Solitary animals have very powerful behaviors that serve to keep them apart from members of their species. Sexual behaviors counteract these behaviors. They allow animals who would normally fight when together to come together and copulate. So these courtship behaviors are very elaborate and ritualized, sometimes involving very distinctive coloration for the male and female.

The wolf and dog, however, are social animals to begin with. It is normal for these animals to live in groups. Thus the male and female are already in close contact, and attachments have already been formed. The only thing to be decided is who is to mate with whom.

A pack of wolves can have up to fifteen members consisting of both males and females at various levels of sexual maturity. It would be chaotic if all males attempted to mate with all females. First of all, in order to maintain a strong viable species, only the most healthy male and females should mate. Secondly, mating behavior is strongly tied to aggression in the male. If all males mated, this would result in a free-for-all.

In order to prevent this, a social hierarchy is formed with a dominant male and female, the "top dogs," so to speak. They are dominant not only in mating but also in many other behaviors. They usually mate only with each other. If a lower-status male approaches and investigates the female he will be attacked by the dominant male and made to submit.

Before the female wolf is receptive, there may be considerable courtship. This behavior consists of "extending the forelegs on the ground while keeping the rear legs semierect and throwing the head to one side with the tongue out" (Scott and Fuller, *Dog Behavior: The Genetic Basis*). This is done by the male and female alternately. Courtship also involves running together and playful wrestling in which the forelegs of one are wrapped around the head of the other. During courtship copulatory attempts by the male are rebuffed by the female, nor will she stand still for the male.

When the female is receptive, the copulatory sequence occurs. Scott and Fuller describe this as follows:

Copulation begins with mutual investigation of the genital and anal regions. The female soon stands still, holding

(120)

her tail to one side, and her vagina may move slightly when touched. The male mounts the female from the rear and attempts to insert his penis while clasping the female with his forepaws. Rapid pelvic thrusts follow insertion, and stimulation of the base of the penis causes rapid enlargement of this region (the bulbus glandis) through engorgement with blood, so that the two animals become locked together. The male then turns around so that the two may stand tail to tail for some minutes while ejaculation goes on. All this behavior is essentially the same as in the dog.

Dogs have basically the same pattern of behavior as wolves with some differences, due mainly to the fact that pet dogs are not kept in groups. Other differences are related to the fact that some of the breeding behavior has been changed through domestication.

These differences conspire to make your pet dog less selective in his mating behaviors. Thus male dogs will mate with any receptive female and are highly attracted by their odor. The fact that dogs do not usually run in packs but are kept alone in homes prevents the establishment of social hierarchies. This would probably have resulted in the extinction of the species had not the domestication of dogs removed the need for extended courtship through selective breeding. Only those dogs who would mate rapidly when they met could be bred. Natural selection supported extended courtship and selective breeding supported abbreviated courtship. This appears to be one of the major effects of domestication of any animal, including the dog. This change in the natural tendency had the "beneficial" effect of producing more dogs but resulted in side effects that are responsible for some of the problems pet owners have with their dogs.

One of these side effects is the excessively aggressive male dog (see section on Fighting). However, it is important to note

(121)

that aggressiveness and sexual behavior are linked. Some male dogs can get very aggressive toward other dogs, people or even its owner in the presence of a receptive female. This aggressiveness is also related to other genetic changes due to domestication.

Other sexual abnormalities are related directly to sexual excesses, deficits and inappropriate control. The most common excess is heightened sexual arousal in the presence of members of the opposite sex. An owner of a male dog will recognize this kind of behavior. You take your dog for a walk in the park. He spots a female and there is no controlling him. If he is a large dog he winds up dragging you across the park. If he breaks loose there is no way to get him to return. You wind up chasing after him as he runs with the female.

It must be pointed out that this is a behavioral excess only from the perspective of the owner. From the dog's point of view it is quite natural. This does not mean it cannot be controlled, and the appropriate control is good obedience training. Your dog should respond to your commands immediately, no matter what is distracting him. The commands that are most important are "Come," "No" and "Stay."

Believe it or not, a sexually excited male can be controlled in the presence of the most alluring female if he has been given the appropriate training. The problem is that most owners don't know how to do this.

Take for example a case I had of a very well-trained male Labrador retriever. This animal could perform all the commands. However, he seemed to forget everything when he was on the scent of a female. The problem was that the owner had trained his dog in the privacy of the backyard. The dog performed perfectly there but nowhere else. Of course the backyard was free of the sexual distractions of the neighboring dogs. The solution was comparatively simple. With the help of a cooperative neighbor's female dog, the male dog was retrained. At first the male was trained in the backyard after the female had been allowed to run through it and apply her scent. When the owner gained control in this situation, an unreceptive female was introduced. The female was kept tied up on the opposite side of the backyard as the male was put through his paces. As the owner maintained control, the male was brought closer and closer to the female. Finally, the owner was able to maintain control of his dog with the unreceptive female running loose. This same procedure was then repeated with a receptive female. The ultimate result was a sexually active male Labrador retriever who would heel, come when called and sit and stay in the presence of the most distracting sexual stimuli. The whole procedure took about one month, with the dog being trained three times a week a half hour at a time. This replaced the usual sequence of chasing the animal, getting angry and beating it for disobeying.

A deficit in sexual behavior is not an important problem for the normal pet owner. In fact, for the owner who is not interested in breeding his dog this can be a decided advantage. However, for the breeder a sexual deficit can be a definite problem, especially if the deficit turns up in a prize-winning animal. Some of these problems relate to improper sexual behavior on the part of the male or female.

Some of the more typical problems involve improper positioning for the male and failure in lordosis (receptive standing) in the female. Pairing an inexperienced animal with an experienced one, at least for the first couple of matings, will go a long way toward preventing these problems.

Another way to prevent this is to make sure that the puppies are raised in a group, as one of the most common causes of this problem is social isolation of the puppy. This happens when the puppy is taken at a young age, five to six weeks, from its litter and raised in exclusive contact with the human owners. Normally the puppy would be romping and rolling with its littermates, performing low-intensity sexual and aggressive behavior. This play activity serves to teach the puppy how to perform these behaviors correctly when it is an adult. There is evidence that if the puppy does not learn the correct sequence of sexual behavior at a critical period during its development, then it will have a difficult time learning it as an adult.

I have had limited success in attempting to redirect improper sexual behavior. A case in point was a prize-winning male standard poodle who would invariably mount all sides of a receptive female, except the backside. This resulted in a protracted mating period and frequent failures. The solution was to train him with a model of a female in lordosis. The model was constructed of wood and padded to look lifelike. The dog was rewarded with praise for approaching and mounting the rear end of the model. He was punished by a strong tug on the leash for mounting any other part. This procedure was very time-consuming since each part of the sexual sequence had to be shaped and rewarded. The dog was first rewarded for approaching the hind end, then for standing up on the hind end of the model with its paws, then for clasping the body of the model with its legs and finally for clasping and pelvic jerks. The word "sex" was paired to all these activities and eventually became a command.

The test came when an experienced, highly receptive female was brought to the dog. The two dogs played and went through the courtship ritual. When the male was sniffing the female's hindquarters and the female was standing ready to receive him, the owner gave the command "Sex." With that, the male looked up, ran to the model and started vigorously copulating with it.

After the male and the model were separated, the model was removed. The command was given again. The dog searched for the model but all he could find was the receptive female. He eventually mounted correctly and inseminated her. On subsequent occasions he was able to perform his duties appropriately and efficiently. However, the model had to be destroyed.

Unlike behavioral deficits in sexual behavior, inappropriate stimulus control of sexual behavior causes the pet owner quite a lot of problems and embarrassment. The two most common complaints are masturbation and mounting humans.

Masturbation in a dog is not a sign of sexual perversion. Many animals including humans and dogs will engage in self-stimulation. This is a quite natural and normal behavior and within reason should be ignored. However, sometimes problems arise when the dog persists in masturbating in front of strangers and friends. This can become a source of embarrassment to the owners.

Male dogs accomplish this masturbatory act through direct stimulation of the genital area by licking or by mounting and performing pelvic jerks on a convenient inanimate object such as a towel, bathroom rug or pillow. This first type of masturbation is generally self-rewarding to the dog. You can only hope to discourage this by saying "No" to your dog when he masturbates.

Some people feel that this type of masturbation is caused by sexual deprivation, but this is completely inaccurate. Sexual behavior is not like thirst and hunger. It doesn't increase with deprivation; it decreases. Sexual behavior increases with stimulation, and if your dog is deprived of any sexual stimulation, including the sight and smell of females, his sexual responsiveness will slowly wane. Thus, trying to cure masturbation by finding your dog an appropriate mate or bringing him around receptive females will only increase the masturbation. This will happen whether he copulates or not. In fact, repeated opportunities to copulate will increase masturbation even more.

The second type of masturbation, using inanimate objects, can be rewarded at times by attention as well as by the act itself. In fact, it is possible that this type of masturbation has been

(125)

intentionally or unintentionally trained by the owner. For example, a friend of mine owned a German short-hair pointer. The owner used to play tug-of-war with his pointer using a discarded throw rug. In the process of playing, part of the rug would fall between the front legs of the animal, who would then clasp the rug with both his front legs and teeth. This resulted in a very peculiar position which the owner found amusing and rewarded with attention.

This position simulated the dog's sexual mounting position and would eventually lead to his performing pelvic jerks and ejaculating on the rug. Since the owner was not going to mate the dog he allowed this behavior to continue, figuring the dog needed some outlet. In fact, the owner paired the command "Hump the rug" with the masturbatory act. This worked very well. On command the dog would run and retrieve his rug and start masturbating. The dog was never cured of this since the owner found the shocked reaction of his neighbors and friends even more amusing than the behavior of the dog.

Owners can also unintentionally teach their dogs to mount inanimate objects and humans. You will recall from the first chapter of the book the dog who was initially trained to mount the arm of the older sister. The older sister, after gaining verbal control of this response, trained the dog to mount her younger sister. This was intentionally rewarded by the older sister and unintentionally rewarded by the mother. In order to help her daughter, the mother would try to distract the dog and this served as a reward. In this case, however, it was not that difficult to train the dog to stop mounting. This was done by teaching the mother to stop rewarding this behavior.

The mounting behavior starts when the dog is a puppy. The puppy is held or scratched in such a way as to stimulate the genital area or he jumps on the leg or arm and starts the pelvic jerks. Since the animal is a puppy this behavior is excused as juvenile, or rewarded by praise and attention because the owners think it is cute.

As the dog matures he starts directing his sexual activity toward humans. With a small dog this can be discouraged. But the problem intensifies and can become dangerous as the dog grows. At sexual maturity a large dog is very powerful and can inflict injury by knocking someone over. Also, the natural aggressiveness that is associated with sexual behavior may start appearing. Thus the dog may mount and if pushed off may attack the person he is mounting.

The best cure for this is to never allow it to begin. When your puppy mounts you, grab the scruff of its neck as a mother dog would. Vigorously shake it and say "No." Then put it down. Call it and praise it for coming to you and not jumping up. Make sure that you do not reward jumping and mounting no matter how cute you may think it is.

FIGHTING

It is typical to think of the dog using his most formidable weapons, his teeth, when he fights. Therefore, many people think fighting and biting are synonymous. However, dogs bite for a variety of reasons.

There are at least three types of bites. One is a predatory attack which is related to securing food. In this case the dog is biting something because he is attempting to kill and eat it. It is extremely rare for this type of behavior to be directed at humans; I have never had the opportunity to examine a dog with this tendency. However, there have been newspaper accounts of packs of dogs running wild, terrorizing neighborhoods. This may be curable but I personally would not recommend it. The best solution is to get rid of the dogs.

The other types of biting are motivated by dominance or fear. The best treatment for fear-biting is to reduce the fear. This will be detailed in the next section.

Dominance-biting refers to the dog's trying to secure or

(127)

maintain its dominant position in a household. This type of behavior may be directed toward other dogs, strangers, friends, members of the owners' family or the owners. The attack may be anything from a growl to a mild snap or severe bite. To understand this type of behavior one must understand the social behavior of the dog's nearest ancestor, the wolf. Most of the wolf's social behavior relates to its maintaining and/or securing a dominant or submissive position in the pack.

The wolf and its canine cousins have formidable weapons for attack and defense. It is of no selective advantage for a dominant member of the pack to kill or maim submissive members. After all, the submissive animals are needed to bring down the prey. No matter how powerful or dominant a wolf may be, it could never bring down a caribou or moose alone. Also, continuous fighting would cause the pack to disperse, destroying any social order that existed.

So wolves hardly ever fight to the finish. In fact, in a well-established pack there is very little if any fighting. Most of the dominance problems are handled by signals that one wolf will give to another. These are called displays. They signal dominance or submissiveness and intentions to attack or run away. It would be helpful for you, the pet owner, to become familiar with these displays. They are essentially the same in the dog and can tell you what your pet is about to do.

COMMUNICATION

The wolf and your dog signal their intentions through body postures and facial expressions. Long before a dog starts barking or growling there will be a characteristic change in the way he moves and stands. These movement patterns are genetically organized and all dogs will interpret the movements the same way. The body postures and facial expressions are a universal language for dogs.

(128)

The problem with this language is that we humans don't completely understand it. Humans move about, have facial expressions and body postures that signal how they feel. This is called nonverbal communication. However, humans also communicate verbally and many times our words tend to hide from ourselves what we are saying with our bodies. Because words are more important to us in our complex society we tend to ignore nonverbal signals.

Since words are relatively unimportant to your dog, he tends to pay attention to your body and facial expression. This is the basis of misunderstanding between pet and owner. The owner is working at a verbal and the dog at a nonverbal level. If the owner's verbal and nonverbal signals are in accord, there is no problem. But, more commonly, the verbal and nonverbal signals are out of synchronization and this can cause problems.

For example, a client of mine had a terrier who persisted in biting when he was caressed and fondled. The owner said that he liked his dog and was just trying to make friends. He could not understand why his dog would turn on him. The problem was that the owner was signaling fear and uncertainty by his movements and body posture. The dog was sensitive to those nonverbal cues and reacted accordingly. The interesting aspect of this case was the extreme lengths I had to go through to convince the owner that he feared his dog. He refused to believe this until I videotaped his reactions to the dog. When we played the tape back with the sound off he was able to see his nonverbal signals, something he was not able to do with the sound on, when he followed only his verbal signals. We could then work on changing his nonverbal cues and decreasing his fear.

Misunderstandings can also arise between pet and owner because human and dog nonverbal signals are not the same. A movement that you may believe communicates good feeling may in fact be a threat posture. Conversely, many owners interpret a dominance posture of their dog as an attempt to be friendly. This misunderstanding can be the source of many dominance problems in the pet. In order to prevent these problems you must understand your dog's signaling system.

The Face of Aggression

Facial expressions play a significant role in communicating your dog's intentions. The most informative part of a dog's face is the position of his ears, eyes and lips, which communicate threat, fear and intention to investigate.

Figure 2 diagrams the various facial expressions of the dog and what they communicate, as originally conceptualized by Konrad Lorenz. As you go from left to right in this figure there is an increasing amount of fear displayed. As you go from top to bottom there is an increasing amount of aggression displayed.

Thus, the lower left-hand corner (position G) shows the facial expression of a very dominant, aggressive, unafraid dog. Very few people would fail to recognize this expression. The basic components are the ears extended forward, the mouth brought forward in an exaggerated pucker. A dog in this state of aggression will usually make direct eye contact with you. He may or may not growl and show his teeth. If you are very close, the teeth will probably be displayed. At greater distances the dog will just stare and pucker and put his ears forward.

This facial expression signals an intention to attack. The dog is saying, "This is my territory and you are an intruder." The next move is up to you. When two dominant dogs approach each other they will both assume this dominant posture. Each will stare, waiting for the other to avert his gaze and submit. Their bodies will be tense and immobile. Any movement could be interpreted as a threat and precipitate an attack.

Figure 2. The Face of Fear and Dominance

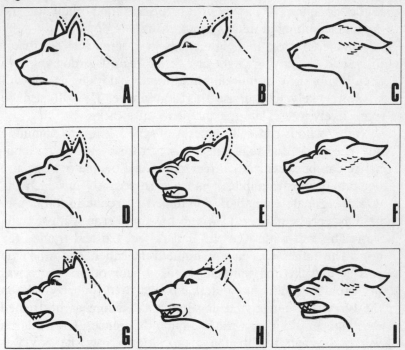

The outcome of this interaction depends on a number of factors. A dominant dog on its home territory will be more aggressive than the interloper. Other factors of importance relate to the genetics and past history of the dog.

There are dogs, such as terriers, who have been bred not to submit and who have a very low threshold of attack. For example, the fox terrier was initially bred to enter the fox's den and attack and harass the fox until it was driven from its den. The pit terrier was bred for dog fights. Two male pit terriers would be placed in a pit and were supposed to fight to the death.

(131)

The modern ancestors of these breeds still possess this tendency to be dominant, so it is not surprising that many of the dominance-biting problems occur with these dogs.

Another factor that influences a dominance or threat interaction is the dog's fight and threat record. A dog who has been highly successful in dominating other dogs or people will be more likely to exercise this dominance. He will also be more likely to escalate the threat to an attack.

A dog who is generally successful will attempt to dominate any person or dog that enters his territory. However, dominance can be specifically directed at some people or dogs and not others. For example, I had a case recently in which the dog, a big male dalmatian, dominated everyone in the household except the mother, to whom he would react with submission. This was natural as she had raised, fed and trained the dog. The father was not at home very much and when he was he and the dog generally ignored each other. There was no problem until the oldest boy entered puberty. When the boy was younger the dog had treated him as he treated the younger siblings, with benign indifference. The children were too small to threaten his position. Now the boy was changing. He was becoming more dominant and wished to take control of the dog. The dog reacted to this potential change in his status with aggressive threats. For example, the boy had trained the dog to perform a variety of tricks such as roll over, beg and so forth, using biscuits as a reward. But the dog would perform these tricks only when the mother was present and would do so with a low guttural growl, his ears forward, lips puckered and baring his teeth.

The mother was concerned about this change in their dog's behavior and confided in the father. The father, a dominant man, would not tolerate this behavior and planned to beat the dog the next time he showed his aggressive tendency. The occasion for this occurred the following weekend. The dog had jumped up and pinned the boy's shoulders to the wall. The father attacked the dog, the dog fought back and the father won.

Instead of correcting the problem this led to more overt aggressive behavior toward the son. The dog also started threatening the other children. With a dominant dog such as this, punishment in the form of aggression can lead only to counteraggression. The only way to deal with this problem is to teach submission to the dog. This was done by rewarding postures and facial expressions that signaled submission with praise or food or both. At first, the mother rewarded submissive behaviors, then the mother commanded submission and the boy rewarded it. Finally the boy alone would reward submission. This procedure was eventually extended to every member of the household. You would think that this would make for a generally submissive dog; however, this was not the case. The dog was submissive to the family members but very dominant and aggressive toward strangers and other dogs. He had learned his place in the family but that did not change his genetic disposition of dominance.

The point is that with care it is possible to change the genetic predisposition of your dog. A dominant dog can and should be made to be submissive to the members of the family. Conversely, if you desire, a submissive dog can be made to be dominant and aggressive. However, the genetic predisposition and past and present history of your dog interact. It is easier to train a dog in the direction of his genetic disposition. When you are trying to reverse a genetic predisposition or past history it takes patience and skill.

The most important skill is the ability to reorganize body postures and facial expressions that signal the aggression/ dominance and submission/fear postures. So far we have discussed the facial expression signaling aggression. However, your dog signals aggression and other intentions in other ways. Figure 3 (page 134) gives a schematic diagram of the body postures related to a variety of intentions.

(133)

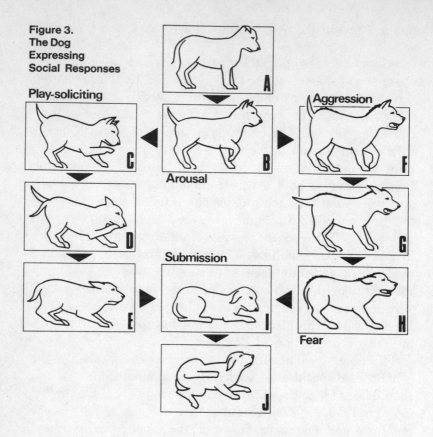

Figure 3.
The Dog
Expressing
Social Responses

Play-soliciting

Arousal

Aggression

Submission

Fear

The Posture and Behavior of Aggression

You can see from Figure 3, position F, that the aggressive posture involves an erect head and tail. The torso is usually leaning forward. The hackles can also be erect. However, the posture is not the only aggressive signal. In addition to biting, a dog has a variety of other aggressive behaviors. One of these is called "standing over." As the name implies, the aggressive animal will stand on his hind legs and place his front legs on the back of a submissive animal. A lower-level form of this threat is when the aggressive animal simply places his head on the back of the submissive animal, forming a T position. The forms of standing over obviously vary with the position of the submissive member of the interaction. If the submissive animal is lying down, the dominant will walk over him and stop when he is directly on top, staring directly into the face of the submissive animal.

Sexual behavior in the form of mounting and clasping and pelvic jerks are also used as threat displays. This is sometimes accompanied by a bite to the scruff of the neck of the submissive animal.

These types of aggressive displays can be misinterpreted by an uninformed owner. I have found that owners who are dominated by their dogs are almost invariably mounted. They may perceive the problem as food or object guarding but on closer inspection you find the dog is also mounting their leg or arm. The dog will usually greet the owner by jumping up, forelegs in the owner's lap and standing over. These behaviors are misinterpreted by the owners as indicating a friendly greeting when in fact they are part of dominance.

Another interesting aspect of these dominance behaviors is that a dog will interpret your behavior in the same way he interprets the behavior of other dogs. When standing erect, an adult human is taller than most dogs standing on all fours. Thus it is virtually impossible for a person to pet a dog without bending over. Dogs will interpret this behavior as "standing over" and react as they typically react to dominance threats. If the dog is dominant and aggressive, he will interpret your well-intentioned pet as a threat and react accordingly, even though you were trying to make friends. This may seem like irrational behavior but it is perfectly understandable when you understand the signaling system of these animals.

Another problem relates to a dominant dog's reaction to children, especially if he is not used to them. A young child has a tendency to try to pick up small dogs and ride larger ones, simulating "standing over." This can cause a dominant dog to react to children adversely. Just because your dog tolerates adults and has never bitten anyone does not mean that he will not snap, growl or even bite a child. This can be a problem when a new baby is brought into a home that possesses a dominant dog.

A recent incident will illustrate this. A young couple called me for advice about their German shepherd. They had married eight months earlier and were expecting a child in three months. The problem was whether to keep their dog, a five-year-old female German shepherd who belonged to the wife before the marriage. This dog was dominant to strangers but protective and submissive to the wife and husband. The husband had a three-year-old male miniature schnauzer. This dog had been spayed and until three weeks before had lived with the husband's parents. When the schnauzer was brought home the two dogs appeared to get along. But the schnauzer was very active and would frequently jump up and place his front paws on the side of the shepherd. The shepherd would react to this "standing over" by a growl or snap which quickly curbed the schnauzer's dominance attacks. The shepherd then started getting more jumpy and the schnauzer seemed to be more active, continuously jumping on and standing over the shepherd. The wife returned home from work one day to find the house extremely quiet. The shepherd was under the table and the schnauzer did not run up and greet her as usual. She entered the den to find the walls and floor splattered with blood. The dismembered remains of the schnauzer were scattered around the room.

Exactly what happened will never be known. What probably happened was that the schnauzer, being a dominant terrier, continually tried to dominate the shepherd. The owners could keep this under control when they were home; however, in their absence the problem escalated. Since the schnauzer was not likely to submit, the threats and counterthreats escalated to a fight, which of course was won by the shepherd.

My advice to the owners was to get rid of their dog—not out of vengeance or retribution, nor even on the possibility that the dog would pose a danger to them, for he remained submissive. However, the dog was potentially dangerous to their expected child.

Facial Expressions, Postures and Behavior of Submission

An analysis of aggressive dominant behavior would not be complete without some statement about its opposite expression. Figures 2 and 3 also depict the facial expressions and body postures of fear and submission. Note that the ears are flattened back, the lips are pulled back in an exaggerated smile and the eyes are averted, as in Figure 2, position C.

The body posture is lowered, the head is down and legs bent (Figure 3, positions I and H). In the most extreme form of submission the dog will roll on its back and lift its leg, exposing its genital area (Figure 3, position J). This may sometimes be followed by submissive urination, which is a signal that the dog does not want to fight and accepts the submissive role.

In another type of submissive behavior the submissive dog does not approach head-on but from the side. The eyes are averted so no direct eye contact is made. The head is lowered and sometimes turned to the side. The submissive greeting may also involve licking of the dominant animal's lower jaw and face.

Quite naturally, submissive behaviors elicit dominant behaviors from the dominant animal. The dominant animal may bite and hold the snout of the submissive animal and he may push the submissive animal over on his back. This is a natural greeting between dominant and submissive animals. Dominant behavior elicits submission. Submissive behavior elicits more dominance. This obviously has the advantage of preventing fights and serious damage.

As a member of a democratic society you might find this dominance-submission relationship of wolves and dogs to be autocratic. This is so. The dominant animal rules with an iron jaw. So if you are to live happily with your dog you must be the dominant member of the pack. You must train your dog that you are dominant and he is submissive, which may sound cruel, unfair and certainly undemocratic. But your dog is not a human being. If you treat him as you treat other humans, he may assume dominance, especially if you are submissive.

This does not mean that you should treat your dog with cruelty. Dominance can be attained without beating or any harsh treatment. All you have to do is to reward submissive behaviors. When your dog approaches you submissively, grab his snout gently, then pet him, praise him or give him a treat. Occasionally, roll him over on his back, then scratch his belly and praise him. By rewarding submissiveness and simulating some of the dominant behavior of wolves you become the dominant animal. This should be done when your dog is a puppy, for he will naturally submit then. This will prevent the problems of dominance from arising. If you do not teach submission to your puppy you set the stage for later problems when he becomes an adult. Most people who have dominance problems come to see me when their dog is about three years old. It is at this age that the dog reaches his peak in strength and maturity and dominance.

DOMINANCE

As the Behavior Problem Checklist indicates, there are three basic ways that dominance can become a problem. Your dog could be too dominant, too submissive or be out of control.

The problem of the overly dominant dog in the household

has already been discussed. Other dominance problems relate to guarding objects and food. My clients in the first chapter had this problem.

To prevent this problem from occurring in the first place you should not take the position that it is natural for a dog to guard his food, a bone or a toy, and just leave him alone. Although it is natural for a dog to guard, it can lead to serious problems. This natural tendency must be modified if the dog is to live with human beings.

A pet dog should allow anyone in the household to remove anything from his mouth, whether it is a toy or a nice red, juicy bone. This is easy to accomplish when your dog is a puppy. Arrange to hand-feed the puppy and stay near him when he is eating and playing with toys or bones. Taking the toy or bone away from the puppy and giving it back as a reward for nonaggressive behavior is usually sufficient to establish good habits.

However, this is usually not done, especially when the puppy has a tendency to guard objects to begin with. Many times I have heard a mother chastise her child for approaching their dog while he is eating. "You know you shouldn't go near the dog when he has a bone." This is the exact opposite of what should be done.

For example, a client of mine had a five-year-old male terrier who would guard any object that he had in his mouth. The dog would growl and rush at anyone, including the owner, who tried to approach it. The owner was a humanistic psychologist with a laissez-faire attitude concerning the dog's behavior. If he wanted to guard objects, she would just avoid him when he had something. She was against controlling the dog's behavior on ethical grounds and certainly could not tolerate the idea of dominating him.

Her attitude changed, however, when the guarding problems escalated from threat to attack. The dog for whatever reason decided that he could no longer tolerate her in a particular room. He would start threatening her with a deep growl. She had to leave immediately or suffer the consequences. She found this behavior capricious and tried to analyze and treat it using her training and experience as a clinical psychologist. But the rules of human psychology did not seem to hold. The more she treated her dog with kindness, love, understanding and respect the worse he got. This kind, loving treatment was interpreted by the dog as submission. The more submissive she appeared the more dominant the dog became.

The treatment involved reeducation of the owner and the progressive regaining of her dominance. The reeducation was simple. The regaining of dominance was more difficult. The dog had had five years training in being dominant. The psychologist had been trained for the same amount of time by her dog to be submissive. The dog was not likely to relinquish his position without a fight. If the owner got in a fight with her dog she would lose, reaffirming the dog's dominant position.

We regained dominance slowly, starting with guarding food. The dog was fed his meals one spoonful at a time, using a long-handled soup spoon. If he growled he would not be fed for five minutes. If he took his food submissively he was rewarded by the continuation of the meal. Three growls terminated the meal completely and he would not be fed until the next day. After three days of missing meals, he submitted.

We then worked with the dog taking biscuits from the owner's hand. He would normally snatch the biscuits very rapidly and then run in a corner and growl while he ate. As this snatching could result in damage to the owner's hand she usually just threw the biscuits at him. She was instructed to hold the biscuit with a pair of pliers. The owner would offer the dog biscuit and say, "Easy." When the dog tried to snatch he would smash his teeth on the metal pliers. He rapidly learned to open his mouth gently and let the owner place the food in. Taking the biscuit to the corner and guarding it was corrected by tying a rope around the biscuit. If the dog tried to run away or growl, the biscuit was yanked away. He could eat the biscuit only if he would eat it submissively at the foot of the owner.

As the owner gained more control she would reward submissive facial expressions and postures by praise, attention and dog biscuits. The most difficult task was training the dog to lie on his back. Like most dominant dogs, this dog had never done so. We first trained the dog to lie down on command, then to lie on his side, and finally to lie on his back, rewarding each step. Through this progressive training the owner was eventually able to gain control of the dog. The entire procedure took three months.

Response Deficit

A rather uncommon complaint is the opposite of too much dominance—too much submission. People with this problem usually have gotten a dog for protection but to their chagrin the dog doesn't protect anything or anybody.

Aggressive behavior can be trained in the same way as submissive behavior. The procedure remains the same but the direction of change is different. One simply has to reward approximations to dominance. First, dominant facial expressions should be rewarded. Praise and reward the dog every time he perks his ears up. Then reward dominant body postures and finally reward barking and growling at strangers.

It would also be best to pair some command with the behavior, such as "Guard." Words such as "Easy" or "Okay" should be associated with submissive behaviors. In this way you tell your dog when to be aggressive and when to be submissive.

A word of caution: If you want a guard or attack dog, you don't want a pet. A dog who has been trained to be aggressive will be more difficult to handle and more dangerous. If you are not expert in training and handling dogs, you could find that you have little or no control over your dog's aggressiveness. If you are not careful, you could transform an otherwise good submissive pet into an aggressive monster. Attack dogs have their place but their place is certainly not in a home.

FEAR

When you think about fear you naturally think about the internal emotional state that you experience when you are afraid of something. You recognize these sensations as unpleasant and usually avoid the things or situations that tend to make you afraid. We don't know if your dog experiences the same internal feelings as you do when afraid, but we do know a lot about the way animals experience fear.

You judge that your dog is afraid of something when he tries to run away or escape the object or situation. We label this behavior as fear since it resembles our own behavior when we are afraid. If we were to monitor his internal processes, we would find that, like you, his heart rate goes up, blood pressure increases, blood vessels in his extremities contract and those in the central part of his body dilate. There is an increase in adrenaline and other hormones in his blood. These hormones, along with a special part of his autonomic nervous system called the sympathetic nervous system, serve to activate the body.

All these body changes are natural genetically organized reactions to pain. They prepare your dog's body to take action. The action may be running away or fighting, depending upon his past experience and the nature of the threat.

These natural reactions to pain become fear when they are associated with something else. This can be very beneficial to your dog. There are many things in his world that are

(142)

potentially dangerous. If your dog did not develop fears, he would be continually injuring himself. The fear allows him to anticipate pain and avoid injury.

Take, for example, the interaction between a puppy and a cat. To a puppy a cat is an interesting toy. The cat may arch and hiss as the puppy approaches but this merely serves to make the cat even more interesting. So it investigates and usually gets a good swat across the nose. Thereafter the puppy associates the cat with pain and avoids cats in the future. This association may stop here, especially if the puppy has limited experience with cats. Or the puppy may develop a more refined discrimination. If your puppy has an opportunity to play with friendly cats it will learn to discriminate between arching, hissing cats (pain) and purring, quiet cats (pleasure).

This fear conditioning is an on-going process. A country dog learns to avoid skunks, porcupines and raccoons. A city dog learns to avoid streets, cars and so forth. The problems arise when the fear is not discriminatory or becomes widespread or becomes associated with a nondangerous situation.

The Genetics of Fear

It is quite unlikely that your dog has genetically organized fears of specific things in his environment. Dogs do not have an innate fear of cats or snakes, for instance. However, there are some general things that can elicit fear or are more likely to be associated with pain. Loud noises and looming objects that cause sudden shadows can elicit fear. If stimuli like these are followed by pain, they become quickly conditioned. Strange and novel sights, smells, and sounds elicit both investigation and apprehension. If these novel situations are associated with pain, they will be quickly conditioned to fear. The behavior and movement of other living things cause investigation and are readily conditioned to pain. Behavior that is similar to the dominance postures and actions of dogs is very easily conditioned to pain.

All these are called "prepared associations." Prepared associations were probably very important to the survival of wolves and dogs before they were domesticated.

There has been no time for your dog to get genetically prepared to fear some of the dangers of modern society like cars, electric fans, electric stoves and ovens. If your dog gets hurt by some of these things he may not associate them with pain or he may associate some irrelevant part of the situation with pain. For example, if your dog gets hurt by the electric fan he may not learn to fear the machine but may learn to fear the humming noise. This may cause him to avoid anything that has a humming noise, like the refrigerator, air conditioner, vacuum cleaner and other electric appliances. This generalization of fear occurs because of the lack of genetic preparation and is called a phobia.

Problems Caused by Fear

One of the most common problems caused by fear is fear-biting. When an animal is being hurt, one of its natural reactions is to bite. This is called "pain-elicited aggression." If you hit or beat your dog to punish him, he will associate what you do just before and during the beating with pain. He will learn to fear you and may try to bite.

The fear bite is somewhat different from the dominance bite. With the dominance bite the dog is the aggressor. The bite is usually more prolonged and savage. The animal may bite, hold on and shake his head from side to side. The facial expression and posture is that of dominance.

The fear bite is a defensive attack. It is usually combined with retreating or escaping. Thus it is a quick snap and then the animal will run away. The facial expression and posture is that of submission. The fear bite most likely occurs when

(144)

the animal is cornered and cannot retreat. However, your definition of being cornered and your dog's definition may differ. Since your dog may hide under things like a table when he is afraid, he may fear-bite at this time even though he may appear capable of running away.

Fear and Submission

Some owners of fear-biting dogs have the mistaken attitude that fear and submission go together. They understand that a dog must be submissive to his owner but they try to make the animal submissive by beating him or treating him very roughly.

For example, a client of mine had a large champion male collie. The owner was well educated; in fact, he was an M.D. The problem was that the dog would occasionally snap at him and had bitten his son. The bite was not severe, it didn't break the skin, but it changed the son's feelings toward the dog. The son felt betrayed and was afraid of getting bitten again. The dog had never attempted to bite the mother and the younger daughter.

With this information I initially hypothesized a dominance problem. A dominance-biter is usually a male dog and usually bites and is aggressive toward the males and not the females in the household. I explored this possibility with my clients. The husband said that he had read somewhere that he was supposed to be dominant with his dog and so had made sure that the dog knew he was the master. He used obedience training to accomplish this and claimed never to have beaten his dog. His wife and children confirmed this.

He and his wife spoke intelligently about their dog's behavior. They apparently had read extensively on the subject. The doctor did not appear to me to be a person who would be easily dominated by his dog. There was no indication from the conversation that he or his son had mistreated the dog. Hoping to solve this mystery, I asked him to bring the dog to my backyard and put it through its obedience paces.

This is when the problem became evident. The doctor would use excessive force when training his dog, feeling that this would demonstrate who was boss. For example, to get the dog used to being handled the doctor would pick it up off the ground by its "mane." If the dog protested he would shake it. He would also forcibly open the dog's mouth with his hands. He would do this with so much force that the dog would whimper with pain. This was done under the rationalization that the dog should get used to its mouth being examined. The amount of force the doctor applied to the dog's rear end when training it to sit was also excessive. He would push very violently and hard.

All these things had conditioned the dog to being afraid of being touched. If you acted as if you were about to touch or pet the dog, it would immediately cower and sometimes turn and snap. The dog was handled very differently by the mother. She was very gentle. Thus, the dog had learned to discriminate between males and females. Being touched by males led to pain but being touched by females did not. It reacted quite understandably.

The treatment involved teaching the husband the difference between submission and fear. The wife was enlisted to help teach her husband how to handle the dog more gently. At the same time the association between being handled by a male and pain had to be broken. This was done using "systematic desensitization," described later under phobias. Since the husband was convinced that the dog had to submit, I showed him how to reward submission with praise and treats rather than forcing submission with rough treatment and fear.

Submissive behavior is desirable but it must be obtained by reward. Treating a dog harshly or beating it will make it a submissive fear-biter. Rewarding submissive behaviors with praise, petting and treats will result in a well-adjusted dog who does not have dominance or fear-biting problems.

Fear-Biting and Fearful Owners

A very common problem associated with fear-biting is owners who fear their own dog. Sometimes the owners have been conditioned to fear their dogs because they were bitten but this is not the usual sequence of events.

The problem usually starts with the owner or a member of the household being afraid of the dog. Males in our society are taught from childhood not to feel fear. So in order to deny the fact that they are afraid they disguise the fear with aggression. Sometimes the denial goes so far that they are completely unaware of their fear. However, their fear affects their nonverbal behavior anyway. Dogs, being very sensitive to nonverbal cues, detect the fear in a variety of ways. The dog begins to fear the fearful owner. This can lead to fear-biting, which accentuates the owner's fear and so on. You can see how this vicious circle can spiral into very serious problems.

For example, a number of months ago I received a call from the owner of a female mongrel dog. The dog, about the size and appearance of a large shelty, had bitten him in the hand and face. He had already decided to have the dog put to death but he was having second thoughts because his nine-year-old daughter was very attached to the dog and was very depressed about its imminent demise.

In order to treat the dog it had to be rescued from the local dog killer. This proved to be very difficult. The killer had already charged $60 to put the dog to death and would not release the dog unless the owner paid him another $30. The owner paid the killer off and got his dog back.

When I arrived I found a very fearful animal chained in the backyard. It would cower and snap when I went to pet it on the head. When I went in and talked to the owner he

(147)

denied being afraid of the dog and acted completely perplexed about the attack. He said that the dog had been chewing on a bone and suggested that this could have been the cause of the bite. He said that he was not afraid for himself but he was afraid that the dog might bite the children.

I assured him that his fear for his children was well placed but I wondered why he was not afraid. Most people tend to fear dogs when they are bitten. After a while he admitted that he was apprehensive of being bitten again. This was something of a breakthrough.

Then he said something that exposed his real feelings. He asked, "Dr. T., I have read about dogs turning on their master or killing children. You know, becoming savage and wild. I have always been afraid of this. Do you think this has happened with our dog?" Upon further probing it became clear that he had always expected this dog to turn on him someday. He would get very tense and tight when the dog approached him or his wife or his children. This fear led him to handle the dog roughly and "test the dog." His tests involved teasing and prodding the dog to see if it would get aggressive. He had taught the dog to fear him and eventually his expectation was fulfilled.

The treatment here involved systematic desensitization of the owner's and dog's fears. I first decreased the dog's fear of being petted. In order to touch the dog on the head without being bitten, I started feeding it biscuits placed on the palm of my hand. Then I would hold the biscuits between my thumb and index finger and invert my hand. This forced the dog to push its nose under the plam of my hand to get the biscuit. When the dog seized the biscuit, I would make a quick pass over the dog's head with my hand. I progressively increased the pressure of the pass until I was able to pet the dog on the head with impunity. I then worked on other sensitive areas, slowly increasing the amount of pressure, associating reward with petting.

When I could handle the dog, I taught the owner to do the same thing. At first he had to wear gloves to relieve his fear but he was quickly able to shed them. As time progressed he became more adept at handling the dog without fear. The dog's fear of the owner was reduced by the reward being associated with petting.

In short, in order to reduce fear-biting you must reduce the fear in both the owner and the dog. If only the dog is treated the biting will eventually return. The owner must learn to accept the fact that he fears his dog and his dog fears him. Without this knowledge there can be no progress.

Phobias

Fear-biting occurs when the dog fears its owners; however, a dog can develop fears of a whole variety of things. If your dog develops a fear of dangerous things, there is no problem. Problems arise when, through some accident, your dog develops a fear of common, ordinary, nondangerous situations or things. This is called a phobia. If the thing or situation your dog fears is not normally encountered, then there is no problem. There is no reason to worry about a dog who is afraid of water if you live in a desert. However, if you live on a houseboat this becomes a decided problem.

Dogs resemble people in the way they develop phobias. I have treated animals with phobias of thunderstorms, noises, being alone, being in small spaces or open spaces, cars or buses, men in uniform, elevators, air conditioners and fans, high places, water, television, refrigerators, beaches, pictures hung on the wall, smokers, telephone and doorbell rings, street noises and country noises, jazz music and electric lights.

There are scientific names for all these phobias. However, the names are unimportant. What is important is that all these phobias have a common cause and a similar treatment.

The cause is usually the accidental association of some part of the dog's environment with pain and fear. Once the fear is conditioned it can spread like a cancer either by association or generalization. If neutral situations are associated with the phobic stimuli they can become fear-producing. If unchecked, the fear spreads.

This fear can affect much of the animal's behavior. Phobic animals may bite, bark, howl, defecate and urinate, destroy property, be completely out of control, refuse to obey commands, run around frantically trying to hide, be overactive or very quiet, refuse to eat or drink or care for their young. However, you cannot directly treat these problems without dealing with the underlying phobia. Of course, these problems are not always caused by phobias. But you must be on guard to determine if a phobia is the cause.

For example, let us examine the case of the phobic Samoyed. The dog was owned by a person who lived on the thirty-fifth floor of a modern apartment building in Manhattan. These dogs are active and inquisitive and difficult to raise in an apartment. But the owner had managed to solve most of the problems related to apartment living.

The only problem that remained was to teach the animal to heel on a leash when going for a walk. The dog was mildly apprehensive about the numerous noises and cars on the street. This caused him to walk in back of the owner and near the sides of buildings, attempting to stay as far away from the street as possible.

To correct this, the owner hired an obedience trainer. The trainer promptly connected a shock collar to the dog. Every time the dog failed to heel he would turn on the shock. Since the dog failed to heel when he felt threatened by a car or street noise he associated these things with the shock and pain. Within two training sessions the trainer had given the dog a full-fledged phobia of the street noises and sights of Manhattan. He became even more uncontrollable and the trainer increased the shock. When the owner noticed how her animal's behavior was deteriorating, she dismissed the trainer. But she was now left with a dog who refused to go out in the street.

Since the owner had to take the dog for walks she wound up dragging him outside with the dog frantically pulling to return to the apartment. This caused the phobia to intensify.

In order to take the dog for a walk, the owner had to walk down the hall, press the button for the elevator, ride the elevator to the lobby, leave through air doors (this is a continuous stream of air blown from the ceiling to the floor that acts like a door, i.e., it keeps inside and outside air separated), and enter the street. She occasionally would take the back exit, when she would have to pass the machine room and an overhead heater.

The dog developed a phobia of the following things: machine noises, blowing air, heaters, the elevator, other small spaces, men in uniform such as elevator operators, doormen and policemen, the arrival of the elevator and the lights in the hall. These phobias were extended to noises from the refrigerator, vacuum cleaner, fan, air conditioner and radiator. The dog was transformed in a matter of weeks from a reasonably well-adjusted pet to a frantically fearful neurotic animal who couldn't be taken for walks and would spend his day hiding in a corner.

The problem was serious. The solution was to apply "systematic desensitization," a step-by-step method of reducing fears. The essence of the procedure is to get the animal to relax in the presence of a mild form of fear stimuli, then work your way up to more intense fears as you conquer the mild ones.

Desensitization Hierarchy

There are two things that are necessary before you start systematic desensitization: a means of relaxing your dog and an identification of a hierarchy of fears. In this case the Samoyed could be easily relaxed by commanding him to lie down and

(151)

by scratching him on the belly. You can also relax and distract your dog by giving him a favorite treat or playing with him. Most people know their pets well enough to choose a good relaxing behavior.

It is necessary to compile a list of all the things your dog fears. The list should be constructed so that the fears are placed in order from the least to the most feared situation. This is a desensitization hierarchy. The list below gives the hierarchy of fears developed for the Samoyed.

1. Putting on the leash and getting ready to go out.
2. Fan, air conditioner, machine noises in the apartment.
3. Walking toward the elevator.
4. Lights in the hall.
5. The arrival of the elevator and the opening of the door.
6. Being in small spaces. The smaller the space and the more it looked like the elevator the more intense the fear.
7. The noises of the elevator fan.
8. People in uniform, such as doormen, elevator operators and policemen.
9. The blowing of the air door.
10. The machine noises in the basement emanating from the machine room.
11. The heater blower in the basement.
12. Street noises.
13. Being close to the street. This included the sight, smell and sound of moving vehicles.
14. Crossing the street in traffic.

Each one of these fears can have its own hierarchy. For example, the louder the fan and air-conditioner noises, the more fear was exhibited. The closer the animal was to the fans, elevator, street, cars and machine room, the more intense the fear. The closer the uniformed people were, the more fear. The smaller the room, the more fear.

Once the hierarchy is constructed all that needs to be done

is to expose the fearful dog to each item on the list, starting from the top and working to the most feared at the bottom. During the exposure the animal should be made to relax as much as possible, using the relaxation technique most appropriate for your dog.

The dog should not be moved to the next item on the list until he is completely relaxed with the item you are currently working with.

With the Samoyed we started by relaxing the dog when we put on the leash. When the dog was calm and relaxed with this, we moved to operating fans in the house. At first the fan or air conditioner was turned on in an adjacent room and the dog was relaxed. Then the dog was brought closer and closer to the fan; we relaxed the dog by rubbing his belly at each step. When the dog could remain on his back completely relaxed, directly in front of the fan and air conditioner, we moved on to the next item, which was household machine noises like the blender or vacuum cleaner. The same procedure was employed, relaxing the dog as he got closer to these things. When the dog was completely relaxed with the household machine noises, we worked on approaching the elevators, relaxing the dog as we got closer and closer. As the fear of each item was conquered we moved on to the next, relaxing the dog in the elevator, in the lobby and nearer and nearer to the doorman. Then we practiced relaxing as we got closer and closer to the machine room in the basement and the air door.

We were eventually able to relax the dog on the sidewalk. Next, we trained him to move closer and closer to the street and the crosswalk. At first we did this during the quieter times of the day when there was little traffic, then when there was more traffic. Finally the dog was able to sit or lie down and let his belly be scratched on a crosswalk during rush hour. The entire procedure took two and a half months, during the summer. Six months later there was a slight but expected recurrence of the street-noise phobia when the seasons changed and it snowed. The owner was able to take care of this in two days by desensitization. There has been no recurrence of the phobia since then.

You may think this a rather elaborate procedure, taking a long time. But this treatment was necessary because the phobia had spread so far before treatment. If the owner had started the treatment at the beginning of the phobia, the whole thing could have taken a few days. The point is to deal with the fears as soon as you notice them. Putting off treatment can allow the phobia to intensify, making your job much more difficult.

Later on I will outline cases of other phobias. A common one is thunderstorm phobia. The logic for treating this problem is the same. However, since you cannot control thunderstorms you must simulate them. I have done this by using a high-fidelity recording of a thunderstorm.

Lack of Appropriate Fear

Another problem which is as common as phobias is the fearless dog. This is the dog who will chew on lamp cords, or stand on the ledge of an open window on the tenth floor barking at passersby, or chase cars, or brazenly walk into a busy thoroughfare, or attack a large dog.

The dog does not seem to be aware of the potential danger that he is in. Owners of these dogs spend quite a lot of time and energy trying to protect their pets from the more extreme dangers.

For the less intense dangers you can let the environment teach your dog the lesson. For example, if your pet has not learned the significance of fire, you can light a candle and let him sniff it. Watch him and don't allow him to burn himself seriously, but let him get close enough to feel the heat and maybe singe his whiskers.

One or two such singes will teach your dog that flames should be avoided. If you pair the word "Hot" with the touching of the flame, he may eventually learn to avoid anything you label as hot. For example, when my dog was a puppy he had a habit of stealing and chewing my cigarette lighter. In order to cure this I heated the top of the lighter with the flame. The top was made hot enough to be uncomfortable to touch but not hot enough to burn. I then placed the lighter on the coffee table well within the puppy's reach and said, "Don't touch, hot." The puppy picked it up and immediately dropped it. I did this a few more times, placing the lighter on the chair or floor. By the third trial he had formed the association between my words and the hot feeling. He avoided the lighter and anything else I labeled as "Hot."

I used a similar technique on the miniature poodle from the first chapter. You will recall this dog had a tendency to steal and eat small inedible objects. We simply placed heated objects in various places where the dog could find them. As he approached and started to pick up an object we would say, "No, hot." This worked very effectively with heatable objects. Other objects were painted with a mixture of Chinese hot mustard powder and ground hot pepper. Again we would say, "No, hot," when he went to pick up these items. In one week the animal had ceased his unorthodox eating habits and would avoid an item that was labeled with the word "Hot." He also learned to drop anything that was in his mouth when the owners said, "No, hot," even if the item was not treated.

These techniques are fine when the danger is not great. But you certainly cannot let your dog find out about moving cars by getting run over. When the danger is great, you must arrange the situation by associating a mild pain with the object.

In one case I treated a large golden retriever who had a habit of walking directly in front of passing cars, forcing them to halt. Then he would jump up with his front paws on the hood or driver's side of a car. This was quite annoying to

(155)

the neighbors and dangerous to the dog. The solution was to make cars in the street signal pain.

This was done by connecting a specially designed laboratory electric shocker between the owner's car and the dog so that when the dog jumped on the car he would complete a circuit and get a controlled low-level shock. With special controls to make sure the fear of cars didn't spread, I was able to eliminate this habit with two shocks.

I would like to emphasize that you, the layman, should not try this. Shock is very dangerous. I used a laboratory model that would deliver a precise amount of current. You cannot use a car battery or plug your dog into the wall socket. If you do, you will wind up electrocuting your dog. The shockers available on the market cannot be used because the shock is imprecise and uncontrolled. They can cause serious skin damage.

In addition to the physical damage, shock can cause serious psychological damage. You will recall that the phobic Samoyed's problems stemmed from the use of shock by an obedience trainer. I, as a professional, occasionally use shock, but I have been trained in graduate school by experts in the field. I have also spent five years studying the effect of shock and fear in my laboratory. I know all the research literature on the subject. In short, in the hands of an expert shock is a useful too; in the hands of an amateur it is a dangerous weapon.

If your dog has a tendency to chase cars, you can pair a variety of annoying things with the chasing. Sudden loud noises, like the blowing of the horn, and a pail of cold water are very effective for many dogs. As the dog starts chasing a car shout "No" and turn on the noise. If he jumps on the car, squirt him in the face with a hose and shout "No."

Another way to cure chasing is to countertrain the chasing response. I had an opportunity to do this with a car-chasing standard poodle. The key was the dog's tendency to balk and pull back when on a leash. Whichever way you pulled the leash, he would pull in the opposite direction. With this in mind, an eight-foot rope was tied to the rear bumper of the owner's car and the dog's collar.

The owner would drive forward. *Very slowly!* The dog would pull back as the car drove forward, associating pulling away with cars. Two such treatments with different cars eliminated the chasing habit. Please be advised that this is a very delicate procedure. The dog was *not* dragged behind the car. The only reason it worked was that the dog had the tendency to pull in the opposite direction, thus associating pulling away with the forward-moving car. If your dog heels and will follow his lead this technique will not work.

For dogs who have a tendency to walk out in traffic, I have used the element of surprise, a long leash (twenty feet) and an unpleasant event paired with stepping in the street. In one case a cocker spaniel would think nothing of strolling into the street. I enlisted the aid of a number of children in the neighborhood. The street was tree-lined, so I had each child hide in a tree armed with a bucket of water. The dog was released but still tied to the twenty-foot leash, which was long enough to allow the dog to enter the street a few feet but not to cross. As the dog stepped into the street, the nearest child was instructed to scream "No" at the top of his lungs and dump the bucket of water on the dog.

We did this on each of the four streets comprising the square block where the owner's house was located. The entire procedure took two days. Each child earned a dollar for his participation. The children thought this was so much fun that they would occasionally scramble up a tree with a bucket of water if they saw the dog coming. If the dog went near the street, they would dump the water. The result was a dog who could be allowed out and would walk only on the sidewalk without attempting to cross the street. For all the dog knew, there was a kid with a bucket of water in every tree.

The essence of this technique is the element of surprise and

(157)

the association of the unpleasant event with the dangerous behavior. I have used everything from a loud shout, horn, firecrackers and water to electric shock. The event should be the kind that can be delivered from a distance without you being present. It should be delivered exactly as your dog transgresses. In this way your dog will associate the event and his behavior. You will not be the signal. The element of surprise prevents your dog from predicting when he will get punished. This is the bolt-from-heaven technique. The dog learns that wherever he is, whether you are in sight or not, he will get punished if he transgresses.

ELIMINATION

Elimination problems in dogs are quite common. But in order to understand this type of problem you must understand the functions of elimination in the dog. The dog and wolf eliminate not only to get rid of waste but also as a means of marking their territory.

A dog's territory may include the owner's house and yard, and, depending on the arrangement of the dog's environment, it can extend a radius of blocks around the house. City dogs who are kept in apartments have smaller territories than do country dogs who are allowed to roam freely. This can cause elimination problems for the city dog, who must be kept on a leash and curbed and thus cannot establish a territory. The dog may have to urinate constantly on various vertical objects in a futile attempt to mark his territory. Additionally, many dogs live in the city, and all of them are trying to do the same thing when going for a walk, that is, mark territory. The sight and smell of excrement and urine is a stimulus for the dog to mark. The poor city dog is faced with the problem of keeping up with the Jones's dog. It is possible that every pole, fire hydrant or other vertical object has been marked by urine many times by other dogs. He may then try to remark those vertical objects, saving his urine so he can hit as many objects in his territory as possible. This can lead to very long walks and frustrated owners.

Another genetically organized behavioral ritual that involves urination is alternate marking. This is part of the social behavior related to territoriality. When two dogs meet, they will usually investigate each other's genital area. Each dog will stand very quietly allowing the other dog to sniff his genitals. This is quite natural, as the smell of urine is the signpost for the dog's territory.

The mutual sniffing may result in a dominance/submission bout, a fight or alternate marking. In the last case the dominant dog, that is, the dog who is on his own territory, will lift his leg and mark some object. Then the other dog will sniff the object, lift his leg and mark it also. This causes the first dog to repeat the procedure. I have personally observed dogs go through this alternate marking for up to half an hour. The owner can become quite frustrated by this alternate marking, especially if he is late for work. A dog raised in the country will not have this problem.

So some of the problems with elimination result from dogs running off a normal pattern of behavior that interferes with the needs or desires of the owners. However, other elimination problems result from the incorrect way owners attempt to change the natural patterns and their misunderstanding about these patterns.

Excesses in Elimination

Encopresis and enuresis are psychological terms that refer to uncontrolled defecation and urination. Normally a dog will perform a number of preliminary behaviors before he urinates. He will sniff, raise his leg if a male, or squat if a female. Many dogs will sniff and turn in circles before defecating. However,

dogs who are enuretic or encopretic do not give any preliminary signs. They just eliminate.

These dogs do not sniff an object and do not even assume
the appropriate posture. An enuretic dog may urinate while
standing erect, or lying down or sleeping, without squatting or
raising its leg on an object. The result is that the urine usually
flows down the dog's leg.

I have entertained a number of possible hypotheses about
this type of problem. It is possible that through some perversion of the breeding process some dogs have lost the genetic
program for the sequence of urination. The other possibilities
are related to potential neurological damage or disease. If your
dog has this problem, have him checked by your veterinarian.

I have treated a few cases of enuresis, all using the same technique. One such case of an enuretic male schnauzer will illustrate it. The schnauzer had had this problem for years.
He would urinate at random without the appropriate preliminary behaviors. The dog would not lift his leg and consequently would get himself all wet. The dog had been
examined by a veterinarian and no neurological damage or
disease could be found. In order to stop this problem the owner
had sent the dog away for two weeks to an obedience training school. The dog returned with a urinary tract infection
and an exaggerated problem.

I was called in after the infection had been treated and
cured by the veterinarian. During the initial interview the dog
urinated. The owners acted immediately, punishing the dog
with a sharp rap on the behind with a newspaper and taking
him outside. Apparently they had been doing the correct
thing—catching the dog in the act of urination and punishing
him immediately. They also praised the dog when he urinated
outside.

Since I was unable to find any fault with how the owners
were handling the problem, I decided to get some preliminary
information on the dog's drinking and eating and urinating

and defecating behavior. The premise is, what goes in must eventually come out. I wanted to know how much and when the dog ate and drank and how long after this he eliminated. The owners agreed to watch the dog, taking careful notes on the time he drank, the amount he drank at each interval, how often he urinated both in and out of the house, how often he was fed and taken for walks and if he urinated and defecated during the walks. They were not to discipline the dog in any way during this recording period.

The amount the dog drank was measured by pouring a precise amount of water into his bowl. When the dog drank, the remaining water was poured into a measuring cup and the difference between the original and the remaining amounts indicated how much he drank.

The owners were able to keep this measurement up for a week. This seems like a lot of work and it was, but it paid off. We were able to tell that the dog drank excessively large amounts of water and would urinate almost exactly forty-five minutes after drinking. The dog had been enuretic fourteen times since they started recording. Eleven times he had been drinking from forty-two to forty-five minutes before the accident. The other three accidents occurred about one hour after drinking. These accidents were unpredictable in the past since a full bowl of water was always available and the dog drank at random throughout the day.

The solution was simple: give water to the dog only about forty minutes before taking him for a walk. If he persisted in his pattern, this would result in at least a 78 percent decrease in the enuresis. So the dog was given water in the morning and evening forty minutes before he was to go for a walk. He was allowed to drink for five minutes and then the water was removed. The dog stopped his enuretic habit and urinated outside from the first day of the treatment. This was after two years of unsuccessful medical, drug and obedience treatment.

I have had two similar cases, and by using the same procedure I got the same results. A six-month follow-up on the first case indicated that the schnauzer had two accidents during the following six months. Both accidents occurred when the owners had failed to remove the water in the morning and left it available to the dog all day.

Excited and Submissive Urination

Some dogs will urinate when they are being petted or scratched, especially if they are rolled over on their backs. This can be a form of submissive display. The problem is that it is not possible to punish this behavior. Punishment will only lead to more submission and consequently intensify the problem.

The dog usually has a variety of problems that are caused by his fears. I have found that when the fear is reduced, using systematic desensitization, the submissive urination is also alleviated.

Submissive urination may also occur with the introduction of a more dominant dog to the household. Pet owners, feeling that their dog's problem stems from loneliness, will obtain a second dog. The idea is that the new dog will be a companion and alleviate the problem. If the original dog urinates in the house, this can cause more problems. For if the new dog is dominant then it is likely that the first dog will submissively urinate and vice versa. It is also likely that the introduction of the new dog will cause a bout of urine marking in the house by both dogs.

Sometimes a dog urinates because he is excited, such as when the owners return home, when the dog is about to go for a walk, at feeding time or when the owners play with him. All these could be instances of submissive urination; however, the difference is that the dog is running about, jumping and nervously anticipating something.

This can be corrected by teaching the dog to behave more calmly. Many people tolerate and like the way their dog gets excited. They reward this excitement by petting, praise and the opportunity to do what he anticipates. Thus, when you are about to take your dog for a walk and he jumps at the door you reward this behavior by opening the door and letting the dog out. You may even try to get there quickly and let the dog out before he urinates on the floor. I have clients who have said, "Once I put the leash on, if I hesitate for even a little bit, my dog will have an accident."

You can solve this by slowly increasing the time your dog must remain quiet before you take him out by use of a stop watch to determine the exact amount of time between putting the leash on and the urinary accident. If your dog's accident time is five seconds, then require at least one to two seconds of quiet behavior before you open the door. You may have to hold your dog still during this time to keep him quiet. When he can remain quiet for two seconds without urinating before going out, then steadily increase the duration of quiet time required.

This can also be done when your dog gets excited when you arrive home or he is about to be fed. When you return home, his reward for being excited is your attention. When your dog is about to be fed, his reward for being excited is being fed. So in both these cases withhold the reward for a few seconds and require quiet behavior before you attend to him or give him food. Then slowly increase the duration of quiet time necessary for the reward.

This decrease in excited behavior will usually result in a decrease in the urination that has been associated with it.

Overcontrol of Defecation and Urination

Overcontrol of elimination is usually associated with the owner's presence. This of course can lead to the dog soiling in the house when the owner is not at home. Many owners with this problem say that their dog is shy or embarrassed and must be left alone to eliminate. These owners confuse a submissive posture and facial expression with embarrassment.

The problem almost invariably stems from the overly punitive and mostly ineffective habit of rubbing the dog's nose in his excrement when he defecates and urinates in the house. What the owners have done is associate the sight and smell of excrement and their presence with punishment. But the actual behavior of defecating in the house has never been punished, as the dog eliminates when alone. People with this problem frequently say that no matter how often they take the dog out he still refuses to eliminate outside.

Since the dog will have to eliminate eventually and since he is conditioned not to eliminate when the owners are present, the only option left is to go in the house when the owners are out. This is a vicious circle. The more the dog soils in the house, the more he gets punished and the more he fears eliminating during his walk when the owners are near.

Since this overcontrol problem is always accompanied by soiling in the house, the treatment will be discussed in the next section.

Soiling Problems in the Home

As previously mentioned, soiling problems in the home could be caused by excessive punishment. However, this is not the only reason for this behavior. It could very well be that the dog has developed a habit of eliminating in a particular location or on a particular surface. In this case the wrong stimuli, those in your house, become the signal to eliminate.

I have previously discussed the use of punishment with this type of behavior. The key to solving this elimination problem is to arrange the situation so that (1) you can catch your dog in the act of eliminating, then punish immediately, and (2) the only place your dog will be able to eliminate is outside.

(164)

This will involve time, effort and some degree of creativity; however, the task will be worth it in reduced damage to carpets and furniture and reduced unpleasantness of cleaning up.

Previously I described a way of predicting when your dog is about to eliminate simply by controlling his intake. This can also be done for the situation where the dog has control of his elimination but continues to soil in the house.

However, the problem can be more complicated if the dog soils at night when you are asleep, during the day when you are out or when you are not around to discipline him. The tendency is to punish the dog when you discover the waste by dragging the dog to it. This rarely works.

A more effective way to handle the problem is illustrated by the following case. The dog was a toy poodle who would persist in urinating on the bedcovers of the oldest son in the household. The boy was fifteen years old and naturally resented this behavior. Consequently he would treat the dog harshly. The mother postulated that the dog's behavior was motivated by spite. She thought that the dog was getting back at the son for his harsh treatment.

What had really happened was that the dog had simply developed a habit of urinating on the son's bed. This probably started because the dog had always been kept in the son's room and had just started doing it there. The problem was complicated by virtue of the fact that the habit had generalized. If the son's door was kept closed, the dog would choose the daughter's bed, and if her door was closed the dog would go to the parents' room. If that door was closed, the dog would use the sofa.

In order to solve this problem the behavior had to be punished in each of the rooms. The dog had to be closely monitored. This was accomplished in three ways. First, he was given plenty to drink. When it was time for him to urinate, one bedroom door was opened. Then a member of the family

(165)

would station himself in a location that allowed observation of the room but prevented him from being observed by the dog. Finally, a Wee Wee pad was placed on the target bed. This is a commercially available device that sounds an alarm if it is wetted with even the tiniest amount of urine. The alarm was a very loud screaming siren which would serve as punishment.

The dog was allowed to enter the room. When the alarm was sounded, the family member would immediately enter the room, pick up the dog and take it outside. The dog would be praised and petted for urinating outside. This was done with each of the beds and the sofa. The entire procedure took four days and resulted in complete cessation of urinating on the beds.

The Wee Wee pad made the procedure somewhat easier but it is not essential. Before I started using a Wee Wee pad I had been able to stop similar problems simply by having my clients watch the dog. When it entered a room where it habitually would urinate or defecate, I or my clients would sneak up and peek in. The instant the dog started eliminating, we would enter the room screaming "No," and perhaps throw a pillow at it. This served to stop it in the act. It would then be brought outside to eliminate.

It may seem cruel to allow the dog to drink a lot of water and then not take him out. It may seem as if you are trying to force the dog to make a mistake. You are! The difference is that you are ensuring that he makes the mistake *only when you can catch him* in the act and correct his behavior.

You use the same procedure to housebreak a puppy. If the new puppy is kept on newspaper it is likely that elimination will become associated with the newspaper. When this is done the amount of newspaper covering the floor should be reduced slowly.

The puppy should be manually positioned on this smaller surface and praised when it succeeds in hitting the paper. Of course, the praise and guidance should occur at the time of elimination. This means that you will have to watch your puppy closely.

The progressive decrease in the size of the newspaper will improve the puppy's aim. The next step is to remove the newspaper and watch your puppy very closely. It may attempt to eliminate in the place where the newspaper was located. When this starts, immediately pick the puppy up and take it outside. It will probably continue its elimination outside.

I was able to housebreak my own dog by removing the paper and tying his leash to the leg of a table, with him attached to the other end of the leash. I stationed myself so I could watch him at all times. Any preliminary behavior that signaled he was about to eliminate was met by a sharp "No." It became apparent, late in the afternoon, that my dog really had to defecate. I could tell this by the way he kept his tail folded between his legs. I took him to the curb and said, "Hurry up." He defecated immediately.

Thereafter I would say "Hurry up" just before he was about to defecate and "Come on" when he started urinating. Eventually, this gave me tremendous control over his elimination. My dog would not defecate unless and until I said "Hurry up." He would not urinate unless and until I said "Come on." The advantages of this type of training to a city dweller are immeasurable. The ability to dictate when and where your dog will eliminate removes all the marking problems, allows you the owner and not your dog to dictate the length of the walk and allows you to curb your dog easily.

The only disadvantage occurred when I went on a three-day trip and had a neighbor walk my dog. I called the neighbor on the second day and found out that the dog had not eliminated in the two days since I had been gone, despite the fact that he had been taken out at least five times a day. Then I remembered that I had forgotten to tell my neighbor the secret words. The problem was solved on the next walk.

EXPLORING

Exploring or investigating objects and places with the senses is a characteristic of almost all animals including man. Exploring can be thought of as stimulus-seeking. The way animals explore their environment is genetically organized, which makes different species of animals investigate their environment in different ways. Usually each species contacts its environment in a way that is similar to the way it feeds. For example, rats explore by sniffing and gnawing, cats investigate by swatting and clawing objects, primates, including people and monkeys, use their hands and eyes, and the dog smells, licks and chews objects.

All species have one thing in common when it comes to exploring. No matter how they do it they usually explore novel stimuli. Novel stimuli usually elicit two types of behaviors, exploring and fear. The more novel the stimuli the more fear is present and the less exploring goes on. However, just because something is new does not mean that it is novel. Novelty is relative to its surroundings. The more familiar the surrounding the more novel the new object will be.

For the dog's genetic ancestor, the wolf, investigating its environment was important for its survival. This allowed it to learn the boundaries of its environment, detect potential dangers, find food and a mate and so forth. The wolf uses all its senses when investigating. However, when man domesticated the wolf he developed breeds of dogs with certain senses sharpened.

This has resulted in strains of hunting dogs that are better than the wolf and other dogs at a particular way of investigating. Thus we have the sighthounds like the Salukis, who use primary vision, and the bloodhounds, who use primarily smell.

Problems

The problems that arise with exploring usually arise from excesses. I have never had a client complain that his dog does not investigate its environment enough. The reason this is included in the Behavior Problem Checklist is that it is conceivable that a problem like this could occur if the dog's function involves paying close attention to the environment, if it is a watchdog, for example. Other problems could arise if the dog's job was to attend to and find very specific stimuli such as the smell of explosives or dope. An inattentive dog could be a serious problem in such a capacity. There are special techniques for improving a dog's attention and investigating abilities; however, these are not important to the average pet owner.

The behavioral excesses of exploring that occur in pets are familiar to most owners. These excesses usually occur in puppyhood and can get the animal in trouble. The puppy who knocks over garbage pails, takes objects out of cabinets, pulls down towels in the bathroom, unravels the tissue paper or chews various objects around the house is just investigating. For a puppy, everything is novel and invites investigation. As your dog gets older, more of his environment becomes familiar and requires less exploring. However, the natural sequence of development can go awry in two ways—overprotection, or sheltering, and rewarding exploration.

Many owners of smaller dogs feel that their pets are too fragile to experience their environment. They protect their dogs from anything that may be even remotely injurious. The animals are raised and kept in air-conditioned apartments, fed specially prepared meals and sometimes not even taken outside for walks. If they are taken out, they are dressed in protective clothing and may be carried around. They are pampered, groomed, not allowed to interact with other dogs and sheltered from strangers. Their entire environment is constant, with little or no changes.

These owners feel that they are being good owners and giving their dogs the best. They are very perplexed when the little pet turns out to be a yappy, snappy, fearful, bug-eyed monster. I have hesitated to use any psychopathological names for dog problems up to now. However, I will suggest that this type of dog could be labeled "neurotic." The dog's neurosis is caused by the owner's overprotectiveness.

This type of problem has a built-in vicious circle that maintains it. By depriving the dog of novel stimuli to investigate they have created a dog who will be frightened by any change in his environment. Even the slightest change is perceived by the dog as very novel, and fearful. This fear reaction supports the owner's original idea that the dog is fragile and better off when protected.

I have been called upon to treat many dogs who fit the above description. The major problem in treating these animals is getting the owners to stop protecting them. Their dog needs things to investigate just as he needs food. The more he has a chance to investigate his environment the calmer he will be.

However, you cannot take a dog like this, who has been deprived of stimulation all his life, and immediately put him into a novel environment. This will simply frighten the dog more and exaggerate the problem. What has to be done is slowly to introduce the dog to greater and greater changes, basically a form of systematic desensitization. The stimulus hierarchy is one of greater and greater change in the environment.

The smaller toy breeds seem to be particularly susceptible to overprotection. A number of months ago I was called on to treat a Yorkshire terrier who had an elimination and biting problem. This Yorkie was a two-pound male that looked more like a shaggy guinea pig than a dog. The problem was, this dog was afraid of anything and everything, including his own shadow. He had been overprotected—raised and kept in a carpeted, air-conditioned den. He didn't even have the run of the house. When taken out of the den, he would tremble with terror and remain completely immobile, his legs and back arched and stiffened like a rock. You could actually pick the dog up and lay him on his side and he would remain in that position. This behavior is similar to the behavior of many wild animals when captured and held. It has been called "animal hypnosis," "immobility" or "death feigning." The opossum uses this response to great advantage to escape its enemies— thus the expression "playing possum."

When I first saw the dog I thought he was having an epileptic seizure, but a neurological examination ruled this out. The problem was extreme overprotection, which caused the fear, which in turn caused the elimination and biting problems.

Systematic desensitization was used to treat the problem. The owners had to relax the dog, as my presence was too fear-provoking. The difference between this case and the case of the fearful Samoyed was that the stimulus hierarchy was two hundred items long and progress through the hierarchy was very slow. For example, in the beginning of the hierarchy minor things such as removing a picture from the wall of the den produced fear. So the first fifty items in the hierarchy involved just moving furniture and objects in and out and around the den. When the Yorkie could remain relaxed with these minor changes, we worked on getting him farther and farther out of the den without fear. After one year of treatment by the owners (I would check on their progress and handle problems periodically), the dog was able to run free in the house. However, he still could not be taken out for a walk and was terribly nervous with strangers.

CHEWING AND DESTRUCTION

On the other side of the coin is the dog who persists in the puppylike behavior of chewing and destroying objects and furniture. Puppies explore by chewing and mouthing objects. However, some owners find this behavior interesting or cute and either tolerate it or actually reward it by attention. This can be done unintentionally if the owner attends to the puppy only when it is chewing a taboo object and ignores it at other times. Rewarding destruction can cause the behavior to persist well into adulthood.

I have known many a disgruntled pet owner who had given his puppy old shoes to chew on, only to find the dog destroying new shoes when it reached adulthood. This problem is exacerbated by manufacturers of dog toys who fashion their rawhide chew toys to resemble household items such as old shoes.

The same problem arises with pet owners who allow their dogs to chew on old furniture or rugs. This will readily be tried out on the new valuable furniture. A dog cannot discriminate between a new object and an old object of the same type.

Most of the chewing, destructive dogs I have treated had been chewers as puppies, and this behavior was tolerated by the owners, who said that the objects they destroyed were not very important. If the owners had corrected this behavior immediately when it occurred the damage could have been prevented.

For example, a year ago friends of mine got a black Labrador retriever as a puppy. The puppy slept on an enclosed porch that was furnished with old junk furniture. They considered it to be the dog's room and he could do pretty much what he wanted to without discipline. When I came to visit I noticed that the puppy was chewing on the sofa, chair and rug of the porch furniture. I explained to them that allowing this chewing to continue could eventually cause problems. They received this information politely and explained to me that they didn't care about the porch furniture. I tried to explain that it was not related to the porch furniture but to allowing a destructive behavior to continue. They listened but it was obvious that they were not going to heed my warnings. After all, free advice is always taken for what it is worth: nothing.

Ten months later they called me for help. Their puppy had chewed all the porch furniture, chewed holes in the wall of the porch and chewed the legs of the chairs of the dining room set.

The day before, they had left the dog home all day, locked in the porch. The dog had managed to get out and he chewed great gaping holes in the new living room sofa and chair and pulled down and ripped the drapes. A few sharp words and a well-directed punishment in the beginning could have prevented this economic tragedy. The situation was serious. The owners were contemplating putting the dog to sleep; in order to save the dog's life drastic action had to be taken. In order to stop this chewing I decided to rig the chairs, sofa, curtains and other objects the dog would destroy so that they would deliver an electric shock. Getting curtains and a sofa to produce electric shock was quite a challenge.

The curtains had to be hemmed with very thin metal wire. The slip covers on the sofa and chairs were covered with strips of aluminum foil tape. The walls that were chewed were also stripped with aluminum foil tape. Miniature brass safety pins were placed in the ends of the shag rug where the dog had been chewing. All these metal attachments were wired to a laboratory shocker that could deliver a precise electric shock to the contacts when the dog bit into them. A device was added to count the number of shocks received.

The dog was then left alone in the house. Before the owners left they would walk around with their dog to each taboo area and say "No, don't touch." The dog was given three days of treatment during which he received eight shocks: five on the first day, two on the second day, and one on the third day. The shocker was left on for three more days but the dog had ceased his chewing since no shocks were counted. The dog has not chewed since then.

I would like to point out that shock was the treatment of last resort. No one reading this book should attempt to do this himself. I have already pointed out the potential physical and psychological damage that can be created by the inexperienced use of shock. It is a powerful tool but only in the hands of a professional.

CARE OF THE BODY SURFACE (COBS)

Care of the body surface consists basically of licking, biting and scratching the hair and various parts of the body. It is elicited by skin irritation, insect bites or matting of the hair. The primary function of this behavior is obvious. Problems arise in the dog especially when the structure of hair has been changed through selective breeding. Dogs have been bred to have excessively long coats (the afghan) or curly coats (the poodle or Skye terrier). However, there have not been any corresponding genetic changes in the way these breeds care for their bodies. Earlier in the book it was shown that bodily characteristics such as hair length and color are unrelated to behavior. So a breeder would have to select those behaviors needed to take care of the new body surface. This, the breeders have not done. Thus, the dog winds up with a brand-new coat without the necessary skills to take care of it. And so the human caretakers such as the owners or the professional groomer must take over where genetics fail.

This results in a number of problems related to COBS. One of the most common is touch shyness; others involve conditioned scratching and self-abusive behavior.

Touch-Shyness

Touch-shyness, as the name implies, is a fear of being touched or petted on various parts of the body. Sometimes this fear is general. The dog is afraid of being touched anywhere by anyone. Other times the animal will allow some people to touch him but not others, or will react only if touched on certain parts of the body. The usual reaction of a touch-shy pet is biting and growling.

The problem can be caused by either fear or dominance. With dominance-related touch-shyness, the dog interprets the petting or touching as a dominance posture. When the human bends over and strokes the back of the dog this simulates "standing over," which, you may remember, is a behavior used by dogs to assert dominance. If the dog is dominant he will react to this petting as a threat to his dominance and behave accordingly. This type of dog will react with aggression to all people he considers less dominant than he is. Thus he may act this way only to strangers or to some family members and not to others. If he is the most dominant member of the family he will react to everyone in the same way.

This behavior is very perplexing to the owners of such a dog. After all, their intention when they were petting the dog was not hostile or dominant; they were trying to be friendly. But good intentions do not count. What matters is the way the dog was programmed by his genetics and environment.

A second cause of touch-shyness is associated with pain. This can happen with the long- or curly-haired breeds that experience painful brushing when they are groomed, or with an animal that has been hit with a hand across the face or nose. When hand movement toward the dog has been associated with pain, the dog is likely to react with biting when someone attempts to pet him.

Sometimes the touch-shyness can be caused by both fear and dominance. This significantly intensifies the problem. It is easy to see how this can happen. As the owner grooms the dog he may elicit a dominance attack in a dominant dog. The owner may then beat or severely punish the dog for this behavior. Henceforth the dog will have a fear of being touched. This may suppress the dominance attack toward the one who hits the dog and could solve the problem. But it may also cause the dog to transfer his aggression to a less dominant member of the family.

For example, about a year ago I was asked to treat a male toy poodle that bit only one member of a household. The household consisted of two older women and their dog. One of the women could best be described as assertive. She was a tall, powerful woman who would not take any nonsense from the dog. The other woman was somewhat smaller and submissive. The submissive woman was the one who cared for the dog's needs and also was the one who was being bitten.

The toy poodle was small but terribly dominant. He would dominate anyone who entered the house by snapping at his heels, barking and growling. When the dog had reached sexual maturity, his dominance increased and he could no longer tolerate being groomed, which usually occurred after every walk. Once the dog tried to bite the dominant woman and she in turn spanked the animal. This suppressed the aggression toward her but caused the animal to start biting the submissive woman. Initially, the animal would jump off the table after grooming and search for the submissive woman. When he found her, he would growl at her. If she went to pet him or pick him up, the dog would bite her.

Eventually the dog began to anticipate the grooming and the threat, and the aggression toward the submissive woman came earlier and earlier in the sequence of going for a walk. Finally the aggression could be elicited by any hint that he was going for a walk. Thus, saying, "Do you want to go out?" or showing the dog his collar, leash or coat would cause him to search for and attack the submissive woman.

In order to prevent the attack, the submissive woman would have to hide in the bedroom when the dog was walked and for at least one hour after his return. The dog learned to stay by the bedroom door and whimper to be let in. If the woman opened the door, she would be immediately attacked.

It was at this point that I was called in. I remember my first encounter with the dog vividly. Wearing heavy leather gloves, I attempted to pet the dog, who was fastened to the end of his leash to prevent escape. He attacked and lashed out violently at anything that touched his body surface. I attempted to use a technique called "habituation" to stop the biting. (I have used this technique to tame wild animals such as snakes, opossums, bobcats and hawks that are also touch-shy.) It means repeatedly and continuously stroking the animal over and over no matter how aggressive it gets. You neither reward nor punish the aggression, just keep on stroking. Eventually the animal calms down and stops biting. But it takes patience, courage and a pair of heavy leather gloves.

I told the owners that this would be a marathon session. I intended to continue petting the dog until he stopped biting, no matter how long it took. The dog continued his violent attacks for the first forty-five minutes of petting. The biting started decreasing after that. As the biting decreased, I increased the intensity of my strokes. The dog completely stopped growling and biting after two hours of continuous petting. I was unable to get the dog to bite even when I tried brushing him and turning him over on his back.

But the dog was not cured yet. When the submissive woman entered, the dog stared at her aggressively. It was obvious that he would attack her savagely if I released him. I directed her to put on another pair of gloves and start stroking. The dog reacted savagely to this, but I had good hold of him. After an hour and a half of stroking by the submissive woman the aggression decreased to zero. Throughout this period I had been relinquishing my hold on the dog to the woman. At the end she had complete control of him. We did one more hour-and-a-half session the next day and both women were instructed to do this once a day for at least half an hour each. Six months later the dog had still not bitten anyone; however, the owners said that he appeared to be more aggressive toward strangers.

Self-Abusive Behavior

If you will recall, the miniature poodle in the first chapter was self-abusive. The dog would chew and bite his forepaws, causing skin damage and bleeding. This is not a very common problem but is more likely to occur with breeds of dogs that have had their hair modified through selective breeding or dogs who have had skin infections.

Dogs normally chew parts of their hair in the process of grooming themselves. But in order for this to become self-abusive two conditions need to be satisfied. The first involves some persistent stimulus, such as an itch or pinch. The second condition is some external reward for this chewing behavior. This can be in the form of attention paid to the animal only when it chews itself, an easily satisfied condition since owners of hair-chewing dogs would naturally try to do something about such behavior.

The problem is that once the habit has started it becomes very difficult not to attend to. If the behavior had been ignored in the beginning it probably would have stopped. However, once it is established, ignoring the chewing leads to an intensification of the habit, greater damage and eventually attention.

What is needed is a way of punishing the animal for chewing without attending to the behavior. This is impossible to do if the owners resort to the standard punishments like spanking or hitting with a newspaper or shouting "No," since all these techniques involve your presence and attention to the behavior.

The ideal punishment should be administered by remote

control without the owners being present. It should associate self-abusive behavior with pain, a quite natural association. The dog should learn that biting hurts, and that if he didn't bite himself he would feel good.

Electric shock best satisfies these requirements. This was used with the miniature poodle and in two other cases of self-abusive behavior I have treated. The technique involves administering a controlled level of noninjurious but painful shock to the area being abused, whenever the animal starts chewing. When the animal is not chewing, he should be rewarded by praise, attention and sometimes by food.

Up till now I have been able to stop the self-abusive behavior with no more than four shocks. Since the shock lasts no longer than half a second, it results in a total of two seconds of shock. Care must be taken so that the shock is not associated with anything else but the self-abusive behavior and perhaps the words "No" or "Stop that." Otherwise, a phobia involving an irrelevant object or situation could develop. In essence, you are training a very specific phobia in the animal—a phobia of abusing itself. This is a very adaptive fear indeed.

Providing rewards for nonabusive behavior is very necessary to the treatment. This serves to maintain the success after the shock is stopped, preventing the animal from slipping back into his old habits.

RESTING

Resting, like any other genetically organized behavior, has a definite sequence leading up to sleeping. The sequence may involve circling on the resting spot, digging the substrate and finally lying down. The circling may serve to test the ground for the softest area. Digging probably serves to loosen the earth, making it softer and cooler.

The amount of resting a typical dog engages in during a

(179)

twenty-four-hour period far exceeds that of the human and the wolf. The dog not only sleeps at night but also takes many naps throughout the day. The amount of sleeping varies with the temperature, the time since the dog's last meal and the amount of stimulation present. For a pet, all these conditions are optimized. The dog does not have to avoid extremes of temperature, or to hunt, and his environment is relatively constant. So he sleeps.

In and of itself sleeping too much is not a typical or important problem. However, a sudden onset of excessive sleeping could signal the beginnings of disease or infection. Excessive sleeping can also mean that you are overfeeding your dog. Overfeeding coupled with not enough exercise is a vicious circle leading to overweight. The more overweight the dog gets, the more he rests, and the more overweight he gets. The rather obvious solution to this problem is to feed your dog less and exercise him more. A decrease in your dog's weight of about 10 percent is sufficient to change his resting habits. This will increase his motivation to work for food reward and result in a healthier, well-adjusted dog.

Resting on Couch, Chairs or Other Inappropriate Places

A dog will naturally rest on the most comfortable surface. If this surface happens to be on a sofa, easy chair or bed, that is where he will rest. Whether you allow your dog on your furniture is up to you. There is no hard-and-fast rule that precludes this. However, it can lead to damage of the furniture.

Your dog's hair is coated with oils from the sebaceous glands in his skin. The oils serve to keep his coat healthy and increase the amount of protection to his body accorded by his hair. However, the oils can readily damage the cloth surface of a sofa or chair. Other potential damage is caused by your dog's behavior before resting. The circling and digging may occur on the sofa and chair, which will eventually result in complete destruction of the furniture. If your dog manages to work a hole in the upholstery, he may continue the excavation, leaving the stuffing all over the house. It is probably better not to allow your dog to find out how much fun it is to dig the stuffing out of your sofa.

The last problem that results from your dog's choice of sleeping places pertains more to country dogs. No matter how much flea powder and spray you use, if your dog runs free he will pick up fleas and mites. These little insects will drop off your dog and onto your sofa, chair, or bed, if he is allowed to sleep there. If they start reproducing in your furniture, you may have a major extermination problem.

If you do not want these problems, I recommend making your furniture off-limits to your dog. This is easily done when you are at home. A quick "No" followed by pulling the dog off the taboo furniture will usually suffice.

However, your dog may learn to discriminate. When you are around he will stay off but when he is alone he will go back on the comfortable chair. To counter this you simply have to make the surface of the upholstered furniture less comfortable and supply a dog bed or other comfortable surface for your dog to rest on. A very simple way to accomplish this is to place tacks up through the sticky side of a two-inch-wide piece of masking tape. The tacks should be about an inch apart. Then criss-cross the upholstery with the tack-laden masking tape so that your dog is not able to rest on the upholstery without encountering a tack. The masking tape can be readily removed when you return home and reused again. It will usually not damage the surface of your upholstery. If you supply your dog with an equally comfortable resting place, he will eventually learn to choose it and the tacks can be removed from your furniture.

Unusual Sleep Cycles

If you maintain some degree of constancy in your daily cycle—going to sleep, feeding your dog, taking him for walks at approximately the same time each day—your dog's cycle will be in harmony with yours.

However, if you maintain an irregular cycle, then your dog will develop a cycle that is different from your own. This can create problems if your dog is active, alert and needs to be taken for a walk when you are sleeping.

Your dog will usually follow whatever cycle you put him on whether it is convenient for you or not. If you consistently get up at 3:00 A.M. and take your dog for a walk, then he will always expect to be walked at this time. The best solution is never to get trapped into doing it in the first place. Feed and walk your dog at an hour that is most convenient for you.

Yawning in Dogs

Yawning in dogs signifies precisely the same thing as yawning in people, that is, conflict between opposing behaviors. When you or your dog awake in the morning you are in conflict between rising and sleeping. At night you are in conflict between staying awake and sleeping. If you are politely listening to a boring conversation you are in conflict between impolitely leaving or not paying attention and politely attending to the speaker, so you yawn.

Yawning can occur at other times too. If your dog is about to chase an animal and you command him to stay, he may yawn. If your dog meets another dog on his territory, he may yawn, not because he is bored but because he is in conflict between submission and dominance. The essence of this conflict is that the two behavior tendencies are about equal in strength.

Many of the techniques used to solve behavior problems in

(182)

dogs involve substituting an acceptable behavior for a problem behavior. Thus, if your dog jumps up on you when you enter, you train the dog to lie down instead. Yawning becomes an indicator of success. If, during retraining, your dog begins to yawn a lot, this means that you are about halfway finished. The problem behavior and the replacement behavior are about equal in strength, leading to conflict and yawning. If you continue the treatment, the new behavior will eventually win out, removing the conflict.

NESTING AND CARE OF THE YOUNG

Evolution has provided wolves and dogs with a complex sequence of genetically organized behavior which functions to nurture, protect and foster the development of the next generation of the species. Without this parental behavior, called the maternal or parental instinct, the species would soon become extinct. However, this term does a disservice to the complexity of the patterns of behavior that are necessary for the maintenance of the young.

Care of the young starts before the birth of the puppies with the construction and lining of a den or nest. Wolves will usually use a den that has been previously used by another animal, renovating it for their own needs. Consequently, nesting behavior is a complex sequence of behaviors involving digging, pushing earth, removing obstructions from the den, lining it with soft material such as maternal hair, and keeping it clean, free of debris and waste when the puppies are in it. There is no possibility for the bitch to have learned these sequences by observation since the nest is already constructed when the pups are born. Learning may be involved in perfecting the skills that are already genetically present and also in adapting the genetic program to the specific terrain when the nest is built.

(183)

The next part of the sequence involves the birth itself and the immediate care needed for the neonatal puppies. Again, this is a complex genetic program that involves being in the den at the right time, expulsion of the neonates, removal of the amniotic sac, chewing of the umbilical cord, ingestion of the amniotic sac, amniotic fluid and placenta, and the licking and grooming of the neonatal puppies which serves both to cleanse them and to stimulate breathing.

Watching the birth process makes one wonder at the marvelous complexity and precision of this event. A bitch giving birth for the first time has never experienced any of the sensations she is now experiencing. She has probably never even seen a neonatal puppy; however, she must distinguish it from the amniotic sac and placenta. As she consumes the placenta and then proceeds to eat her way down the umbilical cord, she must know when to stop and not continue to eat her way right through the puppies.

Anyone who has seen a newborn puppy knows how helpless it is. It is completely dependent on the mother for warmth, nutriment and bodily care. All its behavior appears to be directed toward facilitating the maternal care. Thus it has reflexes and tropisms that direct it toward warmth and enable it to climb up on, find the nipple of, suck and make contact with the mother, and produce a distress call when in pain or away from the mother or just plain cold. This behavior is the signal to the mother to produce the appropriate care-giving behavior. Thus the mother's behavior is supported by the behavior of the puppies and vice versa.

As the puppies develop, more and more complex behaviors unfold. The puppies become more active, opening their eyes at about three weeks, at which time investigating and play behavior start. The puppies start running through some adult behavior sequences during play and actively begging for food. The mother must constantly adjust her behavior to the changes in the puppies' behavior. This meshing of behavior has to work correctly from the very beginning. Learning is involved in the perfecting of these skills and not the creation of them.

Problems with Care of the Young

Given the complexity of the behaviors necessary for care of the young it is not surprising that problems occasionally arise. These problems involve either maternal neglect, in which case the nest may not be established, or failure to groom, feed or wean the puppies. It may involve a deficit in the mechanisms that inhibit predatory behavior and result in the puppies being killed and eaten. At birth a failure to distinguish between the puppy and the placenta and umbilical cord could result in the mother gutting the puppies. Problems also involve inappropriate control and poor meshing of behaviors. The behaviors necessary to maintain the puppies can become problems if they do not occur frequently enough, occur too much or are associated with incorrect objects.

There are three potential causes for the problems: failure of the genetic program, not enough environmental support for the maternal behaviors, and unusual association made with the maternal behavior.

Failure of the Genetic Program

It is quite possible that some aspect of the genetic maternal program will fail from time to time even in the wild canines. In nature if the program fails this will result in the demise and weakening of the offspring and there will be no succeeding generation to transmit this genetic failure. Thus, in the wild there is natural pressure to eliminate these maladaptive behaviors genetically. This is the process of natural selection. Only the offspring of mothers with well-organized maternal behavior survive and are able to reproduce and transmit the adaptive program to the next generation.

When man domesticated the dog, he was able to protect

(185)

his pet from natural selection. He could intervene where the genetic program failed by being a midwife or nurse to the puppies who were not taken care of properly. This intervention has gone so far that some breeds of dogs, due to the reduction in size of their pelvic girdles, can give birth only by caesarean section. This removes even more environmental pressure supporting maternal behavior. Thus, there will be more variability in the maternal behavior of the domestic dog than in its wild ancestors and cousins.

If the offspring of mothers with poor maternal care are saved and allowed to breed, this will lead to more failures in the genetic program. The long-run effects of this human intervention is that more human help is needed for the development of the puppy.

The question then is twofold: Should man continue to intervene, and if so, can a faulty genetic program be repaired by environmental reprogramming or training? For humane reasons I feel that we should attempt to fix the program, and save the puppies. For eugenic reasons I feel that offspring of a mother with a faulty program should not be bred.

If the genetic program can be repaired at all, the repair attempt must be preceded by a detailed analysis of the problem behavior. We must know when, where, and how the mother fails. We must also be able to document the exact sequence of behavior leading to the failure.

For example, I was called upon to help a breeder who had a prize-winning Doberman bitch who had killed four out of five puppies of four litters in a row. I initially advised the owner to stop breeding the dog but eventually consented to try to help when he promised that all the offspring would be neutered before being sold.

From conversation with the owner I was able to determine that the puppies had not been killed immediately. In fact, the first three weeks appeared to be normal. Then the puppies were killed without warning, between the third and fourth week after birth. The owner would just wake up one morning to find the litter had been slaughtered. Nothing unusual had happened the night before. The owner took special precautions not to disturb the mother, especially during the dangerous week.

The puppies were all killed in the same way. Their necks were broken and their skulls crushed, probably by biting down hard around this area. I speculated that perhaps there was something wrong with the mother's ability to inhibit a bite when she retrieved the puppies. After all, the puppies would likely become more active during the third and fourth week, increasing the need to retrieve them to the nest.

We were able to test this hypothesis without damaging any puppies due to the mother's habit of adopting and retrieving inanimate objects during pregnancy and false pregnancy. The bitch appeared to be a very devoted mother both to her inanimate objects and to the puppies. She would repeatedly retrieve both no matter how often they were removed from the nest.

We rigged one of her adopted objects, a stuffed toy dog, with a device able to measure pressure. The device had a thermometer-type readout that could record pounds per inch of pressure. This was easily accomplished by removing some of the stuffing and placing the rubber bulb sensor of the device in the stuffed toy dog.

Then we simply removed the adopted object repeatedly, recording the pressure of the bite each time. Surprisingly, the pressure exerted was always very low. She repeatedly and gently retrieved the toy. We then tried various ways of disturbing her, such as loud noise, running around, running toward her, and reaching for the toy while it was in her mouth. All these failed to increase the pressure of her bite.

Since all the external stimuli we tried had no effect, it was probably some characteristic of the puppy itself that caused the increase in the pressure of biting. In order to simulate struggling we attached a fishing line to the toy and jiggled it while the mother was retrieving, but to no effect. We pulled the toy along the floor to simulate running away, but to no effect. We added fishing weights to make the toy weigh as much as a four-week-old pup. A slight increase in pressure was noted. We then jiggled and pulled the weighted toy. Again another slight increase, but still within safe limits. These increases were reasonable given the increase in weight.

There were only two aspects left that we could try to simulate: the odor and the sound of the puppy. I recorded the distress vocalizations of another litter of Doberman puppies who were about four weeks old. These are the high squeals and yelps that the puppies produce when left alone or when in pain. When the mother was retrieving the toy, we played the distress calls from a speaker in the nest. There was a sharp increase in the pressure, certainly enough to crush the puppies' head and neck.

For some reason distress calls caused the mother to clamp down. If she had a puppy in her mouth it was all over. There was no maliciousness, viciousness or killer instinct. What probably would happen is that she would leave the nest site around the third or fourth week, which is normal for a bitch to do at this time, in an effort to start the process of weaning. The pups would scatter. Hearing the distress call from her pups, she would return to investigate and start retrieving, killing each puppy with the increased pressure of her bite. The last puppy retrieved would be saved since there were no more distress calls from the dead pups.

In order to solve this problem we tried to take advantage of past training. The dog was very gentle. She had been trained to decrease the pressure of her hold on the master's hand or arm with the command "Easy." We simply played the distress recording when the dog had the master's hand or arm in her mouth. If there was any increase in pressure the master would command, "Easy." When she eased up she would be rewarded with praise, petting and attention. After about ten pairings of the distress calls and the word "Easy," the dog would ease up on the master's arm when the calls were played. Then we replicated the same procedure with the toy dog.

When the dog gave birth again, the same procedure was used with the puppies when they were three weeks old. This and the next litters were raised without incident.

So, sometimes the failure in the genetic program can be altered. However, reprogramming is a very tedious job. It involves a complete understanding of the sequence and the exact cause of the problem. In order to reprogram the dog in the previous case we needed to know exactly what caused the increased pressure of the bite. We did not use any human analogies to child abuse, meanness, or any other meaningless terms. The success of the program was mostly a function of the preliminary analysis of the problem. However, I would not recommend applying this solution to your dog if she has a similar problem. The problem may be only superficially similar, but have totally different underlying causes. Without an analysis you could not know this and if you apply the wrong solution you will meet with failure.

Not Enough Environmental Support

Even though maternal behavior is genetically organized, it needs support from the environment to be run off normally. Thus, nesting behavior needs a nest site that is relatively undisturbed by other dogs and people, and one in which nesting materials are readily available. It would be best to make the selection of a nest site yourself with these considerations in mind. Then confine the bitch to that area when birth is imminent.

Other support needed for maternal behavior is appropriate behavior on the part of the pups. This is why a bitch may ignore or kill a sick or deformed pup. If the puppy is not behaving normally, it will not be treated like a puppy. The signal to the mother concerning the identity of the little squirming mass of protoplasm beneath her is mostly the behavior of the puppy. The odor becomes important only when the puppy is separated from the mother.

There is nothing that can be done if a puppy is ignored or killed because it is not behaving normally. There is no way I know of to train a pup to behave normally, and I don't think it is advisable even if it could be done. This mechanism is a natural one that results in the mother culling the unfit puppies from the litter. Behavioral abnormality in a neonatal puppy probably signals some neural damage that would only become more debilitating as the puppy aged. So it may be for the better.

OPERANT BEHAVIOR

Operant behavior is any behavior that works on the environment to produce an effect or consequence. If the effect is a reward, then your dog will do it again. If the effect is a punishment, then your dog will stop doing whatever caused the punishment. In other words, operant behavior is the behavior changed by rewards and punishments.

Operant behavior includes every behavior and behavior problem we have discussed thus far, plus tricks and obedience. Part of the sequence of all genetically organized behavior can be changed by the consequences of the behavior. The part of the sequence that is most changeable is in the beginning, the part that starts your dog off on his route to the end of the sequence, the consummatory act. Thus courtship is more changeable through reward and punishment than is copulation.

The actual structure of the consummatory act, that is, the way your dog copulates or drinks, probably cannot be changed much. However, we have seen that the object at which

(190)

your dog directs his consummatory act can be changed by associating it with something else. Thus dogs can learn to masturbate on rugs, drink dangerous liquids, eat inedible objects and so forth through association.

The problems related to incorrect reward and punishment have been discussed under each behavior class and in the earlier sections on reward and punishment. And it has been demonstrated that anything your dog does naturally can be turned into a problem if it is followed by the wrong consequence.

The behaviors that most people think of when discussing reward and punishment are those behaviors controlled by a command. These are the tricks and obedience behaviors with which dog-training books deal. Although I do not directly treat obedience problems, I have had to deal with them indirectly in the process of treating some other more serious problem.

The problems people have with obedience are the following: (1) Failure of the dog to listen or pay attention to commands. In this case the dog knows what to do but does not listen to the owner. The owner ends up screaming the command in order to get the dog's attention. (2) Failure of the dog to differentiate commands. The dog may sit when commanded to lie down, or, like the dog in the first chapter, go through all the tricks in rapid succession. (3) Failure of the dog to generalize commands. In other words, the dog may sit on command in the house but not in the yard. (4) Disobedience or attending to the command but not obeying it. (5) The dog has never been trained and is thus completely uncontrollable. (6) The dog performs some bizarre behavioral ritual that is unintentionally rewarded by the owner. (7) Barking, whining, demanding behavior.

All these problems are simple to prevent by following some simple rules.

(191)

Rule No. 1: *The Program for a Command*

A command is a stimulus that controls behavior. The stimulus can be a word, gesture, body posture, facial expression or change in the environment, like ringing a bell or turning on a light. Anything that your dog can perceive can be a command simply by consistently giving the command and rewarding the behavior that follows. The general formula for all obedience training is:

Give command—dog reacts correctly—reward dog immediately
Give command—dog reacts incorrectly—no reward given

If you follow these two formulas, your dog will be obedient. The key is to make your dog produce the correct behavior after you give him the command. This can be accomplished in two ways. First, you can wait until your dog is just about to do something you want to control, then give the command as he is doing it and reward him. For example, to train sitting on command the sequence would be:

Dog about to sit—say, "Sit"—dog sits—reward

To train your dog to bark on command you would follow the following sequence:

Dog is about to bark or has just started barking—say, "Bark"—dog continues barking—reward

To train your dog to defecate on command, follow this sequence:

Dog is circling and about to defecate—say, "Hurry Up"— dog defecates—reward

(192)

To train your dog to eat on command, do this:

As you put food dish down on the floor, say, "Eat"—dog eats—reward is naturally the food

To train your dog to come to you on command, do this:

Wait till your dog is walking toward you—say, "Come here," or call his name—dog approaches—reward

If you are impatient, you can gently force your dog into the behavior you want to control as you give the command. This can be done only with locomotive behaviors. For example, to train your dog to sit on command, do this:

Say, "Sit"—gently push down on his hindquarters and up under his neck—dog sits—reward

To train your dog to lie down on command, do the following:

Say, "Down"—when your dog is in a sitting position gently push his front leg forward while holding his hind end down—dog lies down—reward

To train your dog to approach you on command simply tie a long rope to his collar, and proceed as follows:

Say, "Come here" or call his name—reel him in on the end of the rope—dog approaches—reward

It is obviously impossible to force your dog to eat, defecate, urinate, drink, copulate and so forth. But you can make these behaviors more likely to occur by depriving your dog of the opportunity to do them for short periods of time. Then when your dog is really motivated to perform the activity, give him the command, let him do it and reward him.

To train your dog to stop doing things on command, you

simply have to wait for your dog to act, command him to stop, stop him physically and reward him. For example, to train your dog to stop barking, do either of these:

Wait till dog starts barking—say, "Quiet"—hold his mouth shut—reward

Wait till your dog is about to stop barking—say, "Quiet"—dog stops barking—reward

In short, by either waiting for the behavior to occur, making it more likely to occur, or forcing the behavior to occur after a command and then rewarding immediately, you can train almost anything.

The one command that is somewhat different from the rest is the word "no." You want this command to stop any behavior that is occurring at the time you say. To train this you must consistently do the following:

Wait to catch your dog misbehaving—say, "No"—punish immediately

It is perfectly fair to give your dog an opportunity to misbehave but you must give him this opportunity only when you can catch him. So be a devil, tempt him to make a mistake, when he does, say, "No," and punish him.

Rule No. 2: *The Nature of a Command*

The ideal command should be as low in intensity as possible. A verbal command in conversational tones is better than screaming, and whispering is better than conversational tones. A finger movement is a better command than a hand movement, which in turn is better than an arm movement.

The reason for this is that the lower the intensity of the command, the more your dog must pay attention to you in order to get a reward. The premise is basically that of Teddy

(194)

Roosevelt's "Speak softly and carry a big stick." However, I would recommend replacing the stick with a dog biscuit or praise.

This can be accomplished by progressively decreasing the intensity of the command. When your dog listens to your command spoken in a normal voice and obeys it, lower your voice a bit. Do this until he responds to a whisper.

If you are using hand signals, start out with large movements, then reduce the intensity of the movement until you are using just a finger movement for the command.

A good example that illustrates the application of this idea is the porpoise act at Jungle Habitat (a safari park in northern New Jersey). The porpoise trainer would move only one of his fingers a little bit in order to command a particular trick. The group of porpoises would then immediately and simultaneously swim backward on their tails or do some other trick and then return to the trainer to get their fish reward. Then they would stare intently at the trainer's hands. The trainer would fold his hands in front of him, which was a signal to alert the group that another signal (command) was about to be given. He had the undivided attention of his porpoises. The slightest finger movement sent them flying into the next trick.

In comparison, the porpoise act at Great Adventure (a safari park in southern New Jersey) is quite unspectacular. The porpoises seem to be only mildly interested in the trainer's signals. When a command is given, there are usually one or two porpoises that fail to respond or that respond late. The reason for this difference in the acts is the difference in intensity of movement. At Great Adventure, the trainer put his entire body and arm into a signal. And with a great jump he would wave his arm violently above his head. You might think that this would result in better performance, but it doesn't. The porpoises don't have to pay close attention to their trainer, so they don't.

Rule No. 3: *Generalization of Commands*

Practice the commands in as great a variety of situations as possible. If the situations are distracting, then start at the least distracting situation. When you have control in that one, move up to a little more distracting situation. Continue this technique until you can successfully command your dog in the most stimulating and distracting situation. This is basically a variation of systematic desensitization. If you want to be more systematic about the training, make a list of the various areas where you would be taking your dog. At the top of the list have the least distracting situation, such as when you are alone with the dog at home. As you go down the list add situations that are more distracting. At the bottom should be the most distracting situation your dog could encounter, like Grand Central Station during rush hour. Then start the training at the top, moving down a step as you succeed in the previous one. Below is a list of increasingly more distracting situations used for one of my clients' male dog, which will serve as a good example.

HIERARCHY OF DISTRACTION

1. At home alone with dog.
2. At home with dog when familiar friends or neighbors visit.
3. At home with dog when strangers visit.
4. In park at night, no people.
5. In park during day, many people present.
6. When owner is about to take dog out.
7. When owner returns home from work.
8. In park with another dog in sight, at a distance.*
9. In park with a female dog within sight and smelling disstance.
10. In park with female in heat, very close.

* NOTE: The more dogs, the more distraction.

Rule No. 4: *Shaping and Chaining Behavior*

Up to now we have been talking about training simple behaviors. Your dog already knows how to sit, lie down, bark, urinate, eat and so forth. All we wanted to do is get control of these behaviors by a hand movement or word. But what about difficult behaviors or behaviors that take a long sequence of responses? If you tried to wait for them to occur you could get very old.

The procedure for handling difficult behaviors is called "shaping." Shaping means rewarding behaviors that are closer and closer to the goal. For example, let's say that for some reason you wanted your dog to learn how to open the door with his teeth. The following steps will show you how to do this.

TABLE 3. SHAPING OPENING THE DOOR

	Command	Owner's Behavior	Dog's Behavior	Consequence
1.	"Open the door"	Bring dog to door.	Dog approaches door.	Reward
2.	"Open the door"	Touch dog's nose to door knob or put food smell on knob.	Dog smells door knob.	Reward
3.	"Open the door"	Get dog to bite knob by wrapping small piece of meat on knob.	Dog bites knob.	Reward
4.	"Open the door"	Get dog to turn knob a bit, or wait till he does this.	Dog turns knob.	Reward

(197)

| 5. | "Open the door" | Increase amount of turn necessary to get reward. | Dog turns knob more. | Reward |
| 6. | "Open the door" | Dog must turn knob all the way. | Dog opens door. | Reward |

The secret in shaping the "Open the door" response was not to move on to the next step until the dog could perform the previous one. This takes patience and some degree of creativity. You must design the situation so that the dog can perform the task at each step. For example, you may first have to use a door that opens with only a small amount of effort and pressure and place a rubber jacket around the knob to make the grasping easier. Obviously, he is to be rewarded at the completion of each step.

Almost any difficult behavior can be shaped if it is within your dog's physical limits. You can train him to jump great heights simply by starting at low levels and working up, rewarding each level. You can train your dog to walk on a thin beam of wood by starting with a plank and slowly reducing the width of the plank, and rewarding each performance. Care must be taken not to move too fast and not to exceed your dog's current capabilities.

Chaining

To train a long sequence of behavior you have to break the task down into its component parts, then train each part, perhaps using shaping. Finally, connect the parts, starting at the end and working to the beginning. For example, to train your dog to get your slippers you could break down the sequence as follows:

Command: "Get Slippers"
1. Run upstairs.
2. Enter your bedroom.
3. Go to closet.
4. Open closet door.
5. Enter closet.
6. Locate slippers.
7. Pick up slippers with mouth.
8. Leave closet.
9. Go downstairs.
10. Approach you.
11. Drop slippers by your feet.

The eleven steps in this sequence must be hooked together in a chain, each step leading to the next. You would have to make sure that your dog could perform each step before you started chaining them together. Step No. 4 would probably have to be shaped, but the rest of the steps seem to be within a normal dog's abilities.

To chain a sequence of responses you start at the end of the chain and add a new behavior each time the dog masters the previous step. In this case, the first step is to reward the last behavior: dropping the slippers by your feet. The second step would be to reward the dog when it approaches you and drops the slippers. Continue adding behaviors until the entire chain is completed.

Notice that the dog always performs the chain in the correct sequence and is rewarded at the end of the chain. He will not expect to be rewarded at each step but only when he has completed his task.

Using chaining, you can program elaborate sequences of behaviors. All it takes is a good analysis that breaks down the task into its component steps. In order to do this you simply have to run through the task yourself, paying attention to the steps you go through. Then teach it to your dog, using chaining.

TABLE 4. CHAINING "GET ME MY SLIPPERS"

Command	Dog's Behavior Sequence							Consequence
	(1)	(2)	(3, 4, 5, 6, 7)	(8)	(9)	(10)	(11)	
1. "Get me my slippers"							Dog drops slippers at feet	Reward
2. "Get me my slippers"						Dog approaches	Dog drops slippers at feet	Reward
3. "Get me my slippers"					Dog goes downstairs	Dog approaches	Dog drops slippers at feet	Reward
4. "Get me my slippers"				Dog leaves closet	Dog goes downstairs	Dog approaches	Dog drops slippers at feet	Reward
. . . . .								
10. "Get me my slippers"		Dog enters bedroom	(3, 4, 5, 6, 7)	Dog leaves closet	Dog goes downstairs	Dog approaches	Dog drops slippers at feet	Reward
11. "Get me my slippers"	Dog climbs stairs	Dog enters bedroom	(3, 4, 5, 6, 7)	Dog leaves closet	Dog goes downstairs	Dog approaches	Dog drops slippers at feet	Reward

In order to get an obedient dog, all you need is a little patience and a lot of reward, consistency and following the rules outlined in this chapter.

Now that we have covered all the behavior classes separately it is time to put what you have learned into practice. This is the process of diagnosing your problem and setting up a treatment plan. We will cover these aspects in the next section.

5

ANALYSIS, DIAGNOSIS AND TREATMENT
OF PROBLEM BEHAVIORS

Up till now we have dealt with one behavior classification at a time, learning how each behavior can become a problem. This one-problem-at-a-time exposition was done for simplicity's sake. In actuality there is more than one problem occurring at the same time. The first case in the book had thirty-five related problems. In my practice it is typical to find a cluster of three to five related problems.

In order to solve these problems you must know the causes. If there were an obvious, well-known, scientifically documented classification that related typical problems to typical causes, our attempt at diagnosis would be made easier. For example, if I could say that elimination problems in the home are typically caused by severe punishment, then we could speed the process of diagnosis and treatment of elimination problems. Unfortunately, I cannot make these general statments. Neither can anyone else. *Every problem has its unique cause,* just as every dog is more or less different from every other dog. Knowing the causes of the problem can go a long way to helping the owner understand and treat it correctly.

THE NATURE OF CAUSES

When owners try to analyze their dogs' problems, they either get very confused and give up or they make up their minds that only one thing can be the cause. These I have called, respectively, the softheaded and hardheaded problem-solvers.

The softheaded solvers entertain such a wide range of potential causes that they become confused. They usually try to deal with many levels of analysis simultaneously. They will mix up what they know about animal psychology, human psychology, their own personal experience and their unsupported beliefs and attitudes about behavior. Sometimes they will consult a dog-training book written by an obedience trainer who presents his unsupported beliefs and attitudes about dog problems as fact. Or they will consult a book written by a veterinarian who classifies dog problems using human psychological terms like neurosis and psychosis. The softheaded endeavor usually results in confusion and failure but at least these people are open to information. The problem is that they get too much of the wrong advice.

The hardheaded problem-diagnosers are just the opposite: They appear to have only one or two causes for every problem in the world. They say, "It all boils down to genetics" or "All problems are caused by mistreatment; it is the owner's fault." When I try to explain that you cannot make blanket statements, many of them say, "I understand that, but . . ." The "but" is usually their pet cause for all problems. They are not interested in finding out the real cause; they are just interested in supporting their own unsupported beliefs and attitudes.

Many hardheaded problem-solvers also have one or two

solutions to all pet problems. You get statements such as, "If you treat your dog nicely, he will pay you back with kindness," which is sort of a "do unto others" routine, or, "If my dog gives me a problem, a kick in the rear usually straightens things out."

However, causes and solutions are more complicated and almost always unique to the particular dog and the family he lives with. Therefore the owner must analyze the individual problem.

The question remains, how do we know something is a cause? The answer is that causes have some characteristics that give them away. The following will help you decide if something is a cause: (1) The cause must come before the effect. (2) If you take away the cause, the effect should disappear. (3) You should take away only one thing at a time. If you take away more than one thing, you can't tell which thing is the cause. (4) If you replace the thing you think is the cause, the problem should return. (5) There should be a good rationale or reason why the cause works. If you satisfy all these rules, then you know you have located the cause of the problem.

Causes of any behavior problem that have lasted for a while can usually be strung out in a chain. There are things that may have started the problem and things that currently maintain the problem. There is no logical necessity for the primary causes still to be effective in the present. What is important is what is causing the problem now, in the present. The past causes are only important if they continue into the present, either in the memory of the dog or the behavior of the owners.

The relevant present causes of behavior problems in dogs are the behavioral variables that currently maintain the problem. The variables can be remembered by the mnemonic ROCKS. ROCKS stands for Response (R), Organism (O), Consequence (C), Contingency (K) and Stimulus (S). The analysis of any problem is basically asking the right questions about each of these variables. If you consistently keep these questions in mind, you will succeed in diagnosing and treating the problem. The key is keeping an open mind and going through the ROCKS method in a step-by-step manner as prescribed below.

The ROCKS Method

The ROCKS method of analysis will fit almost any problem. It is not a cure but a way of analyzing the problem and deriving a cure. There are no magic cures, no general cures, no magic elixir or pill or miraculous behavioral treatment. There is only good analysis and diagnosis of the problem. If you follow the method you will probably be able to solve your problem.

In order to help you follow the ROCKS method here is an actual case that was analyzed using it. The problem was with a two-year-old male bull mastiff, a beautiful specimen who weighed in at about 185 pounds. The dog had been obtained as a puppy and hadn't been a problem until two months earlier, when he attacked a neighbor who was jogging by the house.

The incident occurred one evening at about 7:00 P.M. The dog was tied by a long heavy chain to a post in front of the house when a seventeen-year-old boy came jogging by for his evening run. The dog apparently rushed at the jogger, ripped the post out of the ground and jumped on and pinned the boy to the ground. The jogger had not been bitten seriously. None of the bites had broken the skin. However, the jogger was quite shaken up, and had many abrasions and bruises from the fall.

In order to prevent this from happening again, the owners, a young couple in their mid-thirties, had a twenty-by-twenty-foot run constructed inside an eight-foot-high storm fence. The dog had free access to this enclosure through a specially designed door in the house, so he could leave the house and enter the enclosure at will. Since both the owners worked the dog was kept in the enclosure all day.

The second incident occurred one month later when a ten-year-old neighborhood boy entered the enclosure to play ball with the dog. The child had played ball with the dog before with no problem. However, this time the dog jumped on the boy's back, knocking him down to the ground. The wife was home and immediately removed the dog. Her impression was that this was an aggressive behavior since the dog's teeth were bared, his hair erect and he was growling.

Three weeks later the third incident occurred. The dog had been barking at a neighbor who was calmly walking by with his dog, an Irish setter. The neighbor had passed without incident and was three blocks down the road when the mastiff smashed open the door of the enclosure, ran after the neighbor and savagely bit him, resulting in eight stitches in his hand. Since the neighbor was a lawyer, the owners were being sued and threatened with loss of their home insurance. This prompted them to seek my help. I reluctantly accepted the case.

(R) THE RESPONSE

The first question to ask when analyzing a behavior problem is, exactly what does your dog do? This may seem rather obvious and mundane, and it is. However, it is necessary to get an exact behavioral description of the problem.

This is more difficult than it may seem. In my practice I find that my clients feel guilty about the problem, or want to assure me that it is not their fault, or they want to place the blame squarely on the shoulders of someone else. For example, one of my present clients began a phone conversation in the following manner:

CLIENT: Before I start, I just want to say that we love our dog. We have never abused it or hurt it.

DR. T: I see. What exactly is your problem?

CLIENT: Well, it probably started when he was a puppy. You must understand this first: you see when he was a puppy we kept him confined in the bathroom.

DR. T: Excuse me, but I won't be able to follow you unless I know what your problem is.

CLIENT: I thought perhaps a little history would help before we get to the actual problem.

It took ten minutes before I could actually get a clear description of the problem. The dog had bitten three people in the last six months.

The second difficulty involves the type of description. Many people are not used to describing behavior in behavioral terms. Instead they use nonbehavioral, judgmental, interpretive descriptions. Sometimes these descriptions are couched in human terms. They describe the problem as being caused by jealousy, spite or hatred. The difference between a behavioral and nonbehavioral description is that a behavioral one describes what your dog actually does, whereas a nonbehavioral one tells what you believe the behavior means. The meaning of behavior is important but not in the beginning. To begin with you must clear your head of the "whys" and focus on the particulars, the "whats" of behavior. Interpretation and diagnosis come at the end of the process when all the particulars are gathered.

The advantage of using a noninterpretive behavioral description is that it prevents you from selecting information that will support your interpretation and ignoring unsupportive information. This is a natural human trait that must be guarded against.

In order to focus on behavior I gave my clients the Behavior Problem Checklist at the beginning of our first meeting. They circled the description under Excess of Fighting and put a question mark after Fear-Biting. I then went over the entire checklist, asking them to describe the behaviors in each behavior classification. This was done because some people cannot recognize aberrant behavior, or excuse it as normal.

The complaint was that their bull mastiff had bitten the neighbors. But what about other behavior?

Feeding. My clients felt that their dog ate normally. When I asked what would happen if they were to take food away, they said, "Oh, we would never do that. We do not disturb him when he is eating."

DR. T: But what if you did?
WIFE: I don't know. But I would never try it.
DR. T: Why?
WIFE: Because he might bite me.
DR. T: What about a bone?
HUSBAND: We cannot get near him if he has a bone. He growls and acts very ferocious. We just leave him alone. Isn't that normal?

As you can see, my clients failed to check Feeding because they felt that a guarding of food and bones was normal.

Drinking. There was no problem.
Sexual. My clients didn't check this but I was able to determine that the dog had a habit of mounting women, especially if they were menstruating. He also masturbated on rugs and pillows. They felt this was normal as the dog was not castrated and had not been mated. They were planning to mate the dog soon, figuring that this would take care of the problem.

Fighting. They described their dog as being friendly toward other dogs in the neighborhood. This was an interpretive description. I asked what they meant by "friendly." They said, "Well, he is always ready to play with other dogs."

DR. T: What do you mean by "play"?
CLIENTS: You know how dogs usually play, jumping on the dogs, and playfully growling.
DR. T: Does he ever bite any other dogs?
CLIENTS: Yes, but he never hurts them. He just bites their cheeks or the backs of their necks.

Upon further probing I was able to determine that the mastiff played using all the dominance postures and behaviors described in the previous section. He would stand over, mount, neck-bite, and so forth. Since he was such a large dominant dog, he had never met a dog who didn't submit.

I found out further that he would jump up on strange men who entered the house. When they stood in the doorway, the mastiff would jump up and place his forepaws on their chest and shoulders. If they were sitting he would go over, put his head in their lap and then stand on their lap with his forepaws. The owners interpreted this as "trying to make friends," when in fact these were dominance behaviors.

The husband would usually roughhouse with the dog. He used to be a wrestler in college and this roughhousing was a wrestling match between the dog and the man. The husband would kneel by the side of the standing dog, put one hand over the dog's back and the match would begin. It usually ended with the husband flipping the dog over on his back and pinning him. This is exactly what the husband should have done to maintain dominance over the dog. It worked. The dog was very submissive to the husband.

Fear. When the husband roughhoused with his dog, the dog would occasionally snap at him. But he had never bitten the man. The dog was also afraid of the vacuum cleaner and car rides.

(209)

Elimination. The dog would roll over on its back and urinate when the husband was about to punish the dog. The dog had occasionally defecated in the house, for which he was severely beaten.

Exploring. The dog was very active and fearless. He would investigate anything new that was brought into the house.

COBS. The dog could not be groomed by anyone but the husband. Two professional groomers had refused to groom the dog because of aggressive behavior.

Resting. The dog would prowl about the house at night and would bark at the slightest noise.

Operant. The dog had been trained with the usual commands: sit, stay, down and heel. He would obey the husband more readily than he did the wife. However, even the husband could not control him if a stranger approached the house.

Nesting and Care of Young. Not applicable.

You can see that all the behaviors taken together form an integrated picture. Now we have enough information to make an interpretation. The dog was very dominant. The problem basically was uncontrolled territoriality. He would guard his territory and attack anyone who entered it. The reason he attacked the three people is that they were not submissive enough. The ten-year-old boy had been patting the dog on the head and back, that is, standing over. The jogger was running, and the lawyer, being a dog owner himself, probably tried to push the dog down when it jumped on him. The solution was to train submissive behavior on command, so that the dog could be controlled, and build a stronger fence.

This interpretation and solution could be arrived at only since I was able to get clear verbal descriptions of the dog's behaviors. I was not satisfied with the original interpretive statements such as "The dog was playful with other dogs." I kept probing until my clients could produce an accurate behavioral description. Then I would relate these descriptions to the known descriptions of genetically organized behavior described in the previous section.

Counting Behaviors

Once you get a clear description of the problem behaviors the next step is to get an estimate of how often they occur. This is done to get some idea of the severity of the problem and to check if the treatment plan is working.

There are two ways to estimate the severity of a problem: a rough estimate from memory, or actually to count the behaviors. The estimate from memory has a value in that it gives you some idea about the severity. However, it is not very useful when trying to evaluate the treatment plan. Memory is replete with omissions and errors. It is also subject to many psychological effects that may make you believe that the treatment plan is working when in actuality it is not or vice versa.

For example, if you truly believe in the value of a solution you may fail to remember or notice the problem. Since you are actively doing something about the problem you may feel better and thus believe you are succeeding. You base this belief on the vague impression that the problem is improving.

On the other hand, the solution may be working but so slowly that you fail to notice it. For example, you are trying to reduce barking and the treatment plan causes a change from one thousand to nine hundred to eight hundred barks per hour in two days. This is a significant drop but it is not very noticeable since the drop in the rate of barking has only gone from 2.8 barks per ten seconds to 2.2 barks per ten seconds. However, it suggests that you will be able to eliminate the barking problem completely in about ten days. If you were not counting the barks, you would have no way of knowing that the solution was working. You would tend to give up before the treatment had a chance to work.

(211)

So counting the behaviors is necessary in evaluating your success. It allows you to continue with working solutions and discard ineffective solutions. We need to count the behavior in such a way that we can estimate the rate (the number of behaviors per unit of time). Rate is much more important than the actual number of behaviors. Obviously ten barks can be a problem when they occur in ten seconds but are not a problem when they occur over ten days. Thus we must count behavior over some period of time. The time base is related to the frequency of the behavior. The more frequent the behavior, the shorter the time base should be. For frequent barking a one-minute or one-hour time base would be effective. For elimination problems a one-day time base would be more sound.

What to Count

Many of my clients want to know exactly what it is that they should count. In many cases you can count each time the problem behavior occurs. For example, if your dog has a continuous barking problem, you can count the number of times he barks in an hour. If he is prone to fits of barking, and then silence, you can count the number of fits per day. A cassette tape recorder is very useful for counting barking, especially if your dog barks when you leave the house. Simply turn on the tape recorder when you leave. You can play sample portions of the tape—begining, middle and end—when you return to get an estimate of his barking rate.

Other problem behaviors, such as jumping on you or eliminating in the house when you are absent, occur only when the dog has an opportunity. Then the most informative count is the number of behaviors per opportunity. For example, you may find that your dog jumps up on you nine out of ten times when you enter the house. By training your dog to lie down when you enter you will probably see that your dog jumps up less and less per opportunity, eight out of ten, then six out of ten and so forth.

If you don't take note of the opportunities as well as the problem behavior, you could make the wrong interpretation of the results. For example, if in the first week your dog jumped on you nine out of ten times, and the second week, ten out of twenty times, the actual number of jumps has gone up but the percentage of jumps per opportunity has dropped from 90 percent to 50 percent. If you just looked at the number of jumps you would come to the erroneous conclusion that your treatment procedure was not working.

There are some behaviors that are dangerous to the dog or to others, and you obviously cannot allow them. My clients with the bull mastiff could not let their dog roam free and count how many neighbors he had bitten in a week. In such cases you must measure some earlier part of the sequence. For the mastiff, growling and barking at passersby was an adequate indicator of his aggressiveness, and this is what we measured. We also recorded how many times the dog would calm down when he was aggressive. The definition of calming down was the complete cessation of barking and growling within two seconds after the command "Quiet" was given. You will recall that the dog was trained to be submissive on command. Figure 4 is a graph of the results of this treatment.

You can see from this figure that before treatment the mastiff growled and barked at about 90 percent to 100 percent of the people passing in front of his house, and would calm down when told only about 10 percent of the time. After twenty days of training to make the dog submissive to the command "Quiet," he was calming down about 95 percent of the time and he would bark at about 5 percent to 8 percent of the passersby. Note the slow but steady increase in the dog's response to the command, and the equally slow decrease in aggressiveness toward people passing by. It took at least five days before any effect of the training was seen. Without recording the behavior, my clients would have given up before the treatment had had a chance to work. So the counting was

(213)

necessary to show them that what they were doing was effective.

How to Count

Counting problem behaviors is as simple as one, two, three. All you have to do is make note of the number of occurrences of the problem per unit of time or per number of opportunities. If the problem behavior occurs very infrequently, you might simply store this information in your head and write it down somewhere at the end of the day. If the problem behavior occurs frequently, it would be easier to have some special method of recording. One device I have found useful in my practice is a plastic adding machine. This inexpensive device is normally used to keep track of your expenditures while shopping. It usually has four buttons, used to enter the price of an

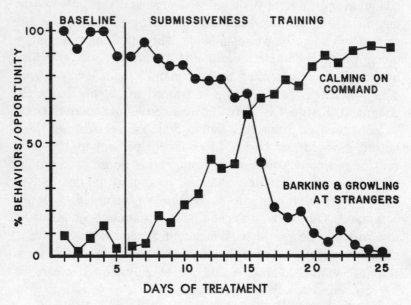

FIGURE 4. GRAPHIC RESULTS OF SUBMISSIVENESS TRAINING FOR THE BITING AND AGGRESSIVENESS PROBLEM OF THE BULL MASTIFF

item in dollars and cents. You can use this device to count behaviors by pressing the pennies button every time the problem occurs. This will automatically count and store the number throughout the day. At the end of the day you can write down the number and reset the adder.

Another convenient device is a golfer's calculator, a device used by golfers to keep track of their strokes during the game. It is small and can usually be worn on the wrist, so it is always available. You simply have to press the little button that advances the count one unit every time the problem occurs. Then write down the count at the end of the day.

Whatever method of counting you use you should have a special place to write down the results. Just writing down the results on an odd slip of paper will not do. It is easily lost or misplaced. A Problem Behavior Diary could be constructed using a spiral note pad. In it you will record the date, your count for the day and whatever observations you have made. Indicate the problems you are having and your attempts at a solution. Indicate any drastic changes that may set you back. If your treatment plan isn't working, try to indicate why and what you intend to do about it.

This may seem like a lot of writing but it takes only about five to ten minutes a day, a small price to pay to alleviate your problems. It is important to have a specific period of time to reflect about your treatment plan. In the quiet of the evening you can evaluate your progress and perhaps come up with a new and better procedure or discard any unsuccessful procedure. My clients find this very useful. They generally report that they get their best ideas during this time.

The Counting Checklist

You may want to include a counting checklist in your diary. There are many kinds of checklists, each for a different purpose. Sometimes it is important to know when the problem occurs during the day. This is especially important if there is some rhythm or cycle to the problem. A cycle can indicate hormonal involvement or some special circumstances that occur at only specific times in the day. If you can establish that there is a cycle, you can observe the problem portion of the day very carefully. For example, a female client of mine found that her male toy poodle became uncontrollable only once a month. This period lasted about a week and coincided exactly with her menstrual cycle. We would never have known this without accurate counting and recording. The problem was that during menstruation my client became less tolerant of the dog and treated him harshly.

Figure 5 gives an example of a counting checklist for a week. You can see that the date and day are recorded across the top and the time of day down the side. In the body of the checklist you record the occurrence of the behavior. This can be done by a check or X if you are recording only one behavior. For many behaviors you simply have to develop an alphabet code, b for barking, g for growling, s for snapping, d for defecating and so on. Just write down the code at the top or side and record the appropriate letter in the cells of the table.

You can elaborate this code to include the situation in which the problem occurs: K for kitchen, B for bedroom and so forth. A two-letter code, K-b, can mean barking in the kitchen.

Other aspects of the ROCKS method include the stimulus situation (S) and the consequences of the behavior (C). These can be recorded using the method presented in Figure 6.

The table itself is self-explanatory. It asks you to record when and where the problem occurred, what you were doing just before the problem, what the problem is, and what you did after the problem behavior. This gets you to reflect upon the possibility that the dog was reacting to something you were doing. If you find consistencies here, you will have a clue to the cause of the problem.

You don't necessarily have to count and record the problem

FIGURE 5. COUNTING CHECKLIST

Name _____   Date _____

Time	Monday	Tuesday	Wednesday	Thursday	Friday	Saturday	Sunday
7–8							
8–9							
9–10							
10–11							
11–12							
12–1							
1–2							
2–8							
3–4							
4–5							
5–6							
6–7							
7–8							
8–9							
9–10							
10–11							
11–12							

FIGURE 6. BEHAVIOR SCHEDULE

Name _____   Date _____

Pet Behavior	Time	Date	Setting	Owner Behavior That Preceded Pet Behavior	Owner Behavior That Followed Pet Behavior	Comments

to correct it. The amount you record is directly related to the mysteriousness of the problem. If you already have a very clear idea about when and where the problem occurs and what to do about it, then the checklist would become redundant. However, if you do not understand the problem, if it is a complete or partial mystery why your dog is biting or whatever, then a detailed analysis will pay off. It will guide your thinking and help you come to the correct diagnosis.

A side effect of counting problem behaviors is that it defuses an explosive situation. Usually a problem behavior in a pet causes a great deal of concern and emotion in the owners. They react with fear or anger and don't understand why their pet is doing this to them. Counting behaviors can clear up this confusion and give the pet owner time to think. Instead of reacting, you record. You try a technique and have good evidence if it's working or not. If your technique is not working you can discard it without emotion and try a new one. You can look at the problem with the cool detachment of a scientist, analyze it and eventually solve it.

A second side effect of counting problem behaviors is that it gives you the patience to get through a treatment procedure that can last a number of weeks or months. By seeing the problem behavior decrease you can see that your plan is working and you can forecast how long it will take to work. You can set realistic goals for progress.

GOAL-SETTING

Once you have established the nature of your dog's problem, gotten adequate behavioral descriptions of the problem and made some estimate of the severity of the problem it is time to set a goal for the treatment.

The goal is basically what you expect to accomplish by the treatment procedure. Most people set a negative goal: they

(219)

simply want the problem to stop. However, this is not adequate. A goal should also specify a time line, subgoals and, if at all possible, be stated positively.

A positive goal is basically a statement about an acceptable behavior that will compete with the problem behavior. For example, if your dog is excitable and jumps all over you when you enter the house, the ultimate negative goal is the complete elimination of the jumping. A positive goal would be the creation of a new competing response when you enter, such as sitting quietly or lying down. This is not just a semantic trick. It is related directly to how you treat the problem. If you set only a negative goal you are left with only one type of treatment: punishment. If you set a positive goal can you reward the competing behavior.

Almost all problem behaviors have acceptable competing behaviors. The idea of a competing behavior is that your dog can't do two totally different things at the same time. He can't lie down and jump up on you at the same time. Licking your hand competes with biting your hand. Submissive behavior competes with dominant aggressive behavior. Resting competes with exploring. Elimination outside competes with elimination in the house. Playing and eating compete with fear. Dropping an item on command competes with stealing or guarding something. Coming when called competes with running away from you.

The point is that most problem behaviors can be corrected by rewarding a nonproblem behavior as well as by punishing the problem. The combination of reward and punishment is much more effective than punishment alone.

In order to reward nonproblem behavior you have to shape it. I described shaping earlier as rewarding successive approximations to the desired behavior. This means establishing subgoals. For example, if you want your dog to stop jumping on you when you enter, your first positive subgoal could be sitting quietly for one second. This may not seem like a long time, but it is for a very excitable dog. When your dog sits quietly for one second (you may have to hold him in a sitting position at first), reward him with praise, petting and affection. When he sits quietly for one second without restraint you can increase the demands. He now has to sit quietly for two or three seconds. If you continue rewarding this quiet sitting, steadily increasing the demands as he succeeds at the easier levels, you will eventually eliminate the jumping problem. As you enter, your dog will immediately sit and wait to be petted or rewarded in some other way.

This technique of shaping competing behavior is especially useful when dealing with an aggressive dominant dog. I have already pointed out that you cannot punish aggression since punishment will cause more aggression. But you can reward submission. At first, reward any sign of submission no matter how slight. A submissive facial expression or posture is a good place to start. You would eventually work up to reward the ultimate submissive posture of lying down on the back with you standing over. This was done with the bull mastiff, with very good results.

Sometimes it takes a lot of detailed observation and a bit of creativity to figure out how to make the animal produce a competing response. For example, I had a case of a two-year-old male Yorkie who would bite the mother of the household. The mother was an elderly woman who fed and cared for the dog. When the dog got excited, he would run to her for protection. If he got even more excited, he would bite the nearest moving object, which was usually the mother. The bites were often serious, breaking the skin. Punishing this aggressive behavior resulted in the animal getting more aggressive, increasing the tendency to bite the mother. Systematic desensitization of the fear and excitement was also ineffective.

What was effective was training a competing behavior to running up to the mother when the dog was excited. The competing behavior I used was backing away from the mother when the dog was excited. This was accomplished by noticing that the dog would pull back on the leash when he was pulled forward.

To train the backing-away response, we would get the dog excited and at the same time the mother would pull the dog toward her with the leash. The dog would fight the leash, pulling backward with all his might. Then when the dog was most excited, and pulling backward his hardest, the mother would say, "Go away," and let go of the leash. This caused the dog to spring backward and run up the stairs. We did this for two 2½ -hour sessions, managing to work in five trials per session. The dog has never bitten the mother since. When he gets excited, he runs and hides under the bed and comes out only when he is calm. The dog will still bite when he is excited, but he is not near anyone to bite. So the competing behavior for this dog was staying away from people until he could calm down.

(O) ORGANISMIC VARIABLES

Organismic variables basically refer to events occurring inside the body of your dog that affect behavior. These events are related to illness, disease, hormonal imbalance, neurological damage, imbalance in blood chemistry and the like. It can be said that almost every illness or internal imbalance can and probably does cause a behavioral change. The changes may be subtle or dramatic.

A bodily infection is likely to cause your dog to become listless and mope around the house. Another nonspecific effect of illness can be a breakdown of behavioral controls, which means that formerly well-trained habits will cease to function. Your dog may start eliminating in the house or refuse to obey commands. The nature of the breakdown is directly related to the strength and generalizability of the behavioral control.

The weaker and less generalized the control, the more likely it will deteriorate when your dog is sick.

This nonspecific breakdown of controls may not be due directly to the illness but to the change in internal sensation caused by the illness. Your dog has been trained to obey commands, eliminate outside, inhibit biting, and so on, when he was healthy. However, this training may not extend to the sensations accompanying being sick. It obviously follows that if you remove the sensations of illness the behavior problems will disappear.

In addition to the nonspecific effects of illness there is a very specific behavioral effect related to the organ or tissue that is damaged or diseased. Infection in the urinary tract causes elimination problems. Brain lesions can cause problems in the behavior controlled by the part of the brain that is affected. An illness-by-illness analysis of behavior change would be a book in itself and beyond the purview of this book.

Suffice it to say that one of the first indicators of illness is a behavior change. If you notice a sudden change in the behavior of your dog, a return of an old behavior problem, or a sudden breakdown of behavioral controls, immediately take your dog to a veterinarian for examination. You should do this before you attempt to treat the behavior using the techniques presented in this book. This is done simply to determine if there is any illness. If there is illness, your veterinarian will deal with it. If not, you have ruled out a physiological cause and you can proceed with a behavioral analysis and treatment.

Even if your dog has a persistent behavioral problem that in all probability has a behavioral cause, I would still recommend a medical examination. This is done to rule out any possibility of a medical cause. For example, a client of mine had a male German shepherd that persisted in chewing the plasterboard walls in the garage. The dog had completely destroyed one wall and was working on another. A medical examination indicated that part of the problem may have

(223)

been a calcium and mineral deficiency in the dog's diet. The dog was probably obtaining some of its needed minerals from the plaster walls. The behavior of chewing the walls could be easily stopped with conditioning techniques; however, that would leave the dog with a dietary deficiency. After the dog's diet was corrected by the addition of the appropriate minerals, wall chewing was stopped by gluing electrodes on the wall and shocking the dog when it chewed.

On the other side of the coin, a purely medical solution to a behavior problem does not always work. For example, veterinarians frequently recommend castration for a male dog that exhibits marking, hypersexuality or excessive dominance problems. This is because these behaviors are partially controlled by the male sex hormone, testosterone, which is primarily produced by the testes. The logic is to remove the source of the hormone and you will remove the behavior problem. The logic is sound but castration alone does not always work. It has already been shown that sexual, dominance and elimination behavior are controlled by other things besides hormones. The more behavioral variables in control, the less likely a hormonal change will work. For example, if a dog is aggressive and dominant, it is likely that the dog is rewarded for this behavior by getting his way. After he is castrated and is still being rewarded when he is aggressive, the problem will not change.

Conversely, a behavior change after castration and other medical procedures may be caused by psychological variables. After the operation the dog may be submissive for a few days to a week due to the fact that he has been taken to the veterinarian and traumatized by the whole experience. This immediate behavior change cannot be attributed to a hormonal change because there is still a large amount of testosterone circulating in the dog's bloodstream. If the owner takes advantage of this temporary submissive behavior and rewards the dog for submission, there may be a permanent change. If

(224)

the owner does not take advantage of the submissive behavior, the problem may return in a week or two when the dog gets over the trauma of the operation.

The point is that a medical treatment of a behavioral problem such as dominance or aggression must be accompanied by a change in the owner's behavior toward the dog. Sometimes this change in the owner behavior occurs unconsciously. Since the dog has been castrated, the owner expects the dog to be less aggressive and behaves accordingly. However, leaving the change to the unconscious or unintentional effects of a change in the owner's expectations is a very "iffy" situation. It would be far better for the owner to take conscious, intentional action to ensure that the medical intervention will be effective. For aggressive problems, this means intentionally rewarding the competing behavior of submission.

The Nonprimacy of Physiology

Many veterinary practitioners feel that the major cause of behavior problems is a biological one. This is understandable given the fact that the problems they usually deal with are medical. However, it is possible for the reverse to be true. Biological or medical problems can have a psychological basis. These are called psychosomatic illnesses.

Many people are confused and suspicious about this. They cannot understand how the "mind" can affect the body. The "mind" is supposed to exist on one plane and the body on the other. But if you think about it for a minute, you will realize that the word "mind" means those structures in the body that control it. This boils down to the brain, central nervous system and endocrine (hormone) system.

All these systems are bodily structures like any others. They are all interrelated in feedback loops; that is, the brain can affect the activity of the endocrine glands and other parts of the body, which in turn can affect the activity of the brain.

(225)

This interrelationship between the brain and the rest of the body permits psychological causes of bodily damage. For example, behaviors like excessive hair-chewing can result in skin damage, which can lead to more hair-chewing and more damage, or starvation and anorexia can be caused by conditioned vomiting. These problems were discussed earlier.

Less obviously, skin inflammation, ulcers and asthma can be caused by psychological as well as physical stress. One type of psychological stress that can lead to bodily damage is restraint and confinement. Another type is the relationship between the dog and his environment.

The stress condition is caused when aversive, painful, fear-producing events in the dog's environment are both unpredictable and uncontrollable. For example, I had a client who would take out his frustrations by hitting his dog. The beatings were not serious and did not cause physical damage. However, the beatings were totally unpredictable. On a good day the owner would tolerate many problem behaviors without reprisal. On bad days, even the slightest disturbance would result in a beating, sometimes hours after the incident. This inconsistency in punishment made it impossible for the dog to determine when and where and for what he was being punished. No matter what the dog did, or did not do, he was punished. There was no way he could reliably prevent or avoid punishment, nor could he escape it. Along with ulcers, the dog developed what is called "learned helplessness."

The dog had learned that he had no control over his environment. This resulted in what can only be described as depression. He spent most of the day quietly resting. He would not initiate any behaviors. He stopped eating and drinking, and had to be force-fed. Eventually, he stopped controlling his other behaviors. He would defecate and urinate while lying down. The owner persisted in punishing this behavior despite my advice against it. The dog died one month after I had seen him even though I was able to reinstate voluntary eating and

drinking, and the ulcer was being controlled medically. The dog died of helplessness.

There can be other types of psychological causes of what appears to be a medical problem. For example, epileptic seizures are caused by an abnormality in the brain called a focus. The focus is a localized part of the brain that acts differently from the rest of the brain tissue. Its electrical activity is much higher and can cause the rest of the brain cells to fire synchronously with it. When this happens, you have an epileptic seizure.

However, there are documented cases of epileptic seizures initiated in a dog who watches another dog have a seizure. This contagious epilepsy usually occurs in hunting dogs when kept together in a pack. These dogs share the same environment, eat the same thing and usually have a common genetic background. You might expect that they would be attending to each other's behavior. It usually starts with one member of the pack having a seizure. Then, one by one, each dog starts to have seizures until nearly all the pack members are convulsing on the ground. The sight of a dog in this state elicits the same behavior in the other dogs. The more dogs that are affected the more powerful the sight, until the most resistant dog succumbs. If the pack is not separated, this activity can last a long time since the first dogs are recovering while the others are still having seizures. The sight of the remaining dogs can reelicit the seizure in the first dogs to be affected, and so on.

Another problem is conditioned epilepsy. I treated a two-year-old male Yorkie who had epileptiform seizures when the kitchen timer bell, doorbell or telephone rang. These stimuli set off the seizures since the owners would get very excited when these bells rang. The excitement elicited the seizures. Eventually the bells were sufficient to elicit the seizures. The seizures were mild, resulting in brief immobility and rigidity for about five to ten seconds, followed by severe rage. During

the rage, the dog would savagely bite at anything that moved near him, including his own body. Thus, if the owners left him alone during the seizure, they would return to find the dog tightly gripping one of his hind legs with his teeth. This self-biting had caused serious damage to the leg. If it continued, it would probably result in permanent damage and perhaps loss of the leg. Since the duration of the rigid part of the seizure was so short, the epileptiform nature of the problem had gone undetected until I had an opportunity to observe the whole sequence. The problem was treated first with ovidone, an anticonvulsant drug. This reduced the number of seizures by one half, i.e., from ten to four or five per week. Then the seizure chain of events was interrupted. This was done by conditioning food rewards to the various bells in the house. First the bells were muffled so that they did not cause a seizure, then they were rung, and the food (cheese) was given to the dog immediately. The muffling was removed in layers, when the dog expected food at the muffled sound of the bells. Eventually, the dog would happily expect food when the bells were rung at full intensity. This dropped the seizure rate to about one per week.

The second part of the seizure—the rage and the self-biting —was treated by delivering a one-second, two-milliampere shock to the neck of the dog when he bit himself or me (I was wearing protective leather clothing and gloves). The shock pulsed at one-second intervals until the biting stopped. Two sessions of shock with five shocks per session resulted in complete elimination of the biting.

Since the dog was treated by drugs and behavioral variables of shock and reward, I am unable to determine which one was the most important. It is possible that they were all necessary for the complete control of the problem.

I have successfully treated four other cases of what appeared to be epileptiform aggression with a combination of anti-convulsant drugs, reward for nonaggressive behaviors and

shock for biting. In all these cases there was a very brief sign of an aura before the aggression. The dogs would remain immobile in a standing, stalking or pointing posture; their eyes appeared glassy and sometimes rolled in the sockets. The aggression was in the form of savage biting and was directed at the owners and me, and seemed to be elicited by movement. There were usually some stimuli that preceded the seizures. These stimuli varied from the activation of machine noises such as a vacuum cleaner, blender or bells to placing the collar or coat on the dog or turning on the TV. None of the stimuli appeared to be threatening but were probably conditioned to the seizure.

Another case, which I was unsuccessful in treating, had no reliable stimuli preceding it. It is possible that in this case the seizure was not conditioned or was conditioned to some internal change in the animal or some subtle external stimulus. However, the apparent randomness of the seizures and biting made it impossible to predict and prevent through the use of contingent reward or shock. The anticonvulsant drug had a mild and transitory effect. The dog was eventually destroyed.

Psychosomatic Behavior Problems

There are many behavior changes that are directly caused by a physiological problem. For example, a dog will limp if his leg is damaged, scratch when he has a skin irritation, vomit if he has a stomach infection or urinate in the house if he has a bladder infection. However, after the physiological cause of a behavior problem is removed, the behavior may persist. This is not common but it can cause quite a lot of consternation on the part of the veterinarian. After all, the bodily signs indicate a cure, but the dog is still vomiting, scratching, limping or urinating.

The reason for the persistence of symptoms after a cure is that the symptoms have been rewarded by attention.

I have treated cases of lameness, vomiting, excessive scratching and urination. Each case has similar characteristics. In all cases the dog would be ignored unless he created a disturbance or had a problem. For example, a case of lameness in a three-and-a-half-year-old female collie started with the dog jumping through the glass window of the storm door. The dog had cut her left front leg severely in the process, necessitating surgery. Previous to this, the dog had been a behavior problem. And most of the problem behaviors were rewarded by attention. In fact, the dog had been shaped to jump on the storm door by attending to her when she jumped up. Now that the dog was hurt, the owners, two elderly women, would cater to her and attend to her when she limped around the house. As soon as the dog began limping or whimpering they would console her and pet her. This was a natural reaction to seeing their pet in pain and perhaps feeling guilty about the whole incident.

In one month, the dog was completely healed. X-rays and medical examinations showed no discernible damage to the bone, cartilage or muscle. However, the dog would frequently whimper in pain and limp around the house. This caused a great amount of concern and frequent visits to the veterinarian. Physical therapy was instituted on the dog's leg under the hypothesis that there was some undetected muscle atrophy during the healing process. This seemed to accentuate the limping and whimpering. The dog would whimper and limp around during the flexation and extension of her leg during the therapy. The owners would pet and console their dog when she whimpered.

The first clue to the fact that this was psychological lameness came when I observed the dog. First, she would only whimper and limp at certain times of day. These times corresponded very nicely to the lunch and dinner hour. The dog would limp to the kitchen, sit and hold up her paw and

(230)

whimper. She was given a piece of meat to console her. Then she would eat the food, hold up her paw and whimper again. When I gave her a large bone during one of these whimpering sessions, she picked up the bone and trotted out of the kitchen. There was no sign of limping. Later she buried the bone in the backyard and did not favor the "lame leg." Subsequently, I noticed that when she limped up to the owners, they would run toward her, pet her and massage her leg. I asked the owners to turn around and run away from her. The dog took off after the owners in full gallop but started limping again when she was about five feet from them.

The solution to the problem was to turn the tables on the dog. The owners were instructed to ignore the dog completely when she limped and to lavish praise and affection when she walked properly. The owners reluctantly complied, resulting in a complete termination of limping in two weeks.

Treatment of Behavior Problems with Drugs

Since the advent of tranquilizers, psychoactive drugs have been more and more commonly employed in the treatment of behavior problems. Some of the miracle chemicals have produced dramatic reversals in behavior problems, especially if the problem is related to a highly nervous, active dog.

However, caution should be noted. There is no such thing as a magic bullet when it comes to tranquilizers. One cannot administer a drug to affect only specific kinds of behavior. When tranquilizers are administered all behaviors are reduced.

The second caution relates to the exclusive use of tranquilizers to treat behavior problems. Just like castration, tranquilizers can set the stage for a behavioral change. But also like castration, you want to reward appropriate competing behaviors. In this way you can wean the dog from the tranquilizer as you get more and more behavioral control.

For example, I recently had a case of a two-and-a-half-year-old hyperactive male German shorthair, referred to me by a veterinarian. When anyone entered the room where the dog was, he would jump and lick and slobber all over the person. The dog would also get very excited when taken on car rides. Tranquilizers had been effective for a couple of months, but the dog needed higher and higher doses. Currently, the only effective dose would lead to sleeping or complete lethargy. The owners complained that using the tranquilizers was like having a stuffed dog around the house. However, if they reduced the dosage, the hyperactivity returned.

The problem was that the dog was rewarded for being active and jumping up on people. This reward was intensified when the dog was drugged. The owners liked the excited behavior of the dog and would encourage it, defeating the activity of the drug.

The solution was to reward quiet behaviors like lying down and sitting when people entered. As control was obtained under high dosages of the drug the dosage was slowly reduced. Each reduction in the dosage caused a return of the jumping behavior that had to be re-treated by rewarding quiet behaviors. This illustrates a problem with training a dog in a drugged state, called "state-dependent learning." The dog may not transfer what he has learned in the drugged state to the undrugged state and vice versa.

The drug was not completely eliminated because that caused such a dramatic increase in jumping and activity that it was impossible to reward quiet behavior. But this progressive decrease in the dosage coupled with the continuous training in quiet behaviors ultimately resulted in the complete elimination of the drug in six months.

The point is that a drug, like a tranquilizer, should not be relied upon to solve a behavior problem completely. The drug should be thought of as only a temporary solution. Tran-

(232)

quilizers can be used to get immediate control of the problem and set the stage for behavioral control. Since the tranquilizer may reduce the problem you have an opportunity to reward competing behavior. If you take advantage of this opportunity you may be able to eliminate the drug eventually. If you fail to take advantage of the opportunity, you will have a drug-dependent dog. Thus the behavior problem will return if the drug is discontinued.

Once you have appropriately defined the behavior problem and ruled out potential physiological causes, you are ready to do a complete analysis of the problem. This involves the stimulus setting (S), the consequences (C) of the behavior and the contingencies (K).

(S) STIMULUS SETTING

When analyzing the stimulus setting of a problem behavior, you are asking what stimuli control the behavior. In order to answer this it is important to take note of when, where and with whom the behavior occurs. Sometimes the answers appear to be quite obvious. For example, in the case previously described, the Yorkie would bite only the mother of the household when he was excited. However, sometimes the answers to these questions are obscure. For example, I had a case of a three-and-a-half-year-old male dachshund who would balk and refuse to enter the elevator. The owner was an elderly lady who could not walk down five flights of stairs. I initially figured that this was a case of fear of enclosed spaces and would try to desensitize this fear. However, the dog was not afraid of entering other enclosed spaces such as a closet or cardboard box. Furthermore, the dog was not continuously afraid of the elevator. Sometimes he entered it and other times would refuse to. The balking seemed to be random. This meant that there were some other stimuli controlling the fear. In order to desensitize the fear, a hierarchy had to be constructed of increasingly more fearful stimuli. This could not be done until the nature of the fear stimuli was known.

The problem of identifying the controlling stimuli was compounded by the many types of events that could potentially control behavior. Not only could any aspect of the external environment be involved but aspects of the dog's internal environment could control and signal the problem. The internal environment consists of changes in heart rate, blood pressure, hunger, thirst, hormones, drugs and illness. Any changes going on inside the body and can be sensed can become a controlling stimulus.

In order to see if internal stimuli might be controlling the fear, I asked my client to use the behavioral checklist presented in Figure 5. She was to take the dog to the elevator every hour and make an X on the checklist if the dog balked. She was also to record an M for meals, D for drinking and E for eliminating. The logic is that internal changes in the dog's body are usually cyclic. If any cycle in the balking was uncovered we could then look more closely at that period of time. But after five days of recording there was no discernible cycle. The dog balked 50 percent of the time whether it was morning, noon or night.

This left some external change that was controlling the balking at the elevator. There had to be something different about the elevator when the dog balked. In order to determine this we examined the elevator closely after the dog balked and when the dog entered freely. The lights appeared the same, the fan had no effect, neither did the presence of the elevator operator. Finally, we discovered the difference. When the dog balked, the elevator was not perfectly lined up with the floor. This caused a widening of the space between the elevator and the floor. This change was very slight, about half an inch.

In order to test this, we placed a small piece of carpeting over the threshold of the elevator door, obscuring the space. The dog would then enter readily.

So the dachshund was afraid of the small space between the elevator and floor. This made sense because of the proximity of this dog to the ground and also because the dog on occasion would catch his nails in this space. The solution was effected with the cooperation of the elevator operator. During the quiet of the afternoon he consented to adjust the elevator so that there was a six-inch discrepancy between the floor and the elevator. This forced the dog to leap up in order to enter the elevator. This was a well-known behavior used frequently and without fear when going up a flight of stairs. The dog performed this leap into the elevator without fear and was rewarded. Then the discrepancy was reduced to four inches, then three, two, one, a half inch. Each time the dog was required to leap in the elevator to get a reward. Within two days the dog completely stopped balking at the elevator. The point is that without adequate identification of the controlling stimulus, treatment probably would have failed.

How Stimuli Come to Control Behavior

There are two ways in which stimuli come to control behavior. The first is through genetics. Genetically organized behavior sequences are initiated by stimuli called "releasers." The dog does not have to learn to recognize these releasers. He recognizes them innately and reacts appropriately. Many releasers have been discussed already in the section on genetically organized and social behaviors in dogs.

After the genetically organized sequence is started by a releaser, it is maintained by changes in the environment. Other releasers are produced by the behavior of interacting animals or the behavior itself. In fact, the sensations created by the behavior can easily serve as stimuli for the next behavior. For example, in some dogs who have barking fits, many stimuli can start the barking, but once started, the barking may continue even if the initiating stimuli are removed. This is because each bark serves as a stimulus for the next bark. This produces a very high rate of uncontrollable barking. It is possible that even the dog may not be able to control the barking once it is started.

Stimuli also come to control behavior through discrimination learning, or teaching your dog to differentiate between things and react accordingly. There are two ways this discrimination training is accomplished, the prediction method and the control method.

The Prediction Method

The prediction method is a natural form of learning that your dog uses all the time. By this method he learns what is going to happen next. All your dog needs to learn by this method is that two events occur reliably close together in sequence. Your dog will learn to predict the second event when he notices the first one. But the only reason he will do this is if the second event is of some importance to him. Thus he will learn to predict when he will be fed, praised, petted or punished by whatever stimuli come before these events.

Those of you who feed your dog canned dog food will notice how your dog reacts when he hears the sound of the electric can opener. He will usually run to the kitchen and anticipate food. The first event, the can opener sound, predicts the second event, eating. However, the can opener may be operated at various times during the day, but only once or twice a day does it predict eating. This is how your dog's discrimination is refined. He will respond to the can opener sound many times and not get fed. Eventually, if you are consistent about feeding time, he will only respond to

(236)

the can opener sound at the time of day when he is usually fed and ignore it at all other times.

The basic paradigm for this type of refined discrimination can be diagrammed as follows:

Stimuli		Event	Response to Stimuli
S + Can opener sound + meal time	$\Rightarrow$	Eating	Anticipates food
S − Can opener sound + all other times	$\Rightarrow$	No eating	Ignores sound and will not anticipate food

The same basic paradigm is at work when your dog learns to anticipate a whole variety of important events. Punishment could be diagrammed as follows:

Stimuli		Event	Response to Stimuli
S + "No" + owner's angry tone of voice	$\Rightarrow$	Swat with rolled-up newspaper	Dog cowers and anticipates being hit
S − "No" + not angry	$\Rightarrow$	No punishment	Dog ignores "No" command

In the above paradigm the owner only punishes when he is angry. Thus the dog will eventually learn to discriminate when his master means business and when he can get away with misbehavior. The dog may not even pay attention to the word "No" since it really doesn't tell him when he is going to get punished. The reliable predictor of punishment in this case is the owner's tone of voice.

Through this prediction method, your dog will learn to pick out, attend to, and respond to reliable predictors of important events in his life whether or not those stimuli are the ones you want your dog to pay attention to. This can result in the problem of inappropriate stimulus control, which will be dealt with later.

The Control Method

The method used by your dog to learn to discriminate between events is the control method. This method not only involves the prediction of good and bad events in your dog's life, such as reward and punishment, but also involves doing something about these events or controlling them. Your dog can learn to control rewards and other good events by predicting under what circumstances they are likely to be given and what he must do to get them. He can learn to control punishment and other aversive events by either escaping them or avoiding them. To avoid them he must be able to predict when they will occur.

Every command that your dog responds to correctly is a product of discrimination learning. The paradigm for the "Sit" command is diagrammed below:

Stimulus	Response	Event
1. "Sit" + (living room)	Sitting	Reward
2. "Sit" + (back-yard)	No sitting	No reward
3. No command	Sitting	No reward
4. No command	No sitting	No reward

Notice that there is only one set of circumstances that leads to reward, that is, the word "sit" followed by sitting. However, in order for the discrimination of the word "sit" to be complete, the sequence 2, 3, and 4 must also happen. Notice also that the word "sit" is followed by sitting and reward in the living room but "sit" is followed by no sitting in the backyard.

(238)

This is very likely to happen if your dog gets excited and runs around when outside. Under these circumstances your dog will learn to sit on command in the living room but not in the backyard.

Every command is given in a context or surrounding. If you train your dog in only one surrounding and not others, he will learn to obey you in only that surrounding and not others.

The same paradigm occurs when training your dog not to do things that lead to bad events. For example, if you were training your dog not to steal food from the table you could use the following method:

Stimulus	Response	Event
1. "Don't touch" + food on table	Stealing food	Punishment—loud noise or bad taste
2. "Don't touch" + food on table	Leaves food alone	No punishment
3. "Don't touch" + food on floor	Steals food	Punishment
4. "Don't touch" + food on floor	Leaves food alone	No punishment
5. No command + food on table	Steals food	No punishment
6. No command + food on floor	Steals food	No punishment

In this case the dog gets punished only if he steals food after you say "Don't touch," no matter whether the food is on the table or the floor. The words "Don't touch" will control whether your dog steals food and not the food's location. This would not be the best discrimination to form.

If you wanted to make the food location the stimulus that controls your dog's behavior, you could do the following:

Stimuli	Response	Event
1. Food on table + "Don't touch"	Stealing food	Punishment
2. Food on table + "Don't touch"	Leaves food alone	No punishment
3. Food on floor + "Don't touch"	Steals food	No punishment

In this case only the location of the food signals punishment. The command "Don't touch" is irrelevant since two-thirds of the time when you say "Don't touch" your dog does not get punished.

The point is that your dog will attend to whatever stimuli reliably and consistently signal reward or punishment. Whether your dog follows your commands or not depends entirely on your behavior. If you arrange that your commands are the reliable predictors, then your dog will learn to discriminate them and obey you.

Unfortunately many owners, due to fatigue, laziness or whatever, do not follow through with their commands. If they say "Sit" or "Down," they do not make sure that their dog sits or lies down on command, nor do they bother to reward immediately following correct behavior. If they say "No," they do not always follow a transgression with a punishment. Thus, their commands become unreliable predictors of good and bad events, and their dog learns to ignore them.

Generalization—The Opposite of Discrimination

Discrimination means that the dog will respond differently to different stimuli. The opposite of this is generalization. Here the dog responds similarly when the stimuli are different. An example of generalization is when your dog will sit on command no matter who says it, whether it is a high-pitched child's voice or a man's deep voice. In other words, the command "Sit" has generalized across various voice qualities. The one-owner dog who obeys the commands of only a single person is an example of lack of generalization.

Even though discrimination and generalization are opposite in their effects, they can occur at the same time. It all depends upon what is to be generalized and what is to be discriminated. You want your dog to discriminate one command from another so he will sit when you say "Sit" and not lie down. But you also want him to generalize these commands to other places besides where you have trained him. A dog that obeys in the dining room but not in the backyard would not be considered obedient.

This failure to generalize commands or other behavioral controls to a new situation is not unusual. In fact, it is a very natural phenomenon. It is so common that I have labeled it the Johnny Carson Syndrome. How many times have you watched the "Johnny Carson Show" and seen an embarrassed owner bring his educated pet on the show. More often than not the pet just sits there and will not perform, or will eliminate all over the stage. This is because the pet has been trained in an environment that is totally different from the TV stage, with its lights, cameras, microphone booms and laughing audience. Its education will not generalize to this new environment.

A general rule is that every time you change a salient aspect of the environment under which the pet has been trained, you reduce the chances that the pet will perform. The bigger the change, the worse the breakdown in control. This will happen no matter how well trained your animal is. In fact, the more training you give your animal under a constant environment, the more likely it is that it will not generalize to a new one. Thus, if you were going on the Johnny Carson Show to show off your dog's new obedience skills and you decided to practice intensively with your dog before the show and you confined this practice to your house or yard, then it is quite likely that your pet would fall flat on his face when he was supposed to perform. The more practice you gave the more likely this would be.

The failure to generalize behavioral controls can be quite a problem for trainers who run obedience schools. For a considerable fee you can send your unruly dog away to school in the hopes that he will return an educated, obedient dog with all his problems removed. If the obedience trainer is honest and knowledgeable, he will succeed in getting control of your dog. When you go to pick up your dog, he will show you his new repertoire of skills. You will be satisfied and gladly pay the bill. If the trainer is more honest, he will give you a few brief lessons on how to control your dog and warn you that you must practice.

You get the dog home and a number of things can happen. First, all the problems can return as if your dog had never been to school. This is because the training did not generalize from the school to the home, and from the trainer to you. The more the school and home environment are different, the less generalization there will be. The more you behave differently from the trainer, the less control you will have. And obviously a kennel is going to be different from your home. And more obviously you, the owner, are going to behave quite differently from the trainer. If you reacted to your dog like the trainer, you probably would have not needed the school to begin with.

The second possibility is that you will muster whatever strength you have and force yourself to conform with the trainer's rules. But just as water seeks its own level, you will return to your old habits and the new behaviors will deteriorate in a couple of weeks. Of course, the last possibility, the most unlikely, is that the dog will behave well from the moment you get him home.

There are basically two ways to prevent the failure to generalize. The first way is to gain behavioral control under the conditions most similar to where your dog must perform. This means to simulate as much as possible the exact nature of the test or show environment and train under these conditions. If your dog must perform in the presence of many other dogs or an audience, lights and cameras, then you must train him under these conditions. An example of a very interesting application of these techniques was relayed to me by a professional circus dog trainer. Of course the trainer knew that he had to train his animals in a simulated circus ring but he added one extra twist. He tape-recorded the sound of applause from the audience. Every time the dogs would perform the tricks properly during the training he would play the recording and follow it with praise and food reward. This made the applause a reward since it was associated with praise and food. By extending the chain of tricks and phasing out the food reward, he was able to get his dogs to work solely for the applause of the audience. This worked very well since the audience would naturally applaud each time the dog performed a trick. In essence, he had trained his dogs to be hams.

The second way to prevent the Johnny Carson Syndrome is to train your dog in as wide a variety of environments as is possible, including the test or show environment. By using a constant command in a variable environment, the command will be the only reliable stimulus predicting reward. In essence, your dog will learn to ignore everything except your command.

How to Analyze Stimulus-Control Problems

There are two reasons to analyze stimulus-control problems: either your obedience commands are not functioning properly or you need to know what is controlling a problem behavior.

Stimulus-control problems in obedience training were discussed in the preceding section. The three type of stimulus-control problems are: (1) Stimulus control too rigid; (2) Stimulus control too weak; (3) Inappropriate stimulus control.

STIMULUS CONTROL TOO RIGID. This will lead to failure to generalize commands. Basically you must answer the question, Does your dog obey every member of the household and obey you in every situation in which he is placed? To answer this you simply have to test the dog. Have each member of the family give the dog a series of commands in a situation such as the living room or the backyard. The procedure is as follows: Each family member gets three chances to command the dog to sit, lie down, come when called, and stay in a sitting or lying position for thirty seconds. Count the number of times each family member is successful in commanding the dog and fill in the number in the figure below.

FIGURE 7. THE OBEDIENCE MATRIX I—PEOPLE

Behavior	Father			Mother	Son	Daughter		Total
Sit								
Down								
Come								
Stay (30 sec.)								
Total								

Thus, if the father of the household gave three sit commands and the dog sat three times, a 3 would be entered in Father—Sit box in the upper left-hand corner. Make sure each person has a turn commanding the dog to sit before you move on to the next command.

When you are finished, you can add the scores for each family member and enter the score at the bottom of the table.

The highest score possible is 12. This means perfect control. An acceptable score is 10 out of 12. This is about 83 percent control. Anything lower than 10 indicates a control problem for that family member. This person should work with the dog more often.

This will also enable you to determine if anyone is commanding the dog improperly. Everyone should be using exactly the same word or hand signal. Also, make sure that everyone rewards the dog for obeying.

In order to test if your dog's commands generalize to other situations, you can follow a similar procedure. You give the dog the commands sit, down, come and stay, in various settings. Try to arrange the settings in order of increasing stimulation or distractability and write these down from left to right at the top of the table below. Then test your dog in each setting, giving him three tries per command. Score a 1 for each time your dog obeys. This will give you a maximum of 3 for each block and 12 for each setting.

FIGURE 8. THE OBEDIENCE MATRIX II—SETTING

Behavior	Setting→Increasing Distractability							Total
Sit								
Down								
Come								
Stay (30 sec.)								
Total								

An acceptable score would be 10 or more, 83 percent, per setting. Anything less than 10 means that your dog needs extra work in that setting.

(245)

STIMULUS CONTROL TOO WEAK.   So far we have looked at the sum of the columns of the table. This gives you an indication about how the commands are generalizing. Another problem is when the stimulus control is too weak. This means that your dog is not obeying the commands when given. This can be assessed by the sum of the rows and dividing by the the perfect score. A perfect score varies with the number of family members tested in the first table and the number of situations tested in the second table. Simply take the number of family members or situations tested and multiply by 3 to get the perfect score. Then divide the perfect score by the sum for each command and multiply the resultant decimal by 100. This will give an estimate of the percentage of control for each command. An 80 percent control or more for each command is acceptable. Anything less indicates that your dog needs more work on that command.

INAPPROPRIATE STIMULUS CONTROL.   This means that your dog is not responding to the command. You tell him to sit and he lies down. This can be easily determined when you are giving your dog the tests for generalization. The problem here is usually unreliable, inconsistent or confused commands. For example, saying "Sit down" can easily be confused with the command "Lie down." Each command should be clear and sound distinctly different from the other. A one-word command of one syllable is the best: e.g., "Sit," "Down," "Stay," "Come," "Easy," "Jump," "Bark" and so on.

If you use hand signals in combination with the command, you may find that your dog ignores the verbal command and pays more attention to your hands. This is because hand signals tend to mask the words and are more salient to the dog. Similarly, pushing down on your dog's rump is more salient than the word "Sit." If you train your dog this way, he may not pay attention to the words and sit only when you touch his behind. One way to handle this problem has been described earlier. Wait until your dog is about to sit or lie

(246)

down, then give the command. When your dog performs correctly, reward him.

Another way to handle this type of problem is to fade out the use of hand signals or the pushing. For sitting, you would first start with using your whole hand, then use only a few fingers, then only one finger, decreasing the pressure of the push on the behind each time. Finally, just place your hand over that area without touching. You can continue this, each time fading your hand more and more out of the picture, until no hand movements are needed.

What Is Controlling a Problem Behavior?

The second reason for analyzing stimulus control is to determine whether a problem behavior is generalized to all people and all situations or if the problem is localized. Earlier in this section I described a problem with a phobic dachshund who turned out to be afraid of the space between the elevator and the floor. This analysis was accomplished by first looking at the time of day that the problem occured. Figure 5 on page 217 provides a checklist that can be used to assess the temporal patterns of the problem. If you find a temporal pattern, try to determine if there is anything different about your dog's environment during that time. For example, ask the following questions:

a. *Do you act differently at that time of day?* There are special times of day when you are most likely to act differently from your usual self, such as meal times, when you are leaving or returning from work, rising in the morning or about to go to bed at night. These are especially bad times for problem behaviors. During these times you are impatient, tired or preoccupied.

b. *Is there anything different about the environment at these times?* Most of the stimuli in your dog's and your own environment run on a schedule. Trains pass by on schedule, there are regular peak and lull hours of car and air traffic,

(247)

smells change regularly during the dinner hour, people return home and leave for work about the same time and so forth. Try to match the cycles in your dog's behavior problem with these cycles and others. This may give you a clue to what may be controlling the problem.

c. *Is there anything different about your dog's internal environment at these times?* This is a very difficult question since you obviously cannot look inside your dog. However, you can note if the problem behaviors change in accordance with some other event that may change your dog's internal environment, such as eating, drinking, eliminating or menstruating.

After you have some knowledge of the timing of the problem, it is time to make a more detailed analysis of the environment. The environment includes the particulars of the setting in which the problem behaviors occur and the behavior of the persons interacting with the dog just before the problem occurs. Figure 9 is a checklist for problem behaviors. Across the top are the various settings in which the behaviors can occur. Down the side are the various people to which the dog can react. Make a √ or X if the problem occurs with any of the combinations of settings and people.

The questions you should ask are: (1) Is there any regularity in the check marks? (2) Does the problem occur with most people in the same place? A "yes" to question (2) would indicate that there is something about the place that is controlling the behavior. For example, the dachshund was afraid of one small aspect of the elevator, the space between the elevator and the floor. This was determined by carefully examining the elevator when the dog acted fearful and when he was unafraid. The determination was confirmed by placing a small rug over the space, which resulted in the elimination of the fear.

d. *Does the problem occur only with some people?* A "yes"

FIGURE 9. A PEOPLE AND SETTING ANALYSIS OF PROBLEM BEHAVIOR

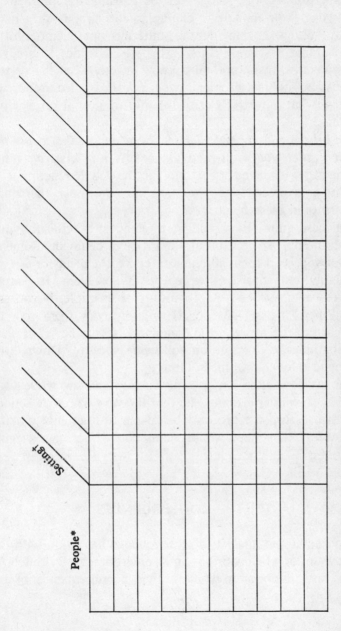

People*

Setting†

* *People*: Write down the names of the people your dog interacts with

†*Setting*: Write in the various settings where your dog could exhibit the problem behavior

to this question would indicate that there is something about the behaviors of the people that is causing the problem. I have given you numerous examples throughout this book of dogs biting, barking at or bothering one member of a household or a specific class of people. In order to analyze this type of problem, you must know exactly what the person did just before the problem occurred. It is also important to know what the person or people did to stop or correct the problem.

e. *If there are no particular places or people that cause the problem, then you must focus on behavior in general.* What are the exact sequence of behaviors in the people reacting with the dog that precedes the problem behavior? Are there any similarities in these behaviors?

All these questions should be directed at specifically what stimuli, if any, are controlling the problem behavior. Remember, all you need for a stimulus to control a behavior is that it reliably and consistently precede the problem. It doesn't have to be logical or even obvious. For example, if you say "Come here" while your dog is running away from you, he will learn to run away to the command "Come here." If your dog continues to jump up on you while you say "Down," the command "Down" will mean jump up.

So pay close attention to what you do and say while your dog is misbehaving. It could be that the very words or actions you take to stop the problem behaviors are actually making them occur. Remember, what is being noticed becomes a signal for what is being done.

(C) THE CONSEQUENCES

The question and analysis of consequence has to do with the effect your dog's behavior has on its environment. By "effect" I mean what happens to your dog as a consequence of his behavior. For example, if your dog aggressively bites you on the hand this may have numerous effects. First of all, the bite may be rewarding to your dog since it is the culmination of a dominant aggressive sequence. Second, the bite may be rewarding because it postpones a counterattack, at least for the time it takes you to overcome the surprise and shock. The bite may also result in punishment. You may strike the dog, deprive it of attention and affection, and deprive it of the things it needs such as food and water. The other consequence of the bite may be a change in your attitude toward the dog. You may begin to fear or hate the dog. This will affect your future interactions with your dog. Other consequences relate to the long-term effect of the bite. You may have the dog castrated in the hopes of reducing aggression, have his teeth removed, tranquilize him, give him away to an unsuspecting family or have him put to death.

All of the consequences affect the future probability of the dog's biting you again. Some of the effects increase the probability of a bite. These are rewards. Others decrease the probability of a bite. These are punishments. The relation between the past and present consequences of the behavior is the ultimate predictor of future behavior. So in order to know what is going to happen in the future, you must analyze the present and past consequences of your dog's behavior. In order to affect the future probability of desirable and problem behavior you must change their respective consequences.

If you have a troublesome dog, the first question you must ask yourself is, "What do I do when my dog misbehaves?" Do you hit the dog? Yell at him? Ignore the behavior? Dream up ways to get back at him? Pet him? Feed him?

Figure 10 gives you a place to record a list of misbehaviors and the number of times they occur per week. After each misbehavior there is a column marked "Consequences." Write down exactly what you do. If there is more than one consequence, then try to write all of them down in order. Estimate

FIGURE 10. ANALYSIS OF CONSEQUENCES OF MISBEHAVIOR

Misbehavior	# per Week	Consequences	# per Week	Time	Feeling	Effectiveness

the number of times per week that you use each consequence. The next column is marked "Time." Try to estimate the time between the misbehavior and the consequence in hours, minutes, seconds or immediately. Make sure you discriminate between the product of the behavior and the behavior itself. For example, if you discover that your dog has defecated, the time should be between the act of defecation and the consequence and *not* between the discovery of the fecal matter and the consequence. The second-to-the-last column is marked "Feeling." Ask yourself how you feel when you are delivering the consequence. Are you angry? Sad? Happy? Do you feel justified? Vengeful? Shocked? If you feel more than one thing, then write them all down. Forget the last column for now. We will get back to it later.

An example of part of a completed Analysis of Consequences for one of my clients follows. The dog would bite, eliminate, guard objects and mount and jump on the owner.

You will notice from the sample that the owner would usually do a number of things when the dog misbehaved. For example, the owner estimated that she discovered the feces hours after the dog defecated, because the dog did it at night and it was discovered the next morning. The owner went through the same ritual each day. She dragged the dog to the waste and rubbed his nose in it. About half the time she also hit the dog. She would then clean him and sometimes pet him when she felt sorry or guilty.

If you do this for each of the problem behaviors of your dog, you will probably find that there are a lot of things you do that you are not totally aware of. By analyzing the sequence of your reactions to your dog's problem behavior you have a starting point from which to change. This may seem like a long, tedious procedure, but it will pay off. Many of my clients find that when they do this, the effects of their behavior become clear. They are readily able to make suggestions on how to change their behavior.

(253)

TABLE 5. ANALYSIS OF CONSEQUENCES OF MISBEHAVIOR

Misbehavior	# per Week	Consequences	# per Week	Time	Feeling	Effectiveness
Elimination on rug	7	a. Rub dog's nose in it	7	Hours	Disgust	
		b. Hit dog	3	Hours	Anger	
		c. Clean dog's nose	7	Hours	Disgust and sorrow	
		d. Pet him to calm	5	Hours	Sorrow and guilt	
Biting owner	5	a. Back away	5	Immediate	Fear and shock	
		b. Yell "No"	5	Within seconds	Fear	
		c. Hit dog	1	Hour	Anger	
		d. Hold his jaws shut and say, "No bite"	3	Hours	Justified	
Growling and snapping when approached if had bone or toy		a. Stop approaching	10	Immediate	Fear	
		b. Say, "Easy, it's okay"	8	Within seconds	Fear and cowardice	
		c. Yell, "No, stop that"	5	Minutes	Anger and indignation	
		d. Throw something at dog	3	Minutes	Very angry	
		e. Stay away from dog until calm	10	Hours	None	

If you find that you cannot remember exactly what you do or what the sequence of your behaviors are, you will have to use Figure 7 on page 244, or keep a behavioral diary. The diary or checklist should be filled out right after you have finished reacting to your dog so that your emotions and re-actions will be fresh in your mind. Do this for a week or so. Then complete the Analysis of Consequences of Misbehavior table based on the diary or checklist.

The next step in evaluating the consequences of misbehavior is to determine the effectiveness of what you are doing. Obviously, the goal of the consequences for misbehavior is to reduce or eliminate the problem. Consequently, the question is, Do the consequences result in the elimination or reduction of the problem behavior? You can answer this question in a variety of ways. First, you can make a guess based on your experience with the problem. How long has the problem existed? How long have you reacted the way you do? If the problem has existed for a number of weeks or longer at about the same level or has increased in severity, despite your attempts at correction, your methods are *ineffective*. No matter how logical or justified they are, no matter where you read about them or who told you about them. Write "ineffective" in the column marked "Effectiveness."

A second method to determine the effectiveness of a consequence of misbehavior is to stop doing anything for about a week. Don't punish, scream, yell, hit, pet or reward. Just act as if the problem behavior did not occur. At the same time take note of how often the behavior occurs before and after you stop reacting. You can do this by using a Behavioral Checklist, Figure 7, page 244, or a behavioral diary. Then return to your original consequences. Did the behavior change? In what direction? Did it get better or worse? Or did it stay the same? If the behavior got better or didn't change, then your consequences are ineffective. Write "ineffective" in the appropriate column. If the problem got worse and you are not unintentionally rewarding it, then the consequences were at least mildly effective. Perhaps there is a way of improving them.

Once you have completed your table of the Analysis of Consequences of Misbehavior you may want to go ahead and start changing things. But before you do, you have one other table to complete: the Consequences of Good Behavior. It looks pretty much like the previous one, except that you will focus on the good things your dog does. Write the good behaviors down in order of goodness, best behaviors at the top and so on. Indicate how many times these behaviors occur

FIGURE 11. ANALYSIS OF CONSEQUENCES OF GOOD BEHAVIOR

Good Behavior	# per Week	Consequences	# per Week	Time	Feeling	Effectiveness

per week, what you do about them, the time it takes you to react and how you feel about them in the appropriate column. If you cannot remember, then consult your behavioral diary or checklist.

An example of part of a Consequences of Good Behavior table for the same client who filled out the Misbehavior table follows:

TABLE 6. ANALYSIS OF CONSEQUENCES OF GOOD BEHAVIOR

Good Behavior	# per Week	Consequences	# per Week	Time	Feeling	Effectiveness
Greets me at door by licking and jumping	10	a. Pet dog, say, "Good boy"	8	Immediate	Pleased	
		b. Ignore	1	Immediate	Tired	
		c. Say, "No, down"	1	Immediate	Frustrated	
Jumps on bed and licks face in morning	7	a. Pet dog	7	Within seconds	Groggy	
		b. Give breakfast	7	Within 30 minutes	Groggy	
Growls at strangers	13	a. Say, "Good dog"	13	Within seconds	Safe	
		b. Say, "Quiet"	10	Immediate	Annoyed	

Now that you have an idea of what your dog does that you like, draw a line on the Consequences of Good Behavior Table and just below it write "Desired Behaviors." This is a list of things you would like your dog to do. Try to include behaviors that would counteract or compete with the misbehaviors. Thus, if your dog jumps up on you and you don't like this, include "staying down when I enter" as a desired behavior. If your dog eliminates in the house, include "eliminating outside" as a desired behavior. If your dog is overly aggressive include "submissive behavior" in your desired list. Also include behaviors that you would like to see your dog perform whether or not they compete with problem behaviors.

Now you have an idea about what behaviors you want to

get rid of, the consequences of these behaviors and the effectiveness of the consequences.

It is time to correct ineffective consequences for misbehavior. You would do well to reread the section on punishment in the beginning of the book. Are your consequences punishments? If they are, do they conform to the rules of punishment? The following is a summary of the rules of punishment presented earlier. For explanation of the rules see Chapter 3.

PUNISHMENT

1. Should immediately follow the start of misbehavior.
2. Should be at an effective dose the first time you use it.
3. Should be ecologically valid.
4. If at all possible, should be administered by the environment and not you.
5. Should be consistent and predictable only by the misbehavior and the word "No."
6. Should be used infrequently and should be varied each time it is used.
7. If you punish your dog, you should find a way to reward him for good or desired behaviors.

Check each one of the consequences for misbehavior against all the rules to determine the problem with your punishments. Remember, punishment has side effects such as teaching your dog to fear or bite you.

After you have analyzed your punishment procedures, try to determine if it is possible for you to conform with the rules. Be creative. Can you sneak up on your dog while he is secretly misbehaving? Can you rig the environment to punish him? If you cannot conform with the rules of punishment, then forget about trying to punish the misbehavior.

A bad punishment that doesn't conform with the rules is worse than no punishment at all. At the very least a bad

a little

far fewe

punishme

as well.

There are

reward the god

ing; (b) using

niques, build and

compete with the n

dog will be so busy p

reward that he will ne

ment will become unnee

a lot happier.

Go over the section on

Chapter 3.) The following n

REWARD

1. Must be under your conscic
2. Must immediately follow the
3. Should suit the behavior as mu
4. Should be as varied as possible fe

Check your table of Consequences of Go

the rules for reward. Do you reward your

genetic

each of these

particular thing t

feeding you can wr

of and if he likes

like. Being pette

Body Surface. If

not conform wi

time you are fi

thing for each

The next s

engage in th

if not stopp

You can

havioral di

frequency

the rewar

"Rank,"

class th

Place a

that o

tinue

rewa

(wh

war

do

he

ard these behaviors more lavishly
ur rewards varied or constant? Do
re they immediate? What could you
behavior your dog does not perform
hape competing behaviors?

uch with how to reward your dog, fill
12. Across the side of the table are the
behavior classes. The completion of
ors is a reward. After each class write the
your dog likes to do. For example, under
te the particular food that your dog is fond
to chew things like bones, rawhide and the
or scratched would go under Care of the
there are things that your dog does that do
h the list, write them under "other." By the
ished, you should have at least one particular
behavior class, the more particulars the better.
ep is to get an idea of how often your dog will
se behaviors per week or how long he will do it
d.

do this by consulting your memory or your be-
ary or checklist. Once you have an estimate of the
and duration of each behavior you are ready to rate
d value of each behavior. Under the column marked
place a 1 after the particular behavior or behavior
t your dog does most often and for the longest time.
2 in the rank column for the next behavior, the one
ccurs a little less frequently or for shorter time. Con-
through the whole list until you have ranked all the
rding behavior, 1 meaning the most rewarding and *n*
atever the number of particulars is) being the least re-
ding. If you have a tie or if you are unsure, then give your
g a choice between the two alternatives and see which one
chooses. The one he chooses first should be ranked higher.
Now you have created an extensive list of rewards for

FIGURE 12. DOG'S PERSONALIZED REWARD LIST

Behavior Class	Particular Behavior	How Often Per Week	Duration of Incident	Rank
Feeding				
Drinking				
Sexual				
Fighting				
Fear				
Eliminating				

FIGURE 12. DOG'S PERSONALIZED REWARD LIST (Continued)

Behavior Class	Particular Behavior	How Often Per Week	Duration of Incident	Rank
Exploring				
Care of Body Surface				
Care of Young				
Resting				
Operant				
Nesting				

your dog. How many of these behaviors have you used as a consequence of good behavior? From my experience, I find that few people use more than one-fifth of the list.

Since you have ranked the behaviors in accordance with reward value, you can use a principle of reward which can be stated as follows: "High-valued behaviors will reward lower-valued behaviors."

This means that the behavior ranked 1 will reward all the lower-ranked behaviors. Behavior ranked 10 will reward lower-ranked behavior like 11, 12, etc., but will not reward higher-ranked behavior like 9, 8, 7, etc. The only necessary condition is that you make the opportunity to engage in higher-ranked behavior a consequence of performing lower-ranked behavior.

The last step is to change your Consequences of Good Behavior Table. Write in new and varied rewards (high-ranked behaviors) as a consequence of good and desired behavior. Make sure you follow through by giving your dog the new rewards as a consequence.

If your dog never performs a desired competing behavior, it will be necesstary to train and shape this behavior. Consult the section on Response earlier in this chapter for a description of shaping and chaining. Consult the section on operant behavior in the previous chapter for a description of training techniques. These techniques and others will be reviewed under the next section, Contingencies.

The Final Test

No matter how carefully you construct your reward list, the final test for a reward is its effectiveness. A reward boils down to any consequence that increases the behavior it follows. If the new reward consequences are effective, then the good and desired behaviors must incrcase. If the new reward consequences are ineffective, then the good and desired behaviors will not increase. If the new reward consequences are in-effective, make sure you are following the rules for reward. If you are, then scrap the new consequences, and try a different one.

The best way to evaluate the effectiveness of new reward consequences is to record the behavior and chart it over days. If the chart line is rising, you are on the right track.

For example, I was called upon to treat a three-year-old female German shepherd who was somewhat dominant and aggressive. She was protective of the members of the family. The owner's main complaint concerned the fact that the dog would jump on them and other people when they entered the house. They had tried some of the standard techniques such as kneeing the animal in the chest when she jumped or step-ping on her hind feet. These techniques were unsuccessful, perhaps because of my clients' lack of physical agility.

Upon further investigation I found that the shepherd also guarded objects by taking them under the table and growling at anyone that approached. The dog had never bitten anyone as yet, but I felt it was just a matter of time.

I decided to work first on the jumping problem and then the guarding problem since the guarding problem would take more skill on the part of the owners. They would develop the necessary skills working on the less dangerous jumping prob-lem.

The jumping problem would be dealt with by conditioning a competing response, lying down, when the owners and others entered. It was obvious that the attention the dog was receiving when she jumped was rewarding the jumping, so it was plausible that having the owners attend to the "down response" would correct the jumping.

This training was tackled in two stages. First, lying down and staying on command had to be strengthened. The dog knew how to do this but would do it only occasionally. Every member of the household, the parents and the two teenage children, was instructed on how to give the "down and stay" command and reward the behavior with praise, petting and a piece of cheese. Each person was to work with the dog for at least thirty minutes per day in as many rooms in the house as possible, and also the backyard. This resulted in over two hours of training per day.

This training regime was carried on for a week. The criterion for shifting to the second stage, the no-jump training, was that the dog had to lie down immediately on command and to stay there for at least three minutes. During the week of "down" training, the owners were to record the number of times the dog jumped up on them, and the number of times the dog growled at them when she was guarding something under the table. The family members were also asked to keep a behavioral diary in which they were to record for each training session the following information: the percentage of times the dog lay down on command, the average duration of time the dog stayed down and any problems or observations they had.

Figure 13 is a plot of the results of the whole treatment. The solid line represents the percentage of times the dog jumped on people when they entered. This number was determined by dividing the number of times someone entered the house into the number of jumps and multiplying by 100. As you can see from the graph, the down training had a small but consistent effect on the dog's jumping behavior. In seven days the dog had reduced jumping by 20 percent. The percentage of guarding represented by the solid line was unaffected by the down-and-stay training.

The 20 percent drop in the amount of jumping probably occurred because the owners characteristically used the word "Down" when they entered the house. As the command got stronger the dog jumped less. The second stage of the treatment was the no-jump training. This consisted of one member of the family commanding the dog to lie down and stay just

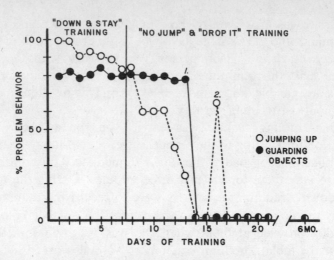

FIGURE 13. RESULTS OF THE TRAINING REGIME. AT POINT 1 THE "DROP-IT" TRAINING WAS USED WHEN THE DOG WAS UNDER THE TABLE. AT POINT 2 RELATIVES VISITED.

before another member was about to enter the house. The person at the door would not enter until the dog stayed down. If the dog stood up as he entered, the person was to step back out and close the door, reentering when the dog remained down. If the dog remained down, the person entering was to approach the dog and reward her immediately for staying down. When the dog mastered this, the time she had to remain down before she got rewarded by attention from the enterer was increased slowly to three minutes. This step took about eight days.

In order to determine if the training was working, the dog was given five test trials per day. On a test trial someone would enter without the dog's being given the down-and-stay command. We wanted to see if the dog would learn to lie down and stay when someone entered. The percentage of jumping up is shown for the next eight days of no-jump training on the right side of Figure 13.

You can see that the dog progressively decreased her jumping so that by the fourteenth and fifteenth day people could enter and the dog would automatically lie down and stay down. No command was necessary. The dog would just lie down and wait to be rewarded.

On the sixteenth day (Point 2), some relatives visited who encouraged the dog to jump up on them. The relatives felt that it was a natural behavior for the dog and were surprised and disappointed when the dog didn't jump up on them. So they called the dog, patted their chest and said "Up," and petted the dog when she jumped. The family was able to regain control of the jumping on the seventeenth and eighteenth days.

On the eighth day of training the treatment of the guarding behavior was started. The treatment consisted of training the dog to bring objects to the owner and drop them on command. First, an object was placed in the dog's mouth and the command "Drop it" was given. The dog's natural reaction to having something placed in her mouth was to drop it, so it was very easy to reward this behavior. The dog was rewarded for dropping the item into the owner's hand. At first the owner placed his hand directly under the dog's mouth. Then the owner moved his hand farther and farther away from the mouth and gave the command "Drop it." If the dog placed the item into the owner's hand she was rewarded. If not, the item was replaced into the dog's mouth and the command was given again.

Within five days the dog would walk across a room and gently place whatever was put in her mouth into the owner's hand. The dog was immediately rewarded for this by praise, petting and cheese.

On the thirteenth day the "Drop it" command was established. The owners were told to use this command whenever the dog was guarding something under the table (Point 1). If the dog had something she was allowed to have (a ball or play toy), the dog was then rewarded for giving it to the owner and then the owners would return it to the dog.

(267)

The guarding of objects completely stopped by the fifteenth day, never to return. As you can see from the graph, both behaviors remained at zero for three days after the end of treatment and were still zero six months later.

(K) CONTINGENCIES

Contingencies refer to how the consequences of your dog's behavior are arranged. This is a "what leads to what" question. Under what condition does a particular behavior lead to a certain consequence?

Life is full of contingencies. These contingencies are the rituals and rules of your dog's and your behavior. These rituals or rules may be intentionally planned, forced on you and your dog by an external agent or the natural environment, or you may unconsciously or unintentionally fall into a behavioral ritual. Every contingency can be put as an if-then statement.

For example, if you drive recklessly then you are likely to get a ticket. This is a planned contingency. If you jump off a cliff, then you are likely to get hurt—a natural contingency. An unconscious contingency for a problem dog is if you enter the house, then the dog will jump up on you. If the dog jumps up, then he will get attention from you.

Basically a contingency is a program for changing or supporting behavior. Up till now we have talked about two types of contingencies. These are: (a) every good behavior should be immediately rewarded; and (b) every bad behavior should be immediately punished.

However, there are many other types of contingencies. Some of them can be used to change problem behavior into desirable behavior. However, there are two types of contingencies that invariably lead to problems. These are TLC, better known as Tender Loving Care, and noncontingent punishment.

TLC

It is important to love, pet, be affectionate to and care for your dog. However, some people believe that TLC is the dog's right. They give unqualified love and affection no matter what the dog does. I have named this contingency the Grandmother Syndrome, after a case I had that nicely demonstrated its effects. The problem was an uncontrollable two-year-old female Irish setter. The setter was owned by a seventy-seven-year-old woman who was the sweetest person you could meet. This woman treated anyone, including her dog, as a member of the family. She never had an unkind word for anyone. She would always focus on the positive and ignore or deny the negative aspects of her dog's and other people's behavior.

The problem was that she showered unqualified affection on her dog no matter what the dog did. The dog would jump on the sofa, run around the house, bark uncontrollably, run away from her, refuse to come when called, chew on parts of the furniture and rugs, defecate and urinate in the house, bark and jump around uncontrollably in the back seat of her car when taken for a ride. The dog would not obey any commands given by her. All these misbehaviors were met by unqualified love, affection and excuses. In fact, the woman only wanted one thing changed: the barking and jumping in the car had ruined her upholstery and it got on her nerves. When I pointed out the other problems, she either excused them or said she didn't mind as long as the dog was happy.

The dog had one redeeming quality: she was devoted to the woman's protection. She would savagely attack anyone who even raised a voice to her. This protectiveness had probably saved the woman's life on three occasions. Once, when she was accosted by some young punks in her backyard and twice more when someone tried to push his way into the house when she answered the door.

When I entered for the first appointment, I found the dog unruly, protective and touch-shy. When I went to pet the dog she tried to bite my hand. I spent the next fifteen minutes rewarding the dog with a biscuit when she came to me when called, petting the dog as I rewarded it. After I could pet the dog with impunity I worked on some basic obedience commands such as "Sit," "Down and stay." The dog took about fifteen minutes to learn these commands and responded immediately when I gave her a command.

When I asked the woman to give the commands the dog completely ignored her. If we both called the dog at the same time the dog would come to me and not her. I had gained control of the dog's behavior in thirty minutes and she had none after two years.

The problem was obvious. The woman had never rewarded the dog's behavior contingently. It did not matter what the dog did or did not do; it was always rewarded by her. Thus the dog had learned to ignore her completely.

The solution was simple: get the woman to start rewarding contingently. It took me six sessions of talking, explaining, and demonstrating before she finally got the message. By that time I had trained the dog to perform an elaborate set of tricks on my command. She would sit, lie down, stay, jump, beg, retrieve, come when called, fetch, bark, be quiet, growl, guard, run around, roll over. The dog learned these tricks in minutes, but the woman still had no control over the dog.

When I gave the woman specific instructions on how to deal with her dog she would invariably forget them. If I wrote the instructions down, she would misplace the paper. This was very frustrating for me as I had to begin over at each session. The woman did not seem to remember what I had told her the last session. This is not surprising given the fact that she was seventy-seven years old.

I finally came upon the solution on the sixth session. I would tell the woman a story or parable. The moral was some aspect of how to deal with her dog. At the end of the story she was to guess the moral, and put it in her own words. This worked! By the eighth session she was rewarding the dog contingently for good behavior and ignoring misbehavior and the problems vanished.

Noncontingent Punishment

It is evident from the previous example that noncontingent reward teaches the dog to ignore the owner. The other extreme is noncontingent punishment. The owner who uses this contingency gives the rationale that he is teaching the dog who is boss. I have previously talked about this in relation to causing ulcers in dogs.

Noncontingent punishment can lead to a behavioral effect called "learned helplessness." The dog can learn that no matter what he does or does not do he will get punished. This results in the dog doing nothing, remaining passive and fearful all the time. This is quite similar to the human emotional problem of depression.

The Beneficial Contingencies

There are many beneficial contingencies. These contingencies are basically programs to solve or prevent potential behavior problems. Many of these contingencies have been studied extensively in the behavioral laboratory and are currently being used as behavior modification techniques for human as well as animal problems. Most of these techniques—such as shaping, chaining or systematic desensitization—have been discussed previously in the context of solving some behavior problems.

In this section each procedure will be outlined in a detailed step-by-step method. Also, the behavior problems most suited to each method will be discussed. However, it must be pointed out that trying to follow the set procedures in cookbook fashion

(271)

without understanding your dog's basic psychology may lead to failure. *No general procedure will exactly fit your specific problem, since no two problems are identical.* You may have to change or combine the procedures to match the specific characteristics of your problem and your life situation. You will be able to make these changes if you develop an understanding of your dog's behavior and the factors that affect his behavior. The previous sections of this book were written for that purpose.

Below is a list of the eleven behavior-change procedures and the pages where these procedures were discussed. Consult these pages before you go on to the procedures themselves.

Partial Reward and Partial Punishment

When you are first trying to train good and desirable behaviors, you should use the most powerful rewards and reward every occurrence of the desired behavior. This continuous reward will allow your dog to learn very rapidly.

Many of my clients say to this, "But what happens when we run out of rewards?" or "That means I have to walk around with a pocketful of dog biscuits." Rewards such as love, attention and petting are basically unlimited, and since you will never run out of them, use them to reward good behavior continuously. Dog biscuits and cheese are limited, and once your dog has learned a new behavior you only have to use the rewards intermittently. This partial reward will not only maintain the good behaviors but will also make them stronger.

The program for partial reward is as follows:

1. In the beginning of the training, reward every instance of a desirable behavior.

2. When your dog has learned this desirable behavior start partial reward.

3. First reward every second instance of a desirable behavior, then every third instance, and then every fourth instance and so on.

4. Continue slowly to decrease the number of rewards for desirable behavior until you approximate a normal or comfortable level.

5. A normal or comfortable level is defined in relation to how many biscuits you would normally give your dog in one day. If you would normally give him five biscuits a day, then spread the ration out throughout the day, using them to reward desirable behavior contingently. You may also reward your dog with his daily meal.

This procedure can be used for every desirable behavior you want to train. There is one caution, however. Many people partially reward undesirable behavior without knowing it. This of course can strengthen these problem behaviors.

(Partial punishment is basically the same procedure using punishment for undesirable behavior.)

(273)

Shaping

Shaping has been described earlier as a way of training hard-to-get behaviors. The basic premise is to reward successive approximations to the desired behavior. A program for shaping is as follows:

1. Make a clear statement of the goal of the shaping, e.g., want the dog to "stay" on command for five minutes.

2. Then break the behavior into manageable levels. Each level should be a little harder than the previous level, e.g., stay for one second, then two seconds, then five seconds, and so forth.

3. Start the shaping at a level that your dog can easily accomplish without failure and reward your dog for accomplishing this level, e.g., if you notice that your dog can already stay for five seconds, then reward this behavior.*

4. Increase to the next highest level only when your dog has completely mastered the previous level. Do not be impatient; go at your dog's pace. Reward your dog for performing correctly at each level.*

5. If you advance to the next highest level and your dog repeatedly fails then:
   a. go back to the previous level and reward him.
   b. create an intermediate step, advance to it, and reward him.* If you have gone from five seconds to ten seconds stay and your dog fails at ten seconds, then return to five seconds. Reward and make an intermediate step of a seven-second stay.*

6. Continue steadily increasing the level of performance, rewarding every behavior that meets the level until you reach your goal.

The shaping procedure can be used to train desirable behavior that will compete with problem behaviors. You can

* Reread the rules for effective reward, page 82.

shape submissive behaviors in an aggressive dog, resting behaviors in an excitable dog, obedient behaviors in a disobedient dog and even aggressive behaviors in a submissive dog.

Once you have shaped the behavior you can use partial reward.

Chaining

Chaining is a procedure used to train short or long sequences of behavior. The idea is that you want to connect one behavior to the next like links of a chain. The first behavior will signal the second, the second will signal the third and so on until the last behavior in the chain is performed. The reward is given only after the last behavior. The steps for chaining are as follows:

1. Write down the sequence of behaviors that you want to chain together. Make sure that each link (behavior) in the chain consists of only one behavior. If a link has two behaviors, make it two links, etc. Example: For guard duty you may want your dog to leave the house, circle the grounds a couple of times (each circle is a link), then return home, enter the house and get rewarded.

2. Run through the sequence yourself as if they were instructions to perform a task. Note if there are any missing links or combined links. Add the missing links or separate the combined links. In essence you should follow the links like a robot or machine. If a link is missing it will become obvious since there will be no way to get from one behavior to the next without ad-libbing a link. Example: For guard duty you may want your dog to check the garage. Then the links would be: leave the house, circle the garage, leave garage, continue circling grounds, return home, enter house, reward.

(275)

3. Make sure that your dog can perform each link before you start chaining. If your dog cannot perform a link, you will have to shape the link using the shaping procedure.

4. Start training the chain with the last link and reward the dog for performing the last link.* Example: Enter house. Reward.*

5. When the last link is well established, add the next-to-the-last link and reward* your dog for completing the two-link chain in sequence. Example: Return home. Enter house. Reward.*

6. Continue to add links, one at a time, backward from the last to the first link in the chain. Do not add a link until your dog has mastered the previous chain. Reward your dog at the end of each new chain for completing the chain in sequence,

7. Don't be impatient. By adding one link at a time, backward, your dog can learn very elaborate chains and perform them in sequence for only one reward at the end of the chain.*

Chaining can be used to create sequences of behavior when they are needed. You probably do this chaining already without knowing it. Many dogs who are given obedience training are taught to perform the commands in sequence—sit, down, give paw, beg, reward—with the reward at the end. Thus when the first command is given the dog will perform all his tricks in the training sequence.

Also unintentional chaining is the source of many behavioral rituals that your dog might go through. If these rituals are a problem, you can use intentional chaining to reprogram the chain to desirable behaviors.

Differential Reward and Punishment

Your dog can only learn the significance of differences in his environment if the differences have different consequences;

* Reread the rules for effective reward, page 82.

this is the procedure of differential reward and punishment. This difference training can allow you to get very precise control over your dog's behavior. You will be able to specify under what circumstances a certain behavior is acceptable and unacceptable.

There are many behaviors that are acceptable under certain circumstances. Aggressiveness is acceptable when directed at a mugger but not when directed at you. Elimination is acceptable outside, but not inside the house. Playful running may be acceptable in the backyard but not in the living room. Chewing bones is acceptable but not chewing furniture. Fear of dangerous things is acceptable but fear of innocuous things is a problem. Sexual behavior among dogs is acceptable but not between you and your dog. Barking at an intruder is acceptable but barking incessantly is a headache.

The program for training differential behavior is as follows:

1. Fill out the following table, indicating when or where or under what circumstances a behavior is acceptable and when it is not.

TABLE 7. BEHAVIORAL ACCEPTABILITY TABLE

Behavior	Situation	
	Acceptable	Unacceptable

(277)

2. Make sure that there are clear distinctions between situations. A distinction such as barking is unacceptable only when I have a headache will not do, as your dog cannot know this.

3. If there is no clear distinction, then make a verbal command be the distinguishing signal.

4. Determine what dimension the distinction is related to. Do you want your dog to bark at everyone that enters your house? Only strangers? Only strangers who frighten or threaten you?

5. Then reward your dog for performing the behavior in acceptable situations and ignore him when he performs the behavior under unacceptable situations. (Note: Punishment may be used instead of ignoring but only as a last resort.)

6. This is not being inconsistent. If the situations are distinctive and you reliably reward or ignore in different situations, your dog will form a discrimination.

7. You may have to use shaping to get your dog to produce the behavior in the acceptable situation. Consult that procedure.

8. You will have to make sure that your dog has equal exposure to both acceptable and unacceptable situations, experiencing the appropriate consequence in each situation. This may take some special effort and creativity, for you may have to contrive the situation. For example, if you want your dog to bark when someone is fiddling with the front door or windows, you may have to request a friend to do this while you reward the barking. Reward silent behavior when no one is fiddling.

Prompting and Fading

Prompting and fading are the natural adjuncts to discrimination training as well as other training. A prompt is a helper

(278)

signal—something that makes the discrimination easier or the behavior less difficult. It is used in the beginning of training to insure that the dog will perform the correct response and get rewarded. A good prompt makes it almost impossible for the dog to make a mistake. For example, many of the training routines for obedience are based on the principle of prompting. To train your dog to sit, you may push gently on his hindquarters and push up under his neck. This is a prompt, forcing the dog into a sitting position when the command "Sit" is given.

Although the prompt is helpful in the beginning of training, it is usually undesirable to continue the prompt. You want the dog to respond to the command and not the prompt. Thus fading the prompt is the next step. Here you make the prompt less and less perceptible. For sit training you would push easier and easier on the dog's rear end, until no pushing is necessary.

A program for prompting a submissive behavior in an aggressive dog is as follows (this assumes that your dog will not bite the trainer):

1. When your dog acts aggressive by perking up his ears, puckering his mouth and showing his teeth, say "Easy" and gently push his ears and lips back in a submissive expression. Reward the dog immediately while still holding him.

2. Next, let go of ears and lips (fading). If they stay back for one second, then reward the dog.

3. Gradually increase the time the dog must maintain a submissive facial expression to get a reward, and gradually decrease the pressure on his ears and lips (fading).

4. Eventually your dog will produce a submissive facial expression to the word "Easy." This will also lead to a more submissive attitude.

An example of the use of prompting and fading to paper-train a puppy is as follows:

PROMPTING

1. Have a large area approximately 3′ x 6′ covered with newspaper.
2. The prompt: the instant the puppy shows any sign that he is about to eliminate—i.e., sniffing, squatting, circling, etc.—immediately and gently pick him up and place him on the paper. Keep him there until he eliminates or five minutes are up. Then remove him from the paper.
3. The puppy should not be allowed to do anything but eliminate on the paper. Playing with, sleeping on or chewing the paper should be immediately stopped by picking the puppy up and removing him from the paper.
4. If he eliminates on the paper immediately reward him.

FADING   (When your dog successfully eliminates on the large area)

5. Slowly decrease the size of the papered area by removing one square foot at a time.
6. Guide your dog so his elimination aim is accurate under the smaller area. Reward him immediately upon accurate elimination.
7. When the puppy can accurately hit the smaller area, decrease the size again, remembering to guide the dog and reward him.
8. Continue to decrease the size of the paper until it is 12 x 18 inches square, guiding the accuracy and immediately rewarding accurate elimination each time.

At this point the newspaper will have very good control of where your dog will eliminate. If you pick up the newspaper

(280)

and place it outside, your dog will eliminate outside on the paper.

9. Continue fading the size of the newspaper placed outside. Eventually you can fade out the newspaper completely.

Extinction

One of the simplest techniques to use is extinction. This means that if you fail to reward a trained behavior for a long enough time, the dog will stop performing the behavior. This sometimes boils down to ignoring a problem behavior that you previously had unintentionally rewarded with attention.

This technique, as simple as it sounds, is often very difficult to use for a number of reasons. First, a problem behavior may be rewarded by a variety of consequences beside attention (see the section on the types of reward, Chapter 3), so just removing attention, that is, ignoring, may not always work. Second, if the problem behavior is rewarded by attention alone, then the behavior will be very powerful in getting your attention. It is very difficult to ignore these attention-getting behaviors. The third reason relates to the process of extinction. When an animal is not rewarded when he expects to be rewarded, he initially escalates the problem behavior. Thus the process of extinction involves an initial increase in the problem behavior followed by a precipitous decrease in the problem behavior. Many people give in during this initial increase and reward the behavior. This makes the behavior even stronger and harder to extinguish next time.

Just because extinction can be hard to use does not mean that it isn't used. You use it unintentionally all the time when you fail to recognize, attend to and reward desirable behaviors. Thus, in many cases of a troublesome dog the owners have extinguished many desirable behaviors. It is best to use extinction intentionally. What follows is a program for ex-tinction.

1. When you have identified the problem behavior, do an analysis of consequences (previous section) to determine what if anything could be rewarding the behavior.
2. Then completely remove all identified sources of reward for the problem behavior. This means removing all conse-quences, including any type of attention. The behavior must result in nothing, *no* change in the dog's environment.
3. Accept an initial increase in the behavior problem. This increase does not mean failure. It means that you have been successful in removing all rewards and the behavior is begin-ning to extinguish.
4. Don't give in. No matter how exasperating the behavior becomes, it will eventually decrease. If you give in before the behavior is completely extinguished, this will result in an im-mediate return of the problem at full or greater strength.

Extinction can be used to decrease any behavior problem that is maintained by external reward, and can be combined with other techniques such as shaping and rewarding com-peting behavior to increase the speed of change. Extinction will not work if the behavior problem is intrinsically reward-ing. For example, the actual act of being aggressive may be rewarding for a very dominant dog, scratching an itch is re-warding for an itchy dog, eating is rewarding for a hungry dog, exploring is rewarding for a restless dog. In these cases other techniques such as punishment, habituation or rewarding competing behavior may be more effective.

Punishment and Relief

Punishment has been discussed elsewhere in the book (see Chapter 3). The one aspect of punishment that can cause trouble is the rewarding effects of relief. Every punishment, to be effective, must be something your dog would not normally choose to experience. In fact, a punishment is something your dog would normally escape or avoid if given a chance. This is one of the reasons punishment works. Your dog escapes punishment by stopping the problem behavior or avoids punishment altogether by not performing the problem behavior.

But this escape and avoidance aspect of punishment can lead to problems. Any behavior that terminates punishment or prevents it is rewarded by "relief." The trouble arises when the behavior that terminates or prevents punishments is a problem behavior in itself. The two problem behaviors that are most likely to succeed in getting relief from punishment are aggression and running away.

If you are punishing a problem such as furniture-chewing, and your dog turns and bites or snarls at you and you stop the punishment, you have done two things. You have punished chewing and rewarded biting or snarling. The dog will stop chewing and start biting. If you punish the act of eliminating in the house and your dog runs away from you, stopping the punishment, you will stop elimination but train running away. This is why a dog who has been beaten can get to be very aggressive or very timid. It all depends on what the dog has done in the past to escape or avoid the beating.

Thus there are two guidelines for punishment:

1. Try not to use it if possible.
2. If you must use it then make sure your dog doesn't perform another problem behavior to escape or avoid the punishment.

Systematic Desensitization

This technique has been described in the previous chapter. It is used to decrease fears in a phobic, timid or anxious dog. The steps in progressive desensitization are as follows:

(283)

1. List of fears: Identify all situations or events that cause your dog to be afraid. Make the list as long and comprehensive as possible. Do not try to put the fears in any particular order. The first question is, what does your dog fear?

2. List of likes: Identify and make a list of the situations, events or activities that your dog likes. These things will be used to counteract the fear so they should be as strong as possible. The longer the list the better.

3. Order your dog's list of fears from the least-feared situation to the most-feared situation. The most-feared items go at the bottom of the list.

4. Examine each item on the list to see if it can be broken down to smaller items or parts. For example, fear of being on the street can be broken down to fear of cars, car noises, crowds of people, traffic smells and tall looming buildings. Fear of being in an elevator could be fear of vertical movement, the elevator operator, the noises in the elevator, the blowing fan, enclosed spaces or crowded spaces.

5. Examine each item to see if there is a greater to lesser dimension implied in the item. For example, a dimension for fear of machine noises could be related to how close the dog is to the machine or how loud the noises are. A dimension for fear of being enclosed could be the size of the enclosure.

6. Order the newly discovered smaller items and dimensions, from least- to most fear-producing within the list.

7. Now expose your dog to the least-feared item at the top of the list at the same time you are relaxing or distracting him with an activity or item from your list of likes. The activity should be powerful enough to block or inhibit extreme fear and will cause him to engage in the liked activity.

8. If your dog becomes very frightened he will not be able to engage in the liked activity and you will not succeed in reducing the fear. In this case reexamine the hierarchy of fears to see if there is a less fearful situation that can be used first.

9. Continue exposing your dog to the feared item in com-

bination with the liked activity until there is little or no fear shown to that item.

10. Then move on to the next item on the list, continually exposing the item until the fear dissipates.

11. Repeat steps 9 and 10 for the entire hierarchy of fears.

Helpful hints:

a. Obedience commands, such as "Down and stay" can be used to desensitize a fear, especially if the commands are very strong and the dog is rewarded for obeying.

b. It is best to vary the liked activity as much as possible and then use as many activities as possible. For example, if your dog likes biscuits, cheese, playing ball and being rubbed, command him to lie down and reward him with a piece of cheese or a rubdown while you expose him to a feared item.

c. A very pleasurable event or situation may be used to desensitize a fear. If your dog loves the beach but fears loud noises, expose him to gradually louder noises while he is playing on the beach.

d. Don't move on to a higher fear unless you have conquered the previous lower fear. Be patient; let your dog tell you when he is ready for the next fear exposure.

e. If you find that you have made a mistake in the order of the hierarchy, so that your dog gets to a certain item and will not progress, reexamine your hierarchy. You may have left something out or failed to identify the culprit or dimension of a situation of a fear. Adjust the hierarchy to accommodate this realization.

Counter-conditioning

Counter-conditioning is a general term referring to the idea of training your dog to produce a competing response in the presence of events or situations that normally produce the problem behavior. The competing response is a desirable behavior. The idea is that your dog cannot perform the competing desirable behavior and the problem behavior at the same time. If you increase the strength of the desirable competing response through reward, the problem behavior must decrease.

Counter-conditioning is used in shaping, chaining, differential reward and systematic desensitization and will be explained under each of these techniques.

Flooding

For very intense complicated fears that result in your dog being terrified and uncontrollable, systematic desensitization is the best technique. However, for mild fears another technique called flooding can be used. This technique is based on the fact that many things become fear-producing because they are associated with pain or some other noxious event. In order for your dog to lose his fear this association needs to be broken. However, your dog will not do this on his own. He will run away before he has a chance to find out that the feared event or situation is not dangerous.

Thus, if you force your dog to experience the mildly fearful situations in such a way that he cannot escape them and if you make sure that nothing really dangerous happens during this exposure, the association will be broken and his fear will extinguish.

The flooding technique is thus an extinction technique and the procedure is as follows:

1. Determine what your dog fears and if there is any dangerous aspect about the event or object he fears. If the event is truly dangerous and can cause pain do not use flooding.

2. If the dog fears innocuous objects and the fear is mild, then arrange the situation so that your dog must experience the feared object for some time. For example, if your dog is afraid of the vacuum cleaner, simply leave the vacuum on for an hour

and go about your business. If your dog has a mild fear of the noise of the air conditioner, just turn it on and behave normally.

3. Do not act differently when you are flooding your dog. This difference in your behavior may scare the dog and accentuate his fear.

4. If the fear appears to be getting worse instead of better, then it was too strong for flooding. Switch to progressive desensitization.

Habituation

This technique is like extinction and flooding but it is used with unlearned or genetically organized behavior. The premise is that if you repeatedly elicit a genetically organized behavior the behavior will decrease as if it were fatigued. This technique has been known by animal handlers for thousands of years. To "man a hawk," one simply attaches the wild hawk to a leather thong and places it on one's arm. The point here is to keep the hawk there until it stops struggling and starts eating. This may take many hours. To tame a python or boa constrictor one simply picks it up and holds it over and over again. Initially the snake tries to bite but if you wear protective clothing it doesn't hurt. After picking up the animal many times the biting gradually decreases. Most people are familiar with the procedure of breaking a horse. The cowboy first places the saddle on the horse. The horse's initial response is to buck; however, this eventually stops. The cowboy keeps getting on the horse until it stops bucking completely.

This technique is so simple that no step-by-step procedure is necessary. Simply continue eliciting the behavior until it stops. I have used the technique with great success when dealing with epileptiform aggression in a poodle. The dog would react with fits of rage if touched. I simply continued touching the dog until he stopped trying to bite.

I have also used this technique with two Yorkies who would

(287)

fight if left together. I muzzled both dogs and put them together. The first fight lasted two hours, the next for about one hour. The third fight lasted twenty-three minutes. The fourth lasted fifteen minutes, the fifth and sixth ten minutes and the last fight for three minutes. Throughout the whole procedure, which took three days, the dogs could go for longer and longer periods without fighting until fighting completely stopped.

There are some helpful hints with this procedure:

1. Make sure you know what is eliciting the behavior and then repeatedly and continuously elicit it.

2. Make sure the dog and you are adequately protected. Muzzle a fighting dog and make sure his adversary is muzzled. Wear protective clothing and heavy leather gloves for a biting dog.

3. This is a very violent procedure. It is not advisable for dogs or owners who might have coronary problems or any other medical problems that might be exacerbated by the violence.

4. Make sure you never reward the dog, trying to calm it down or attending to it, during the habituation.

5. This is a procedure of last resort. It doesn't always work and if not done properly can lead to further problems. Use it only when everything else has failed.

THE SOLUTION

In the previous section a large number of general methods or contingencies were outlined. However, the separation of these techniques is a convenience. In reality more than one and perhaps as many as ten are employed simultaneously. Each technique is modified to suit the demands of a client's life situation and the specific problem behaviors. Care must be taken to make sure that all the techniques are complementary or at the very least that they don't contradict each other. Thus the program I outline for my clients is individual. It is hoped that by reading this book that you will be able to design your own individual solution to your pet's behavior problem.

In general, each solution involves some sort of counter-conditioning. We substitute a desirable behavior for each problem behavior, using reward for most of the techniques.

For the dog in the first chapter, the first problem tackled was the behavior related to eating. Dry dog food, which was harder to swallow and caused more chewing, resulted in slower eating. The dog was also given "Easy" training with biscuits and his own food. The easy training is basically differential reward for taking the food slowly and easily. The food was dispensed one spoonful or biscuit at a time, preceded by the command "Easy." If the dog attempted to take the food rapidly or vigorously, the food was removed. He was given the food only if he took it easily. At first, any sign of taking the food easily was rewarded. Then the definition of "easy" was increased slowly, using a shaping procedure until the dog was required to be very gentle when taking the food.

Food-guarding was combatted at the same time with hard dog biscuits attached to a two-foot nylon string. The dog was given the biscuits, preceded by the word "Easy." If the dog tried to walk or run away with the biscuit, it would be pulled out of his mouth by yanking on the string. This resulted in the dog gnawing the biscuit at my clients' feet. The dog was made to come closer and closer to my clients and eat while lying down, by shortening the length of the string, which was securely held under their feet. This was continued until the dog would have to lie down six inches from my clients' feet and allow them to pet him (a form of desensitization) while chewing the biscuit.

In order to counter-condition the barking demand for food the dog was shaped to wait silently for each food ration after the command "Easy" was given. After he would take the food easily on command, the time between the command and giving the food was gradually increased. Initially, one second of silently sitting and waiting was rewarded. The silent time was increased by three- or five-second steps until the dog could silently wait for up to seventy-five seconds and then take the food easily when it was offered. If the dog barked or snapped at the food, the mother or daughter would put the food away and lock the dog in the kitchen for three minutes (i.e., extinction) and then return for the next trial.

So, just by rationing the dog's daily meal and giving each bite of food as a consequence of patient silent waiting and easy taking of the food, my clients were able to reduce dramatically some of the persistent feeding problems. At the end of shaping, the dog was required to sit quietly when the meal was being prepared and stay seated for two minutes after the bowl was placed on the floor. When the command "Easy" was given, he was allowed to approach the food slowly and eat. Any violation in a meal resulted in a loss of the meal for that day. This was designed to extinguish any remaining feeding problems.

Furthermore, the dog was always fed in the kitchen and never in any other part of the house. Hopefully, a discrimination would be formed that eating occurred only in the kitchen.

Rapid excessive drinking and demanding water was another problem with this dog. To combat this, he was given forty-eight ounces of water in three sixteen-ounce amounts thirty minutes before a walk. At first all sixteen ounces were given and the dog was allowed eight minutes to drink it. He usually consumed the ration in three to four minutes. Any demand for water at unspecified times was ignored. This had the effect of dramatically reducing his urination in the house.

In about a week and a half the dog had accustomed himself to this new drinking regime and we took advantage of this to continue training quiet behaviors. The dog was now given his sixteen-ounce ration in four- to eight-ounce portions. The owners said, "Do you want a drink?" and placed the dog's water bowl on the floor. If the dog sat quietly by his bowl for one second, the eight-ounce portion was poured in. The time of quietly sitting by the bowl was gradually increased in five-second steps to seventy-five seconds in the same way as waiting for food was shaped. If the dog barked, the bowl would be removed for three minutes.

Drinking from the toilet was cured by aversive and avoidance training. After each flush, the toilet water was doctored with quinine powder which gave it a very bitter taste but would not hurt the dog. The toilet seat was adjusted so that it would fall if it was jarred, making a loud noise and hitting the dog on the head. Thus the toilet was delivering the punishment and not the owners. The toilet drinking stopped after two bops and one bitter drink.

To stop the pica (that is, eating inedible objects) it was necessary to make the dog react to these objects as if they were dangerous. The objects themselves must deliver the punishment and not the owners. The owners would only warn the dog that the object is dangerous. This was done rather easily by installing electrodes on various objects that could be used to deliver measured electric shocks. Other objects that could not be electrified were heated until they were uncomfortable to touch. Objects that could not be heated or electrified were coated with a paste of Chinese mustard and Italian red pepper that produced a burning sensation on the tongue.

There were seven conditions that had to be met for treatment with shock to be successful and not have bad side effects. First, the electrodes and the wires had to be small and inconspicuous so they would give no clue to the presence of the shock apparatus. Thus the dog would not be able to discriminate which inedible objects were electrified. Second, the objects electrified had to be as varied in shape and construction as possible. Thus the dog would not be able to predict which class of objects was dangerous. For all the dog knew, all inedible objects might be potentially dangerous. Third, the location of the electrified objects had to be as varied as possible to prevent the dog from forming a discrimination based on place. Fourth, the owners' behavior should not change during the treatment to prevent the formation of a discrimination based on their behavior. Fifth, there should be no change in the dog's environment, no furniture moved, and the like, to prevent a discrimination about the shock to be based on environmental change. Sixth, there should be only one clue to the shock, the owners' warning, which was, "No, don't touch!" The owners were not to approach or chase the dog, just say those words from wherever they were standing. The owners' position in relation to the electrified objects was also varied, sometimes close, sometimes far, either standing, walking or sitting.

With these conditions in effect inedible electrified objects were placed around the house. When the dog went to pick up an object, the owners said, "No, don't touch," in a neutral tone of voice. If the dog picked up the object, he would get a two-milliampere shock from the electrodes. At other times the dog was not warned in advance and if he picked up the object the owners said, "No, drop it," and a shock was turned on. The dog's immediate reaction was to drop what he had in his mouth. The dog received a total of eight shocks, each about one-tenth of a second duration and the behavior was completely eliminated.

Now when the owners said, "No, don't touch," the dog immediately stopped and would drop anything he had in his mouth on the command "No, drop it." This takes us to the seventh condition for the use of shock. The owners were required to lavishly reward "Not touching" and "Dropping" on command with food, praise and petting. This was done to keep the behavior strong after the shock was removed.

All these precautions were necessary when using as powerful a punisher as shock. Other precautions involved the use of a laboratory shocker that produces a "clean" shock, one that is precisely controllable and whose characteristics are specified and known. The shock devices currently available to the public are very dangerous and can cause psychological damage to the dog. I use shock only as a last resort and only with great care and knowledge.

The word "No" was used intentionally during the shock training to build up its stopping power. It was hoped that the "No" command would generalize with a little help to other behaviors. This in fact was what happened. The word "No" was able to stop a whole variety of problem behaviors.

Demanding food from the owners at meal time was solved by the effects of the silent-wait training used when the dog was fed and watered. And now the strong inhibitory "No" was used to further silence training.

Silence training involved waiting for the dog to start barking, saying "No, quiet," holding the dog's muzzle shut for three seconds and then rewarding him with praise and food. Holding the dog's muzzle was a behavioral prompt ensuring that he would respond correctly. As the dog responded to the command correctly the amount of pressure on his muzzle was reduced (fading the prompt) and the length of time the dog had to be silent was increased (shaping).

When the silence training was pretty well established, the owners were instructed to reward with praise but only partially reward the silence with food until the food reward was given only occasionally. At this time the owners were instructed to engage in "mock" meals in the dining room. The mock meals were used to generalize the silence training to when the owners were eating. (Up to this point the owners were still eating all their meals in restaurants.) They would sit down at the table and begin eating. When the dog barked they were to say, "No, quiet." If the dog stopped barking, they were to reward him with praise and a bone immediately. If the dog continued barking, they were to hold his muzzle for three seconds and then reward with praise. The silent time necessary for the praise reward was steadily increased. At no time was the dog ever to be rewarded with food during the owners' meals.

Barking at the daughter, which was the original complaint, was corrected by a combination of fading and reward for silence. You will recall that the dog would bark at the daughter whenever she said, "Mom, call Sebastian" and the mother would reward the consequent aggressive barking. To turn the tables on this we faded in the words, "Mom, call Sebastian." At first the daughter was instructed to say "Mom" in a low voice. If the dog remained silent, he was rewarded. If he barked, his muzzle was held for three seconds and then he was rewarded. Then the girl was instructed to say, "Mom, call," and then "Mom, call Sebastian," raising her voice each time and rewarding silent behavior. When the dog stopped barking at the girl in these situations, the mother was instructed to participate. The girl would say, "Mom, call Sebastian," and the mother would reward the dog for silence.

Aggressive mounting was corrected by counter-conditioning with a "Down and stay" command. At the same time the obedience chain was disrupted. Both the mother and daughter were instructed in how to train various obedience commands with special emphasis on "Down and stay." The commands were given in a scrambled order and reward was given after each correct performance. Incorrect performances were ignored and not rewarded. When the "Down and stay" was well established, it was used whenever the dog mounted the daughter. The dog was rewarded for lying down. If the dog refused to dismount and lie down, he was told "No" and forcibly removed from the girl's leg; then the command "down" was given and the dog was put in a down position and rewarded.

The dog's hair-chewing was punished using a shock procedure similar to the one used with pica. In fact, the dog's foot was considered another inedible object. The shock was delivered to the dog's neck via a specially made collar when the dog started chewing his feet. The words "No, don't touch" and "No, drop it" were paired with the foot-chewing and shock. The same precautions were used with the punishment of this self-abusive behavior as was used with the pica. The foot-chewing was eliminated after three shocks. The speed of the change was probably due to the transfer from the previous shock training.

Defecation in the house was never treated by me. This problem disappeared about one week after the shock conditioning. When I discussed this with my clients, they said that they were using the "No" command when the dog was caught defecating in the house. This usually stopped the dog in the act. Then they would immediately take the dog for a walk and reward him for defecating outside. Both these techniques were successful and were generated by my clients with no advice from me. I had figured that the defecation would be one of the hardest problems to deal with and was waiting until the easier problems were conquered first.

The initiative on the part of my clients was very rewarding for me. It showed that they had learned their lessons well. They were dealing with problems independently of me. This is the ultimate goal of the treatment. I was confident that they could deal with any other problem that might arise.

They had become their own animal psychologists.

Bibliography

American Kennel Club. *The Complete Dog Book.* New York: AKC, 1956.

Beck, A. M. *The Ecology of Stray Dogs: A Study of Free-Ranging Urban Animals.* Baltimore, Md.: York Press, 1973.

Eibl-Eibesfeldt, I. *Ethology: The Biology of Behavior.* New York: Holt, Rinehart, and Winston, 1975.

Fox, M. W. *Canine Behavior.* Springfield, Ill.: C C Thomas, 1965.

————. *Abnormal Behavior in Animals.* Philadelphia: Saunders, 1968.

————. *Behavior of Wolves, Dogs and Related Canids.* New York: Harper & Row, 1971.

————. *Understanding Your Dog.* New York: Coward, McCann and Geoghegan, 1972.

————. *The Wild Canids.* New York: Van Nostrand Reinhold, 1975.

————, and Bekoff, M. "The Behavior of Dogs." In *The Behavior of Domestic Animals,* edited by Hafez, E. S. E. Baltimore, Md.: William and Wilkins, 1975.

Heidiger, H. *Wild Animals in Captivity.* London: Butterworth, 1950.

Levinson, B. *Pets and Human Development.* Springfield, Ill.: C C Thomas, 1972.

Little, C. C. *Inheritance of Coat Color in Dogs.* Ithaca, N.Y.: Cornell University Press, 1957.

Lorenz, K. *King Solomon's Ring.* New York: Crowell, 1952.

————. *Man Meets Dog.* London: Methuen, 1954.

————. *On Aggression.* New York: Harcourt, Brace and World, 1966.

Lyons, M. *The Dog in Action.* New York: Howell, 1972.

Marler, P., and Hamilton, W. J., III. *Mechanisms of Animal Behavior.* New York: John Wiley and Sons, 1966.

McCay, C. M. *Nutrition of the Dog.* Ithaca, N.Y.: Comstock, 1946.

Pfaffenberger, C. J. *Training Your Spaniel.* New York: Putnam, 1947.

————. *The New Knowledge of Dog Behavior.* New York: Howell, 1963.

Reed, C. A. "Animal Domestication in the Prehistoric Near East." *Science* 130 (1959): 1629–36.

Rheingold, H. "Maternal Behavior in the Dog." In *Maternal Behavior in Mammals*, edited by Rheingold, H. New York: John Wiley and Sons, 1963.

Rutter, R.J., and Pimlott, D. H. *The World of the Wolf.* Philadelphia: J. B. Lippincott, 1968.

Saunders, B. *Training You to Train Your Dog.* New York: Doubleday, 1952.

Schmidt-Nielson, K. *How Animals Work.* New York: Cambridge University Press, 1972.

Scott, J. P. *Aggression.* Chicago: University of Chicago Press, 1958.

————, and Fuller, J. L. *Dog Behavior: The Genetic Basis.* Chicago: University of Chicago Press, 1965.

Seligman, M. E. P. *Helplessness.* San Francisco: W. H. Freeman, 1975.

Tinbergen, N. *Curious Naturalists.* London: Country Life, 1958.

Van Wormer, J. *The World of the Coyote.* Philadelphia: J. B. Lippincott, 1968.

Index

Behavior, inherited, of dogs, 58, 60–66

Behavior of aberrant dog, 16–17, 25

Behavior of dog with professional dog handler, as opposed to behavior with owner, 8

Behavior, operant, 4, 190–200

Behavior Problem Checklist, 103–104 (*tables*)

Behavior problem, stimulus setting of a, 233–235

Behavior problems of dogs, types of, 100–109

Behavior, sexual, between dogs, 42–44, 102, 119–127

Behavioral diary, 17, 18

Behavioral rituals, happy fits as, 44–45

"Behavioral trap" and barking, as fault of dog's owner, 12–14

Behaviorist, an animal psychologist as a, 53–56

Beneficial contingencies, and dog's behavior, 271–272

Biological and medical causes of dog's behavior problems, 225–226

Birth process, and immediate care of the neonatal puppies, 184–185

Biscuit trick to stop barking, 6

Bitches, wild canine, removal of body waste by, 19, 30

Biting by dog, caused by fear, 144–145, 149

Biting by dogs, three types of, 127–130

Biting own feet or paws raw, by the dog, 39, 41

Biting problem, 73, 144–145

Biting your face, as result of giving unintentional reward, 77–78

Biting your mother-in-law, as result of giving dog an unconscious reward, 78–80

Body postures and facial expressions, as means of communication by dogs, 128–130, 134

Body surface of dogs, care of (COBS), 174

Booby-trapping, creative, to scare or punish dog, 93–94

Borchelt, Drs. Peter and Diana, *xiv*

Breeds and genetics, 65–68

Breeds, different, AKC description of, 60

Bribery of dog, 47

Calcium and mineral deficiency, possible cause of, 223–224

Can opener trick, 21, 23, 25

Car chasing by dogs, curing habit of, 155–157

Care of dog's body surface (COBS), 174

Care of the young, and nesting, 183–190

Carpets, soiling of by dog, 26–27

Castration, 224–225

Changing behavior of dog, technology of, 74–77

Chaining of dog (perhaps using shaping), 197–199, 200 (*table*), 201, 275–276

Chewing and destruction of objects by dogs, 172–174

Chewing by dog, on his own feet, 38–39

Chewing or eating by animal, leading to attack of persons disturbing him, 110

Chewing plasterboard, as possible calcium and mineral deficiency, 223–224

Children, dominant dog's reaction to, 135–136

Clients, problems of, and discussions of solutions with animal psychologist, 14–17

COBS, care of body surface of dogs, 174

Command to dog by owner, 191
generalizations, 196
"Get slippers," 199–200 (*table*)
hand signals, 195
nature of, 194–196
rules for program of, 192–194
verbal, 194–195

Communication by dogs through body postures and facial expressions, 128–130, 134

Conditioning and forming of fixed-action habits, 96–99